COPPER CRUCIBLE

COPPER CRUCIBLE

HOW THE ARIZONA
MINERS' STRIKE OF 1983
RECAST LABOR-MANAGEMENT
RELATIONS IN AMERICA

SECOND EDITION

JONATHAN D. ROSENBLUM

ILR PRESS AN IMPRINT OF
CORNELL UNIVERSITY PRESS
ITHACA AND LONDON

First published 1995 by ILR Press
Second edition published 1998 by ILR Press/Cornell University Press

Printed in the United States of America

Library of Congress Cataloging-in-Publication Data

Rosenblum, Jonathan D., b. 1958
Copper crucible: how the Arizona miners' strike of 1983 recast
labor-management relations in America, 2d ed. / Jonathan D. Rosenblum.
p.   cm.
Includes bibliographical references and index.
ISBN 0-8014-8554-1 (pbk.)
1. Phelps Dodge Corporation Strike, Morenci, Ariz., 1983–   2. Strikes and
lockouts—Copper mining—Arizona.   3. Industrial relations—United
States.   I. Title.
HD5325.M73   1983M677   1994
331.89'28223431'0979151—dc20   94-27852

Cornell University Press strives to use environmentally responsible suppliers and materials to the fullest extent possible in the publishing of its books. Such materials include vegetable-based, low-VOC inks and acid-free papers that are recycled, totally chlorine-free, or partly composed of nonwood fibers. For further information, visit our website at www.cornellpress.cornell.edu.

Paperback printing 10 9 8 7 6 5 4 3 2

To my mother and my father

Contents

Preface to the
Second Edition, 1998

When I accepted the invitation to update *Copper Crucible* for this second edition, I first planned to write about large themes of industrial labor relations at the millennium. Let me offer, instead, a rain check. I got sidetracked—or, really, "mainstreamed" into the heat of a current conflict. What's happening today at Phelps Dodge preempts any millennial summing. Alex Lopez is the one who led me back to the crucible one more time. Although he retired from the Steelworkers in early 1998, Lopez showed me that a set of events in western New Mexico in the 1990s put Phelps Dodge on a new collision course with a union and U.S. union history. Between 1996 and today, the turbulence has been building in Silver City, New Mexico, in a decertification and contract clash between the company and renowned Steelworkers Local 890, also known as the "Salt of the Earth" union. So I have written a new epilogue of the Phelps Dodge–union saga. It picks up after Morenci Local 616 president Angel Rodriguez's eulogy for the Phelps Dodge unions in Arizona (in the conclusion, "Angels and Demons") and takes the title "Life after Death?"

I dedicate this new edition to my newly arrived son, Simon; to my partner, Jane Larson; and to the late professor and friend Richard Snyder, whose conversation and criticism on early drafts informed so much of this book.

J. D. R.

Madison, Wisconsin
August 1998

Acknowledgments

If my brother Keith had not choked back the tear gas that day in June 1984 to tell me about the riot between copper miners and state police in Clifton (and to write his stories for the *Arizona Daily Star*), I might never have undertaken this project. His accounts, delivered as I worked as a reporter-researcher for the *New Republic* magazine in Washington, D.C., drew my attention to the situation of Arizona's striking copper miners and eventually led to this book. To Keith and his wife, Elizabeth Bradshaw Rosenblum, I owe a special thanks for their help, lodging, *carne asada*, Circle K Thirst Busters, and concern for my sanity. A number of other Arizonans have, likewise, generously given me shelter and/or their best creative input: Nicholas Hentoff, Marguerite McIntyre, Louis and Jane Rosenbaum, Richard and Marjorie Snyder, Tom Miller, Diana Rix, Wade Jensen, Kathy Boyd, and Francisco, Juanita, and Bobby Andazola. My appreciation also goes to the Rode Inn Motel of Clifton, Arizona (which allowed me frequently to stay past checkout time), P.J.'s Restaurant (for its sustaining green chile omelettes), and to my Clifton landlords, Antonio and Josephine Rivas, who taught me a lot about local union history and Clifton hospitality.

Elsewhere in the world, I have benefited from the wise counsel of Jane Larson, Joseph Ferguson, E. J. Flynn, Jason DeParle, Julie Brown, Bruce Payne, Nadine Epstein, Daniel Levy, Susan Lehman, Dirk Olin, Patrick McMahon, Cornelia Grumman, Leon Fink, John Hoerr, Stephen Goldberg, Jeanne Brett, Tina Rosenberg, Leonard

Rubinowitz, Richard Meeker, Gail Ross, Benjamin Aaron, Alison Irvine, Duncan Campbell, the Peter Handler poets society, the *Germinal* reading group (Karen Curtis, Loic Picard, Anne McLeod Trebilcock, and Roberto Bedrikow, with the creative guidance of Emile Zola), Shauna Olney, Alan Gladstone, all the Kohns, and Lucy McNair.

Among the subjects in this book, I would like to extend my special appreciation for their willingness to make time for me to the following officials: from the unions: Frank McKee, Robert Petris, Mary-Win O'Brien, Alex Lopez, Angel Rodriguez, Ray Isner, and the late David Velasquez; from the Morenci Miners Women's Auxiliary: Fina Roman, Anna O'Leary, Carmina Garcia, Boo Phillips, Irene Diaz, and Shirley Randall; from Phelps Dodge: George Munroe, Richard Moolick, William Seidman, John Bolles, Pat Scanlon, and the late Phelps Dodge private counsel, John Boland, Jr.; from the Arizona state government: Ronnie Lopez, George Britton, Andrew Hurwitz, Brian Devallance, and former Arizona Governor Bruce Babbitt, now U.S. Secretary of the Interior. I would also like to thank here the unnamed sources who provided me with important firsthand insights into the workings of Phelps Dodge, the unions, and the Phoenix office of the National Labor Relations Board.

I could never have completed this project without the funding assistance of the Dispute Resolution Research Center of Northwestern University; the generous provision of office space and conversation from the School of Public Affairs at Arizona State University; the research time granted by Mead Data Central for its Nexis/Lexis system; the library and microfiche support from the *Arizona Republic* and *Arizona Daily Star* newspapers; the archivists, especially Christine Marín, at the Chicano Research Collection at Arizona State University library; and the pure inspiration of the International Labor Organization in Geneva, Switzerland, where, when I wasn't examining complaints about violations of freedom of association or bothering the librarians for books, I could consult with the great 1930s copper statue of a pick-swinging hard rock miner.

Now, for the people who have lived with this work more than just about any others, I would like to thank my parents, Victor and Louise; my sisters, Susan, Ellen, and Laura (whose loans got me through the days when I hardly had a copper penny); my brothers (besides Keith), Peter, Warren, and Joshua; the staff of Cornell University's ILR Press (who generously agreed that such a big family meant that the author should get a few extra complimentary copies), and in particular, Frances Benson, Patty Peltekos, Andrea Fleck Clardy, Faith Short, and freelance copyeditor Jane Margaret Hunt. Without the encouragement of all of the above, I probably would have opted for more conventional pursuits after law school and would never have finished this book. If the author must (and does) take complete blame for factual errors, misconstructions, malapropisms, and excessive highway references, I nevertheless hold these individuals responsible for much of my staying power.

One disclosure: I worked in Arizona state government as a writer and policy aide to then Governor Babbitt in 1985–86. At that time, the strike was two years old and alive only in legal briefs and aid applications by permanently replaced workers. I did not participate in any way in the Arizona government response to the conflict, but I did see enough of the community fallout from the strike to see that someone needed to investigate its background, causes, and effects. I decided to write this book in 1988, and I intermittently conducted my research and interviews while I was working as a reporter-researcher at *Time* magazine, attending law school, and practicing law. Some portions of the book are adapted from my articles that appeared in the *Wall Street Journal*, the *Arizona Republic,* and the *Arizona Daily Star* and from my senior research paper at Northwestern University School of Law entitled "Getting to No: The Phelps Dodge–United Steelworkers Strike of 1983–86."

Finally, a note to the reader about my documentation. For the sake of flow, I have not used footnotes in the text. However, a complete set of source notes, with occasional elaboration on the text, appears in the back of the book, beginning on page 247.

COPPER CRUCIBLE

Crucible: A container . . . that can resist great heat, for melting, fusing, or calcining ores, metals, etc.; the hollow at the bottom of an ore furnace where the molten metal collects; a severe test or trial.

[Etymology: From Old English, cruce, *pot, jug . . . plus suffix* -ibulum *(as in* thuribulum, *censer) but associated by folk etymology with Latin* crux, *cross, as if lamp burning before cross]*

—Webster's New World Dictionary of the American Language

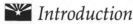

Critical Conditions

They had prepared for this battle by the book. One hundred state troopers marched around the mountain curve on June 30, 1984, toting riot shields, wooden bullet guns, and tear gas, backed by armored vehicles called "batmobiles." Their badges announced the Department of Public Safety (DPS), and their shoulder patches displayed the great copper star of the state of Arizona. Mission "Restore Peace" was about to begin against striking copper miners. But well-armed as they were, the last thing these riot troopers expected to find blocking their way was a naked man.

Bobby Andazola was somewhat surprised as well. He had walked out onto the highway fully dressed, intending to ask the state troopers a question: Why were they entering his family's town? After all, this was Clifton, Arizona, the union town. The only disturbance here was a crowd of strikers leading a shift-change picket line. The troopers had been stationed in the company town of Morenci, four miles up the highway. In Morenci, these DPS foot soldiers had been assigned to protect replacement workers at the mine gate, epicenter of the statewide strike against Fortune 500 copper mining giant Phelps Dodge Corporation. Now marching military-style into Clifton, the troopers clearly hadn't come to answer questions. So former copper miner Bobby Andazola stood on the scorching blacktop in the center of U.S. Highway 666, his arms outstretched like a martyr on the cross. He yelled furiously at the troopers, wishing the whole world to hear: "In the name of Lord God, Lord Jehovah, would you do this to your own brothers and sisters?"

〜❦〜

This day was an anniversary. A year earlier, at midnight on June 30, 1983, Bobby Andazola's father, brother, and nearly twenty-four hundred other copper mine, mill, and smelter workers had gone on strike against Phelps Dodge Corporation. The workers were protesting cuts in wages, vacation time, and medical benefits. Copper prices were bad, but every other major producer in the United States had agreed to a bare-bones contract proposed by the unions: wages would be frozen and the workers would get cost-of-living increases only. A coalition of unions, led by the United Steelworkers of America, had pitched the deal as "Strike-Free in '83"—a promise of the first bargaining in fifteen years without any strikes in exchange for the wage freeze. But Phelps Dodge, or "PD," as this New York–based company was called locally, refused to sign the contract. Instead, the company carried out its cuts and, as federal labor laws allowed, began permanently replacing strikers with outside hires. Within a few months, the strikers at Phelps Dodge mines in Morenci, Bisbee, Ajo, and Douglas, Arizona, as well as strikers at a refinery in El Paso, Texas, had lost their jobs to replacement workers.

To strikers and supporters like Bobby Andazola, an anniversary rally and fish fry to protest the company's action was certainly no breach of the peace. The rally was, rather, a display of solidarity in an old and, to their minds, never-ending struggle for justice against Phelps Dodge.

The Andazola family had been a fixture in these eastern Arizona mountain towns since 1905, when Bobby Andazola's grandfather moved the family from Chihuahua, Mexico. But being a fixture in a mining town certainly didn't mean being well settled. Metcalf, the town where those first American Andazolas lived, was wiped off the map by Phelps Dodge and replaced with a rock crusher. The family moved to the company town, Old Morenci, where Francisco and Juanita Andazola raised three sons, Frank junior, Peter, and Bobby. Then Old Morenci, too, was swallowed by the mine. Everything, including the high school that the boys had attended, was buried under hundreds of feet of rock.

To mining families, the cuts and slashes made by mine machinery, the smelter's stench of sulphur, and the vast slag heaps signified mostly economic strength. Living off the rock, they had to adjust to the consequences—a periodic erasure of place and past. "We built a house," said Francisco, "but Phelps Dodge owned the ground." The last time he heard that mine expansions would take his home, Francisco tore down the house and moved his family (lumber and all) four miles down the highway from Morenci to Clifton, from the company town to the union town. He rebuilt the house there, never asking for reimbursement.

Life in Clifton gave the miner at least the illusion of independence from Phelps Dodge. Cactus-sprinkled red cliffs towered over brick and wood-frame houses. The San Francisco River rolled right through the center of town. Here, families who could afford it purchased land of their own and settled. The natural surroundings were so much a part of life in Clifton that residents continued to refer to one of the downtown streets as "Chase Creek" even after the creek that once ran alongside it was dammed by Phelps Dodge for its mining needs.

Clifton and its 4,250 inhabitants also had created a lively small-town democracy, led by the town council, a seven-member body elected at large with a part-time mayor. The family-owned town newspaper, *The Copper Era*, had published without interruption since the 1890s. About half the population was of Mexican descent, a result of recruiting efforts early in the century by Phelps Dodge and other copper companies who sent agents to Mexico to bring back miners— and sometimes whole families. The Andazolas had first come to the Phelps Dodge mines as a result of such recruiting efforts.

Four miles up the road in Morenci, the sign at the entrance to town said, "Unincorporated," yet Morenci, Arizona, population two thousand, was one of the most fully "incorporated" towns in the world. Phelps Dodge not only made copper in Morenci, the company sold the ice for the icebox and bread for the breadbox. (Each loaf came in a Wonder Bread–like plastic bag with the insignia "Phelps Dodge.") Everything from electric power to police service to the dirt under residents' feet was either owned or administered by Phelps Dodge. Company administrators, virtually all of them Anglos, lived on the highest hill in Morenci. Below, in a cluster of small but comfortable frame houses owned by Phelps Dodge, lived most of the employees who couldn't afford to live in Clifton. The "mayor" of Morenci was the mine superintendent.

Morenci's vast open pit, although it sometimes consumed and haunted the miner's world, was also a source of pride. The Andazolas liked to take first-time guests for a visit. From an overlook, visitors saw a curving, jutting mountain of mesquite and prickly pear to the south, all rising to an irregular sort of nipple. But directly below, the earth opened into two miles of blasted, stepped rock—a mountain bleeding wild tones of blue and green and red. Mining engineers call the first dynamite blasts "uncapping the mountain," and Phelps Dodge uncapped its first mountain in these parts in 1881. By 1981, according to a blue Phelps Dodge sign at the overlook, the company had extracted more than two billion tons of copper-laden ore. Thousands of miners, stretching through four generations, built their lives out of this rock and a PD paycheck.

Just east of the overlook still stands a reminder of some of these generations of Phelps Dodge workers. Graves of Mexican-American miners, marked with crosses made from metal pipe or wood and baling wire, lie along a steep incline buttressed by stone walls and wooden slats. The gravestones bear dedications such as *"Aquí descansan los restos de Luciano Ramirez el que fue victima de una traición escirola durante la huelga de Morenci November 15, 1915* (Here lie the remains of Luciano Ramirez who fell victim to a treacherous scab during the 1915 strike in Morenci . . .)." Under the social segregation of the early copper era, Mexicans were separated in death as in life from the Anglos in Phelps Dodge mining towns.

Francisco Andazola's first job started after the depression, when he got on at the mine as a "mucker," the lowliest laborer. "Mexican work," such jobs were called then. Eventually he was promoted from shoveling out muck to a technician's job with PD's water and light company. Francisco earned a better wage than relatives who were farming or mining back in Mexico. He convinced himself—and told his children—"If you'll be good to the mine, the mine will be good to you." When the strike began in 1983, Francisco was one year short of a forty-year pension, so he faced a tough choice. He joined the strike, he said, "because the union had gotten us all the raises," and perhaps also because "it was getting kinda rough around here."

Like his father and two older brothers, Bobby Andazola had gotten his first job at the Morenci mine. In the early 1970s, he worked at the rock crusher, monitoring machines that pulverized boulders into copper-laden dust. But Bobby was the black sheep of the family— more philosopher than miner. He had honed a strong instinct for justice as an altar boy at Holy Cross Church in Morenci and through literature that the priests might have missed, like *Lord of the Rings* by J. R. R. Tolkien. Bobby used to take pensive, meandering walks through the mining dumps. Old pieces of the buried towns—

medicine bottles, porcelain vases (from the early Chinese workers), medallions—rose up there like driftwood on a beach. He began a collection. His favorite piece was a Mexican coin, dented and worn, but with the date, 1897, still visible. It was minted only a few years before Andazolas first arrived in Arizona from Chihuahua. Bobby gave the coin to his grandmother a few years before she died.

Mining didn't suit Bobby, so he left for the burgeoning "sunbelt" economy in Phoenix, four hours away. There, he took a job in construction.

⟩⟩⟨

On the steamy afternoon of June 30, 1984, a full year into the strike, Bobby Andazola was back in Clifton to look after his parents. As a salsa band played a festive set, strikers formed a highway picket line to harass the strikebreakers driving home at the afternoon shift change. Bobby was sitting with some friends on his parents' tin roof lunching on catfish caught in the San Francisco River and drinking beer when he heard a strange percussion echoing in the canyon. Well beyond the rhythms of the band's bass fiddle, the troopers were announcing their arrival by hitting plastic shields with wooden batons. When Bobby saw them round the mountain, heading on a line toward his parents' house, he turned to his friends and said, "No, no, there's something wrong here. This is an invasion force." His father and brother had already lost their jobs to strikebreakers. Did the troopers now want to erase their dignity as well?

There were still a few hundred feet of highway between the advancing cadre of troopers and what strikers called the "heckling line" when Bobby suddenly appeared out of the crowd and stood between the strikers and one hundred armed riot troopers. Fully dressed, he threw his hands up and yelled at the state troopers to turn back, to "get the fuck out of my town." He was abusive, but also moralistic as he beseeched them to leave Clifton alone. No one in the crowd of strikers and picnickers knew then that the troopers had been ordered to break up the picket line after an unmarked DPS car had received a slap on the trunk from a striker. But when a bottle flew out of the crowd, the troopers quickly revealed the full scope of their mission. They surged forward and began to launch gas canisters at the crowd.

Bobby angrily threw things back at the troopers. First his shoes.

Then his shirt. ("All I had to throw was my clothes," he said later.) Then he heaved his pants. Then there was nothing more to throw.

A deep silence insulated by smoke fell on Route 666. The salsa band stopped and the picketers drew close together. A few news photographers in town for the anniversary recorded the apparition: a short, brown man stark naked in an otherworldly fog standing alone against one hundred heavily armed state troopers backed by shielded batmobiles. Then the moment passed, and the officers swarmed over Bobby, pounding his body with their plastic shields and hauling him to a waiting van. He was arrested and charged: indecent exposure and unlawful assembly.

The crowd reacted to the invasion with fury. Picketers and picnickers waded through tear gas and wooden bullets to launch a hail of rocks at the troopers. The whole scene could stand as a union portrait for the 1980s titled "Labor's Last Stand."

Twenty strikers and their supporters were arrested; many more were overcome by tear gas, including a seventy-two-year-old man with a pacemaker, a two-year-old child, and a woman eight months pregnant. On the other side, six troopers were injured by flying rocks. Even Father Joseph Lombardo, a Catholic priest who had come down to the Route 666 confrontation in an effort to mediate, was felled by a blast of tear gas and helped to safety.

During the first year of this strike against Phelps Dodge, strikers had shut down the mine by force and had been replaced by strikebreakers, deluged by a flood of the San Francisco River, and evicted from their homes—but this battering by state troopers was perhaps the strikers' harshest test yet.

To look now at these towns and the conflict these mining families lived for more than two years (and many still live) is to begin to understand why some two thousand Arizona copper workers sacrificed so much only to see livelihoods, friendships, and even communities dissolve.

A Century of Struggle

To look to Clifton and Morenci is also to see the lines of a broader historic conflict between American labor, management, and government. The dismal condition of organized labor in the 1980s and 1990s can be explored in its rawest form by tracing Phelps Dodge's relationship with unions, from the birth of the unions to their death.

The relationship went back decades. Early in the twentieth century, labor strife at Phelps Dodge attracted revolutionaries like Mother Jones and peacemakers like Felix Frankfurter, President Woodrow Wilson's envoy. Later, New Deal labor laws like the National Labor Relations Act helped promote a worker's right to organize and collectively bargain, and they protected, at least on paper, a union's right to strike. These laws helped establish a balance of power and an uncomfortable entente between Phelps Dodge and a union coalition, led since the mid-1960s by the United Steelworkers of America.

The 1980s brought two new challenges to that balance: volatile world economic conditions and conservative national political leadership.

Like many basic American industries, copper mining faced a difficult challenge from foreign competition and a sour economy. Because copper was traded on world exchanges, the industry had always adjusted to global forces more quickly than other sectors, like steel and automobiles. Still, in the early and mid-1980s, market volatility and a worldwide recession combined to create depression-level prices. Third world countries were producing copper below cost in order to pay growing debt burdens. U.S. monetary policy, meanwhile, was pumping up the dollar, which meant that anything made in America, including copper (the United States was the world's second largest producer), was more expensive on the foreign market. Experts attempting to make sense of the market expected terrible conditions in the short term. But, as one trade publication put it, "Seeds are being sown today . . . [for] perhaps record profits for the industry by the mid-1980s."

An always difficult relationship between labor and management in copper met its greatest test in 1983. The challenge was much bigger than mere sectoral bargaining issues, however. With the election of President Ronald Reagan, national labor policy began a shift to the right. This was the decade when workers learned a harsh lesson of American law: the once-vaunted right to strike became, as Supreme Court Justice (and, coincidentally, Arizona copper region native) Sandra Day O'Connor put it in an opinion, "a gamble." Losing the gamble meant being permanently replaced by nonunion workers.

President Reagan opened the decade by firing the nation's striking air traffic controllers, an act that would embolden companies fighting their unions. But it took a private action on the order of Phelps Dodge to show that companies had the muscle to execute—and that an

American public would tolerate—large-scale replacement of unions as a means to end a strike. Though isolated in location, the Phelps Dodge strike had a nationwide effect. It helped perfect a new logic in labor relations: If you can't live with a union, then kill it, legally, with permanent replacements.

When the balance between modern corporate, labor, and government hierarchies collapsed in 1983, communities like Clifton, Arizona, were crushed. Faced with novel circumstances, Phelps Dodge, the unions, and the state government all set their courses hard and fast. Company president Richard T. Moolick said he was "born with the thought that you cross a picket line. You've got that right." Phelps Dodge enlisted the help of one of the country's premier business schools, the Wharton School and its Industrial Research Unit, to help the company draw workers across that picket line. As for the unions, the top Steelworkers official in copper, Frank McKee, believed that Phelps Dodge was attempting to destroy the unions, and he stood resolutely opposed to concessions. Finally, in response to the fires that the company and union officials' fierce positions kindled, Arizona Governor Bruce Babbitt committed a Democrat's cardinal sin against organized labor: he sent in the troops.

All around, positions hardened. Characters clashed. Police power intervened. Traditional antagonism met nontraditional circumstances, yielding chaos. And all around, there was a strange anticipation of blood—if not direct violence, then lethal economic wounds to the union or the company.

When the dust (and the last court challenges) had settled more than two years later, Phelps Dodge had wiped out thirty union locals made up of more than two thousand workers. Its antiunion stand destroyed the entire bargaining structure in the copper industry. After three lean years, from 1982 to 1984, Phelps Dodge became an emerging "superstar," in the words of an admiring business press, churning out record profits.

It is no tragedy, of course, when an American business prevails over uncertainty, creates jobs, and makes profits for new investments and shareholders. The tragedy is in the wounds to families and communities that sometimes result from capital's triumph. An inquest into the Phelps Dodge strike reveals that the strike needn't have happened the way it did. The company could have flourished, and the unions could still have survived. Instead, a more than two-year-long strike was marked by failures of understanding, iron fists, broken laws, and damaged lives. Solidarity was crushed, perhaps forever. The Phelps Dodge strike sounded a call for communities of workers to take a more activist role in their unions and their industries. The strike, and others like it in the 1980s, pushed companies to communicate with their workers. And it led to a stormy debate in the U.S. Congress over the death of unions in America.

The conflict also led to a two-page spread in *Life* magazine—the naked man, Bobby Andazola, and one hundred stiff-jawed riot troopers. It was a stunning scene, as well as an emblem of the times: union families stood bare and vulnerable, nowhere to go. From the Machinists locals to the Boilermakers to Morenci Miners Local 616 of the United Steelworkers of America, union power was being cut down by the decertification campaigns of replacement workers.

This, then, is a book about a company in the throes of change, about people who work the copper rock, and about the life and death of union locals in America.

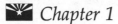 *Chapter 1*

Workers of the World and Copper in Arizona

> *He opened the shaft of the bottomless pit, and from the shaft*
> *rose smoke like the smoke of a great furnace, and the sun*
> *and the air were darkened.*
>
> —Revelation 9:2

Route 666 rides the rugged eastern seam of Arizona from the Petrified Forest, south, across the Zuni River, through the Apache National Forest, and into the mountain mining towns of Clifton and Morenci. Unlike the straightforward, gentle passage of retired Route 66 ("America's Highway"), U.S. 666, its descendant, is tortuous, wild, and as strange as its name. In little more than one hundred miles, the surrounding altitude ranges from twenty-nine hundred feet to more than eleven thousand feet. With some four hundred twisting curves in one sixty-mile stretch, the road has sent more than its share of travelers crashing off cliffs. If, as Nat King Cole sang, drivers get their kicks on Route 66, they take their risks on 666.

From the time it was numbered, people who lived along the road worried over a possible connection between ancient symbolism and their modern fate. For those nearest the Phelps Dodge copper mines in Morenci, the allusion was obvious: the beast in the Book of Revelation rose from a pit with the markings "666" to signal the apocalypse. At the road's dedication in the 1920s, local Apaches reacted with curiosity to the white people's numerology; they performed a ceremony called "the Devil's Dance." Residents regularly wrote the highway department and their congresspeople to change the highway number. After all, an Arizona car owner cannot even purchase a vanity plate with the number "666" on it—the state won't permit it. But highway routing follows its own science (666 indicates that the road is an extension of Route 66) and "the complaints were not on a logical level—they were emotional," explained Arizona traffic engineer Dennis Alvarez. Although the signs regularly disappeared due to vandalism, the numbering stayed.

In fact, the highway does have a hellish past. From the Painted Cliffs near New Mexico, rising to Alpine, Arizona, and plunging again to Morenci, the highway traverses millions of years of lava flows, shifting tectonic plates, and what geologists call "plutonic bodies." Water once coursed through these formations, gradually concentrating the metal content. Some of this metal found its way to the surface as native copper for cowboys to stumble over. But millions of years of percolation also created what are known as porphyry deposits, a widespread but less obvious copper presence in much of the area rock. This sort of geological activity occurs elsewhere as well—copper-laden regions worldwide include the vast "ring of fire" around the Pacific Rim and large regions of Africa, especially Zaire and Zambia, as well as the former Soviet Union. (Copper mining began on the island of Cyprus, from whose name the word "copper" derives.) But in all, Arizona's rock contains the most copper in the United States and the United States has the second largest copper reserves in the world.

In 1540, the celebrated Spanish explorer Francisco Vásquez de Coronado and his chronicler Castañeda became the first European visitors to what geologists now call the Clifton-Morenci mining district. They followed a route from northern Mexico in search of the magical "Seven Cities of Cibola," cities they believed were paved in gold. To Coronado's distress, the explorers found mostly Apaches and cactus. Three hundred years later, as the Industrial Revolution was taking shape, a posse from New Mexico chased horse thieves into the area and found deposits of the red metal. A copper boom followed.

Industrial America needed copper urgently. Growing cities required huge amounts of electrical power, and the wire that conducted electrical current best was usually made from copper. In the 1880s, the telegraph, the electric light, and the electric tramcar all became fixtures of modern society. To produce five thousand kilowatts of electricity for a city, a single generator employed more than a ton of copper. More locally, the typical house was built with about six hundred pounds of copper just for the infrastructure of pipes, wiring, and so on. In mid- and postindustrial America, add an average of more than twenty copper-wound electric motors, ranging from clocks to refrigerators to furnaces to the personal computer fan. A car contains from thirty-five to fifty pounds of copper. Copper also resides at the very soul of America: the Statue of Liberty is clad in one hundred tons of copper ⅒th of an inch thick. Then, of course, there are the pennies filling America's mason jars.

Squeezing this kind of honey from the Arizona rock took some imagination, technology, and thousands of workers willing to give their lungs, their limbs, and sometimes their lives.

In open pit mines, where most copper is mined today, the work goes something like this: blast away a few thousand pounds of porphyry rock, load it into a giant 150-ton dump truck, and crush it under the force of a giant bell-shaped bearing. Crush it some more under finer bearings, send it away in train cars or conveyors, then mix with water and chemical agents to isolate the copper particles. Now, bake at two thousand degrees, drop in a mammoth ladle and separate the waste material (slag) from the copper, and send the copper through flaming moats for processing into slabs called "anodes." From one hundred pounds of rock, this gargantuan process produces barely twelve ounces of copper. Now send it off to a refinery, purify it into 99.99 percent pure copper cathodes, and finally wire and pipe America (and the world) with it.

On the Job

Work at a copper smelter means mastering "a hard, hot, gassy job," said Ralph Martinez, who ran a crane in Morenci from the late 1960s to the early 1980s. If shafts and pits are the belly of copper mining, then the smelter is its hearth and heart. Martinez operated from about sixty feet directly above the glowing, steaming, rumbling furnaces, moving the cab along a track like a spider on a long web. He worked from a standing position day or night, pulling levers, pumping pedals, and keeping an eye on everything through a window designed to separate him from the fumes. Below, the lives of workers depended on his precision. When the copper reached two thousand degrees in the furnaces, Martinez moved in with a ladle about the size of a freight elevator. He transferred a load of fifty to sixty tons of liquid copper from furnace to converter, knocking the ladle against a wall in order to keep the copper from crusting. Sparks and molten copper shot about. Sulphur fumes and dust created a mist that, struck by rays of light from the high smelter windows, looked like "rain when the sun is shining through," Martinez said. The effect was starkly beautiful, but it was also purple, poison rain.

"The window seals of the crane cab leaked," said Martinez. "And the filters for air conditioning wouldn't work because of the heat. In fact, they would suck gas in." When the gas burned especially badly, Martinez went to the company hospital where "they would give you eye wash."

Reports on injuries in copper smelters regularly noted that workers were exposed to dangerous levels of arsenic, as well as sulphur dioxide, lead, cadmium, and silica. "There is greater health and safety regulation for mine equipment than for miners," warned the 1979 study *At Work in Copper*. The same study pointed out that time lost due to illness and injury in smelters was nearly double that of American industry as a whole.

Andrés Padilla worked for more than thirty years at the Morenci mine, most of it punching pipes into a converter to aerate the molten solution. "The temperature where you were working was over 120–130 degrees. You just went in there and got out when you couldn't stand it. You'd cool off and go back in." His father worked at the mine, too, until the day when, repairing the mechanical rod of a "roaster" (an older smelter), the equipment caught a piece of his clothing and "got a hold of him," mutilating his arm. The elder Padilla had to have the arm amputated and replaced with a hook. He received the company's version of workman's compensation for four years, until the coverage ran out, and then he worked at odd jobs to support the family.

Residents of Clifton and Morenci, if they owed their livelihood to copper, came over the years to know victims' names as if they were war casualties: Pete Chavez (amputated leg), Conrad Navarrete (arm), Max Navarrete (dead), Concepcion Pompa (dead), Ray Merino (dead). Similar lists were compiled in the other copper towns. Trains, conveyors, slurry pools, crushers, furnaces, acid, arsenic—mining operations produced extreme dangers as well as dollars.

Birth of a Copper Baron

From the early days of the American copper industry, one of the largest investors in Arizona copper mining was a New York City import-export firm called Phelps, Dodge and Company. In the mid-1800s, processed copper was imported from England and used locally for purposes such as ship bottoms, percussion caps (for weaponry), and copper kettles. Using this imported copper, Ansonia Brass and Copper Company, a Phelps Dodge subsidiary in Connecticut, fast became the largest manufacturer of copper and tin plate in the United States. In 1849, the company was already capitalized at $1 million and showed a profit of 30 percent.

Phelps Dodge gave the concept of an American corporate culture unique depth. The company was launched in New York in 1834 by Protestant families whose legacies are still revered in speeches by management and in portraits hung throughout the Phelps Dodge headquarters. When the Carnegies, Rockefellers, and Mellons were just beginning to build their fortunes, Anson Greene Phelps, the company founder, had already attached his name to the towns of Ansonia in Connecticut and Pennsylvania. Phelps himself was named by his father after two trailblazing heroes—an English sailor who traversed the globe (Anson) and his father's Revolutionary War commander (Greene). The combination of ruggedness and patriotism in Phelps's names became hallmarks of the company.

Phelps Dodge supplied the copper wire for America's first transcontinental telephone line, built many of this country's important railways, and provided tin for a generation of kerosene lamps (marketed by the young John D. Rockefeller). Phelps Dodge products could be found in mercantile stores "from Maine to Mexico," Robert Glass Cleland wrote in *A History of Phelps Dodge*, a book published in 1952 to celebrate the company's first one hundred years.

Phelps Dodge began to mine its own copper in 1881 after a timely visit to New York headquarters by a hard-luck southwestern mine owner. The man wanted Phelps Dodge to invest in his mine by buying a share of the Morenci property and providing heavy machinery and rail lines. After sending engineer James Douglas to Arizona to examine the claims, Phelps Dodge bought a $30,000 interest in Morenci and invested another $40,000 in a mine that turned out to be a motherlode in Bisbee, Arizona, about ninety miles south of Morenci. The company purchased the Bisbee mine a few years later for $1.25 million.

Phelps Dodge managed its mining investments closely, transforming into a modern, orderly business what had sometimes been a boom-and-bust world of whiskey-drinking grubstakers. (Even sheriff's deputy Wyatt Earp and his quick-drawing friend, Doc Holliday of Tombstone, originally came to Arizona to stake mining claims.)

Just a few years prior to the Phelps Dodge purchase, a local dreamer named George Warren had owned a substantial share of the Bisbee claim. But in 1878, Warren offered his claim as the ante in a bet with another man that Warren, on foot, could outrace a horse for a hundred yards around a post. Warren lost the race and his share eventually produced about $20 million worth of copper—for Phelps Dodge's new Copper Queen mine. (In a rather ironic footnote, the mining district was named for Warren). In 1890, Phelps Dodge properties produced fourteen million pounds of copper. In another ten years, that output more than tripled to forty-five million pounds. In 1906, when the company announced to mercantile customers that it was phasing out portions of its retail business "to devote our time and attention to the mining and selling of Copper," the word deserved a capital "C." By 1913, the company's output had tripled yet again to more than 157 million pounds, and the profits were fabulous even by later standards.

Phelps Dodge directors and managers, meanwhile, played a role in the intrigues of the Industrial Revolution. In addition to their bold investments, they were indicted by the federal government on charges that included selling arms to Mexico to forestall revolution, conspiring to deprive workers of their civil rights (while breaking strikes), and violating customs laws (they once tried to conceal imported metals as works of art by having them molded into Roman gods and goddesses). They escaped convictions on each of these, but paid a $270,000 settlement to the government for the "works of art." Such activities established an unmistakable pattern that persisted into the 1980s: in the American corporate frontier, Phelps Dodge officials sometimes conceived of the company as a government unto itself.

Yet, on the whole, Phelps Dodge was a remarkably stable and enduring business in an unstable world of metals. It bred talented, inventive engineers and hired executives from the top schools in the country. One of these engineers and a future Phelps Dodge president, James Douglas, helped invent a copper extraction process that increased production by 30 percent and made Arizona mines the most productive in the country. Phelps Dodge leaders were also deeply imbued with the Protestant work ethic. According to biographer Cleland, the founders followed "the stern, militant, uncompromising creed of John Calvin and John Knox." William Dodge—the "Dodge" in the company name—married into the family by courting one of Phelps's daughters after prayer meetings at church. Dodge was so protective of religious values that, as a player in the family fortune, he refused to bankroll railroads that operated on Sundays.

A corporate philanthropic mission also drove the company founders. Cash-rich Phelps Dodge officials provided much of the backing to establish American University in Beirut, Union Theological Seminary in New York City, and even the nation of Liberia for freed slaves. The company extended its Protestant ethic to the mining camps as well. In exchange for harsh conditions and long days (and nights, since copper mining went on twenty-four hours a day), workers found decent housing, company-sponsored churches, and mercantile stores only too happy to furnish credit to miners. In the Arizona mining towns of Bisbee and Morenci, Phelps Dodge built and owned virtually everything.

Over the years, Phelps Dodge developed vast properties in Bisbee, Ajo, Morenci, and Douglas, Arizona. These early twentieth-century mining towns were crucibles of ethnicity and ideology. Their work forces included a colorful mix of Cornish ("Cousin Jacks"), Welsh, German, Swedish, Spanish, and Italian craftsmen, with laborers from China, Mexico, and the adjacent American states as well as the Navajo Indian reservation. The Mexican workers, who made up as much as 80 percent of all laborers (exclusive of craftsmen), were considered by many the best smelter workers. The names of Clifton and Morenci's turn-of-the-century bars tell the same story: Dennigan's Last Chance Saloon, Sirianni's, Spezia's, La Mariposa, the Club Verde. When Arizona legislators passed early "America-first" laws regulating these workers (one law limited the percentage of foreigners allowed in the mines), the copper-domed capitol in Phoenix became a virtual United Nations of activity, with telegrams and foreign consuls arriving from all over the world to protest the laws.

A growing American union movement also came to Clifton and Morenci to attempt to organize these workers. At the vanguard of the western labor movement were unions like the Industrial Workers of the World ("Wobblies") and the Western Federation of Miners. The Wobblies, led by Big Bill Haywood, declared their goal of a United States run by workers and guided by "One Big Union." The famous union songwriter Joe Hill was one of these southwestern Wobblies, and he hopped trains through Arizona, Utah, Montana, and California advocating unions and strikes. Hill was executed in Utah in 1915 on a murder conviction that labor leaders claimed was trumped up

by the copper companies. Hill's execution, which brought protest
letters ranging from the King of Sweden to American President
Woodrow Wilson, was described in a famous song:

> *The copper bosses killed ya Joe,*
> *They shot you Joe, says I.*
> *Takes more than guns to kill a man,*
> *Says Joe, "I didn't die."*
> . . . .
> *And standing there as big as life,*
> *Smiling with his eyes,*
> *Joe says, "What they forgot to kill*
> *Went on to organize."*

At the turn of the century, the copper dome of Arizona's state capitol
served as a beacon to robber baron and laborer alike. Aside from
ranching, there was only one "real" business and one "real" job in
Arizona—hard rock mining. One in every five Arizona men was
employed in mining-related work. By 1910, the state had become the
nation's largest copper producer, surpassing Utah and Montana,
with nearly $40 million in annual revenue. The first elected governor,
George W. P. Hunt, a former copper miner and labor supporter, was
lauded by labor radical Mother Jones as "a most human and just
man." When Arizona became this country's forty-eighth state in
1912, residents chose for their state flag a radiant copper star against
a backdrop of dark blue and a setting sun. Eventually, that shining
copper star not only flew from Arizona flagpoles but also found its
way onto auto bumpers, supermarket banners, professional football
jerseys, and the shoulder patches of state troopers.

Phelps Dodge and the Unions

Phelps Dodge's relationship with labor unions in Arizona began as
it ended—with National Guardsmen, feuding union and company
officials, and national media attention. In 1903, exactly eighty years
before the strike that ended unionism in Clifton and Morenci, Mexican laborers united in "Mutualistas" or mutual aid societies to protest
a 10 percent wage cut. The "cut" was really a reduction in hours, a
response to the sweeping national movement for eight-hour work-

days. But although the mining companies effectively gave the all-white craft workers an hourly raise, the laborers, mostly minority workers, lost both hours and wages.

One morning in early June 1903, some two thousand miners took to the Morenci streets in protest. The companies defensively attributed the strike to "agitators from outside [who] got the Mexicans and Italians excited," according to economic historian George Leaming. "The strike was finally broken by the arrest of the strike leaders and the use of the territorial militia and five companies of federal troops." Mexican leaders were rounded up and deported. The strikers were chased out by sudden torrential rains, which caused horrendous flooding and killed fifty people. Yet, as another study of the 1903 action noted, "The strike did not end labor difficulties in the Clifton-Morenci district."

A year later, the company (and community) antipathy toward laborers recruited from Mexico became even more pointed, although the conflict did not take the form of a strike. In September 1904, the Sisters of Charity in New York City sent forty abandoned or orphaned children, ranging in age from eighteen months to five years, to be sheltered and raised by Clifton and Morenci families. The New York Foundling Hospital had organized this program for sending children to foster families throughout the country and, at the request of a Clifton priest, the foundling hospital placed these children with Arizona families "of the Spanish race." The children were white or light-skinned children, curiously described in Arizona Supreme Court records as being "of unusual beauty and attractiveness." The children arrived at the Clifton train station, where the conflict began: "It having become a matter of notoriety in Clifton that a number of children were to arrive, to be distributed to Mexican families, a crowd of Mexicans gathered at the station on the arrival of the train, together with a few American women of good families; the latter being attracted by curiosity and a desire to see the children, who, they supposed, were Mexicans."

After the children were delivered, a crowd that swelled from twenty-five to three hundred white residents (it is not clear from the court records whether the people in the crowd were American or specifically Caucasian) went to some of the Mexican homes and demanded that the children be turned over to white families. The host families apparently complied with the demands. The crowd then went to solicit the support of the Phelps Dodge superintendent, identified only as "Mr. Mills, one of the leading citizens of the town." Mills led a visit to the Catholic clergy in Clifton to demand that all the children be housed in white homes. "As a result of these remonstrances, and a statement by Mr. Mills, that the American residents of Morenci would not suffer the children so to remain, the priest and the agent . . . visited the homes of the Mexicans having the children and obtained the surrender of them."

The New York Foundling Society, which oversaw the adoptions, quickly filed suit against those who had taken custody of the children, demanding their return to the society or to the Mexican families. Upon the testimony of copper company employees and white Morenci residents, the Arizona Supreme Court refused to return the children and described the Mexican families as "the lowest class of half-breed Mexican Indians . . . impecunious, illiterate, unacquainted with the English language, vicious." The Foundling Society pursued its appeal all the way to the U.S. Supreme Court, in the first of many cases that emanated from Phelps Dodge–related events to the highest court of the land. The Supreme Court backed away from what could have been a strong stand for civil rights. It held that the children's personal freedom had not been denied by the white families and that federal law therefore did not provide jurisdiction for it to rule on the dispute. The Arizona Supreme Court ruling stood. At the time of the 1983 strike, this story was still remembered by Mexican-American families in Clifton and Morenci as an example of the way Phelps Dodge historically had disregarded the rights of Mexicans.

In September 1915, with wartime demand raising copper prices, more than four thousand workers at several western mining companies, including the Phelps Dodge properties, called for a wage increase and recognition of the national hard rock miner's union, the Western Federation of Miners (WFM). At that time, white laborers earned approximately $2.80 a day, and Mexicans earned even less, $2.39 per day. (Both white and Mexican laborers earned more than the average national manufacturing wage of about $11 per week but shift bribes and inflated rents in company towns cost laborers as much as $25 per month.) Operating under the name Detroit Copper Company, Phelps Dodge was determined to keep the new union out, and, along with the Arizona Copper and the Shannon Copper companies, refused to negotiate. All of the Clifton-Morenci district was idled by the resulting strike. The mine managers agreed to hold talks only after their employees promised not to demand recognition of the WFM, which Phelps Dodge regarded as an outside agitator. (The company was said to be more willing to negotiate with the American Federation of Labor because it had no interest in organizing the common laborer). Even with the employees' guarantee, managers rejected the miners' contract demands and broke off the talks.

Then Arizona Governor George Hunt, the bald, roly-poly former miner, stepped in. Considered a friend of labor, Hunt wanted to avoid any incident like the tragedies a year earlier in the Colorado coalfields. On April 20, 1914, miners had struck the Rockefeller-owned properties in Ludlow, Colorado. Federal and state troops who were sent in opened fire on strikers and their families and set the workers' tent village ablaze. That massacre left thirty-nine workers and family members dead, including two women and eleven children. On September 15, 1915, a few days after the Arizona strike began, Governor Hunt took the train into Clifton in an effort to restore calm. He addressed the Clifton strikers in a speech at the town square: "Those people who had the temerity to stand up for their rights are heroes and not traitors," Hunt declared to a cheering crowd.

Apparently hoping to draw public attention to the company cause and enlist strikebreakers, the mine managers then declared to newspapers (many of which the companies owned) that they were in imminent danger of a revolt. After staging a flamboyant "escape" on railcars from Arizona into New Mexico, the owners set up a worker's camp that was expected to be used to organize strikebreakers.

At this point, Governor Hunt called in the National Guard—and ordered them to keep strikebreakers out of town. This was an unprecedented move in favor of the union movement by an American governor. National political journals like *The New Republic* and the *Nation* quickly praised the handling of the strike as a model for the nation, and nationally known labor leaders made the difficult trek to these isolated Arizona towns to add their support for the strikers. Among these was Mother Jones, the well-known Illinois labor radical most often found among midwestern and southeastern coal miners. In her 1925 autobiography, she observed, "The strike of the miners in Arizona was one of the most remarkable strikes in the history of the American labor movement . . . [The miners] received large increases in wages and a standing grievance committee was recognized which was to act as intermediary between the operators and the miners." Mother Jones chose this opportunity to give a rousing, though perhaps sardonic, speech on unionism in the United States:

> I know that every man and woman here is a loyal member of the union. I refer to the United States, the union of all the states. I ask then: if in union there is strength for our nation, would there not be for labor! What one state could not get alone, what one miner against a powerful corporation could not achieve, can be achieved by the union. What is a good enough principle for an American citizen ought to be good enough for the working man to follow.

Although she praised the strike, Mother Jones also criticized the strikers for failing to stay with the new union movement. She noted in her writings that the miners "agreed to give up their charter in the Western Federation of Miners in return for a standing grievance committee. Thus they sold their birthright for a mess of potage. They were without the backing of a powerful national organization."

The Arizona miners' strike entered the national political consciousness when *The New Republic* magazine described the action as a model of peaceful negotiation. The 1915 Arizona settlement, the magazine wrote, might reverse the process "by which a handful of owners in New York, Boston or Edinburgh can impose upon ten or fifteen thousand men and women the choice between surrendering their liberties or starving." The magazine predicted that the same kinds of peaceful industrial actions could be replicated "if only the government protects the strikers in their rights." Walter Douglas, president of Phelps Dodge, wrote a scathing response, accusing the magazine of "half-baked philosophy from the highbrows." Governor Hunt responded in turn with an attack on Douglas in a subsequent issue, suggesting that Phelps Dodge officials had attempted to intimidate him into taking actions favorable to the company.

Back in Arizona, meanwhile, Hunt declared that this peaceful resolution of the strike "had no parallel in the industrial history of the United States." But to management at Phelps Dodge, the outcome was not a precedent worth repeating.

Following the 1915 strike, Phelps Dodge executives decided that, if the company was subject to control by state officials, it would have to take a larger role in determining who those officials were. First the company pushed a no-confidence referendum against Hunt that nearly unseated him prior to the 1916 elections. Next, according to

James Byrkit, author of *Forging the Copper Collar*, a highly regarded study of the early Phelps Dodge:

> The counteroffensive by management grew to include the control of every aspect of Arizona life—economic, political, social and even religious. The mining men intimidated editors, threatened ministers, bought sheriffs, seduced lawmakers and bullied union leaders. They rigged elections and manipulated the legislature. . . . Between 1915 and 1918, the companies, led by Walter Douglas, completely reversed the direction of Arizona politics and destroyed the liberal influence in the state.

By a disputed margin of thirty votes (out of nearly sixty thousand votes cast) Progressive George Hunt lost the 1916 gubernatorial election to Republican Thomas Campbell. Campbell, a former county tax assessor who liked to wear a ten-gallon Stetson, had drawn the strong support of the copper companies. With Campbell in office and King Copper gaining control of the legislature and media, Phelps Dodge began to test the new political machine. In 1917, the newly named International Union of Mine, Mill and Smelter Workers (formerly the Western Federation of Miners) and the Wobblies organized a strike in Bisbee to gain a bigger share of the wartime copper price windfall, which had doubled Phelps Dodge profits. The two unions were in competition with each other for members, leading to a heavy surge in organizing activity. The IWW also opposed U.S. involvement in World War I. One prominent historian has written of the organization's ideological goals that although the IWW "often denounced capitalism in strident terms . . . the Wobblies remained in practice a remarkably non-ideological, pragmatic group, who succeeded in organizing thousands of unskilled workers long ignored by [Samuel] Gompers and the American Federation of Labor."

But Phelps Dodge, in language that sounded like the pretext for its own battle, called the IWW "an organization founded on principles inimical to good government in times of peace and treasonable in times of war." Company president Walter Douglas, who was quoted as saying about unions that "you cannot compromise with a rattlesnake," quietly planned one of the most remarkable attacks on labor ever devised. He arranged for union members who worked at Phelps Dodge to be rounded up and herded into cattle cars at dawn at the point of machine guns. This was Phelps Dodge's answer to Hunt's boast only two years before of an action that "had no parallel in industrial history." A kind of company-enforced "Trail of Tears," this action would be the largest forced migration by a private corporation in American history.

The Bisbee Deportation

The deportation began on July 12, 1917. Wearing white armbands, vigilantes under the leadership of Bisbee sheriff Harry Wheeler went house to house in the ramshackle mining community, rousing anyone who had been blacklisted as a "supporter" of the strike against Phelps Dodge or any other "suspicious-looking person." The so-called Loyalty League members were armed and authorized to shoot if necessary. One union miner and a deputy were killed when the miner opened fire rather than yield to authorities. In all, more than twelve hundred men and a few women (no exact count was made) were rounded up and marched to a baseball field for processing. All but the women and those who publicly swore allegiance to the company were then pressed into cattle cars still laden with manure and shipped across the state line to Hermanas, New Mexico. Company biographer Cleland wrote, "According to the testimony of the superintendent of the El Paso and Southwestern [Railroad], orders for the actual deportation by the railroad were issued by Walter Douglas, president of Phelps Dodge."

The *New York Times*, which only a few weeks earlier had encouraged formal deportations of antiwar radicals from the United States, called the action an "inhumanity" and wrote, "Bisbee had the right to defend itself against violence, not to do violence." The deported workers were left stranded without sufficient water or food in the New Mexico desert until federal troops were summoned to give them provisions. Meanwhile, the Loyalty League established kangaroo courts to "try" alleged union supporters who wanted to work in Bisbee in the future, including any who attempted to return from the desert. There is no record of how many of the deportees ever made it back to Bisbee.

Years after the incident, Bisbee resident Katie Pintek recalled in an interview that "people were standing and crying. It was like the army had prisoners. If they saw someone about to run, they were going to shoot. Two did get killed that day. . . . What kind of America was that?" she asked.

President Woodrow Wilson—whose closest friend and biggest contributor was Phelps Dodge director Cleveland Dodge, a Princeton classmate—wired Arizona governor Thomas Campbell, stating somewhat diplomatically that "I look upon such actions with great apprehension. A very serious responsibility is assumed when such precedents are set." Wilson's presidential letters show an unusual gap during this period, suggesting that his usual written correspondence with Dodge was removed and destroyed. (Dodge family members have told the current editor of President Wilson's papers, Professor Arthur Link of Princeton, that no correspondence exists, a hole that Link calls "puzzling." Link's view is that President Wilson "loved [Dodge] as a friend" but that the president kept the friendship separate from business issues).

Rather than issue orders for U.S. troops to enforce the deportees' return, President Wilson ordered the troops to shelter the deportees. He later dispatched a team of mediators to investigate the Bisbee incident and other western labor strife. Whatever President Wilson's immediate response to the events, the mediators were ultimately empowered to make a thorough investigation.

Felix Frankfurter's Great Adventure

Felix Frankfurter, then a Harvard law professor on loan to the War Department, led the five-member President's Mediation Commission, which departed Washington by train in late September 1917. The trip was for Frankfurter a sometimes romantic, sometimes harsh ride through the landscape of early American labor history. Then thirty-seven years old, Frankfurter was at the outset a bit testy about this assignment from the president, complaining to his future wife, Marion Denman, that "I'm . . . sort of a dry nurse for various pets of this administration." But Frankfurter wrote later that, as he traveled "deeper and deeper into these marooned outposts of the country," he came to believe that the mining town strife challenged "our American striving to realize the democratic faith."

Members of the commission spent hundreds of hours listening to testimony from miners and traveled to all the same Arizona towns that Mother Jones not long before had stirred with her speeches. Frankfurter was obviously affected by these visits, mailing off a remarkable series of letters to various prominent Easterners, from Supreme Court Justice Louis Brandeis to federal judge Learned Hand. His curling script appears on letterheads ranging from the Copper Queen Hotel in Bisbee to the Dominion "European Plan" Hotel in

Globe, Arizona, as well as on War Department stationery—some extra pages Frankfurter apparently had left over from a recent assignment in Spain.

Historian Michael Parrish presents these Arizona letters in a biography, *Felix Frankfurter and His Times*. A future Supreme Court justice, Frankfurter wrote to Judge Hand about the Bisbee deportation that "the thing is so shallow and so pathetic, as well as brutal. These old bags, who have fought labor and unions as poison for decades, now wrap themselves in the flag and are confirmed in their old biases and . . . obscurantism by a passionate patriotism. Gee—but it's awful and then they wonder at the fecundity of the IWW."

Frankfurter and the commission examined the mining companies' claims that the IWW was fomenting worker rebellion in order to stall the war effort. The commission found that, to the contrary, the workers had legitimate grievances. Frankfurter wrote Justice Brandeis that the miners' complaint "is as to their position as wage-earners. It's . . . a fight for the status of free manhood." Waxing even more philosophical in another letter to Marion Denman, Frankfurter wrote that the mine managers "control a quarry and forget it's also a community. . . . In a word, there is no fellowship for [the miners] in the great industrial enterprise which absorbs them."

The Mediation Commission remained in Arizona for nearly two months, "sleeping and eating in railroad cars, endlessly listening to and negotiating with managers, workers, public officials, and ordinary citizens, who filled stenographers' notebooks with testimony that exhibited their hatred, fear and ignorance." At one point, Frankfurter himself was reportedly accosted by a Bisbee deputy sheriff, who walked into Frankfurter's private railcar with a six-gun in his holster. The deputy, Frank Johnson, told the presidential aide, "Well, Mr. Frankfurter, you Jewish son-of-a-bitch, I just called to tell you, you had better be out of this town by six o'clock tonight." The source of this story, Bisbee resident Frank Cullen Brophy, said that Frankfurter did leave Bisbee soon after, and Brophy asserted that "Bisbee had little use for Wobblies or presidential investigators."

Under Frankfurter's guidance, the Mediation Commission produced a document geared to calm labor radicalism as well as corporate vigilantism. Frankfurter believed that the federal government should co-opt the IWW and other labor radicals by providing support to more moderate labor unions. Government conciliation and negotiation machinery could be set up, he recommended, through the American Federation of Labor.

Frankfurter's personal appeals to mine owners brought provisional agreements to allow arbitration on wage and other disputes, but little in the agreements was ever executed. "Wherever possible, the mine operators purged [American Federation of Labor] members as well as Wobblies, rejected out of hand consideration of their employees' grievances, subverted the elected grievance committee and refused to adjust wages to the cost of living," writes historian Melvyn Dubofsky.

Essentially, Phelps Dodge had already gotten what it wanted: control over copper production and Arizona law. Working with the federal government could only be a step backwards.

Despite the commission's mild report and recommendations, a high-level war of letters began between Frankfurter and former President Theodore Roosevelt, who, to say the least, disagreed with the Frankfurter report. Roosevelt wrote Frankfurter on December 19, 1917, and accused him of taking "on behalf of the Administration an attitude which seems to me to be fundamentally that of Trotsky and other Bolsheviki leaders in Russia, an attitude which may be fraught with mischief to this country." Roosevelt wrote of the IWW, "These are the Bolsheviki of America and the Bolsheviki are just as bad as the Romanoffs and are at the moment a greater menace to orderly freedom." It is not insignificant that the leaders of the Bisbee Loyalty League had been Roosevelt Rough Riders.

Frankfurter responded at length in a letter to "My dear Colonel Roosevelt":

> When opportunity offers I should like to go over with you in detail the whole industrial situation in Arizona and to make you realize the clash of economic forces that are at stake, and make you realize the long, persistent and organized opposition to "social justice," to the establishment of machinery for the attainment of such justice, which culminated in strikes in the Arizona copper districts last year. It is easy to disregard economic abuses, to insist on the exercise of autocratic power by raising the false cry of "disloyalty."

Phelps Dodge executives and others were eventually indicted on federal criminal conspiracy charges for the Bisbee deportation. But in those days, even a corporate conspiracy to imprison and deport workers across state lines was not fully addressed by federal laws. A federal trial court dismissed the charges, calling them a matter for state courts alone to examine. On appeal, the U.S. Supreme Court in *U.S. v. Wheeler* (the Bisbee sheriff, Harry Wheeler, was represented by future Supreme Court Justice Charles Evans Hughes) agreed that there was no federal authority to prosecute such alleged criminal offenses. (Under today's law, Phelps Dodge officials could be prosecuted under several provisions of the civil rights and criminal laws). State charges were eventually filed, but the trial of Sheriff Wheeler in Tombstone ended not only in acquittal but with jurors publicly applauding his actions.

The Bisbee deportation thus marked the ascendancy of Phelps Dodge as copper king. Industrial unions like the International Union of Mine, Mill and Smelter Workers and the IWW entered a long period of stagnancy—in fact, the federal government followed Phelps Dodge by arresting and imprisoning IWW leaders in Chicago and elsewhere for opposing World War I. Arizona labor power ebbed throughout the 1920s and 1930s.

Labor Law Outlaw

It would take America's first national labor legislation and another war to renew labor organizing activity at Phelps Dodge. In 1935, Congress passed the National Labor Relations Act, providing for the first time federal protection of the right to organize a union and to strike. In the 1940s, demand for copper in military production suddenly turned good management-labor relations into a national security priority. Arizona mines were federalized, with some workers serving seven-day shifts on army commissions. With such an increased demand for labor, industrial unions for the common laborer finally made inroads.

Some craft unions under the American Federation of Labor had remained at Phelps Dodge after the tumultuous early century brawls, preserving union representation for machine and rail operators, boilermakers, and other so-called skilled workers. But these were exclusive organizations, often working in tandem with the company to keep the better jobs away from racial or ethnic minorities and unskilled whites. Company supervisors expressed this caste system by referring to Mexican-American, Native American, and southern white laborers, respectively, as "Chilis, Indians and Okies," according to Andrés Padilla, a Phelps Dodge smelter worker who retired in 1977 after thirty-four years. The slurs were intended as a slap at the

Congress of Industrial Organizations (CIO), which strove to bring equal rights and pay to all these workers.

Birth of a Union

Padilla and future union president David Velasquez hauled the very first ore out of the new Morenci open pit in the 1940s. Despite several years of college in Tucson, Velasquez was limited by the company and craft unions to the lowliest labor jobs because of his Mexican ethnicity. "I walked the shovel through town, up Burro Alley, the main street, then climbed a ridge to get it all to the pit," remembered Velasquez, a tall, charismatic man. When the first bulldozers replaced the electric shovels, Velasquez had a job assisting those operators. Again, Mexicans were blocked from the higher-paying operator jobs.

"The fact that I was working with bulldozers meant that I would be in the Operating Engineers union of the American Federation of Labor [AFL]," Velasquez said. "So I signed up and paid the dues. A day or two later, the business agent called and told me, 'We think you Mexican boys should be together in a different union.' " It was called the Federated Labor Union, also under the AFL.

The company went along with the unions' racial preferences for whites, again blocking the way for craft promotions. "That was the end of my interest in the AF of L," said Velasquez. "I never did go back." Instead, he helped organize a branch of the CIO, which promoted equal opportunity for all races. The union organizers met secretly at spots along the Gila and San Francisco rivers outside Clifton—what Velasquez called the *tules*, Spanish slang for "the boonies." At the first meeting, a regional activist from the International Union of Mine, Mill and Smelter Workers (Mine-Mill) told workers that a union could mean better wages, improved safety, and pressure on both the company and craft unions to turn over valuable apprenticeships to minorities.

With Padilla and Velasquez leading the sign-up campaign, the union garnered strong support, especially among Mexican-Americans. After two years of organizing, the union won a certification vote in 1942. The long drought for laborers was ended, and the new union was designated "Morenci Miners Local 616 of the International Union of Mine, Mill and Smelter Workers." The victory was a cause for celebration and songwriting in Clifton and Morenci. For nearly a

year, Mine-Mill represented the entire labor force of more than
three thousand employees at Morenci, because all workers had been
included in the bargaining unit vote. But the celebration was soon
muted. White craft union leaders and the company encouraged
competition to deny Mine-Mill a solid bloc of supporters. Later in
1942, a dozen craft unions reasserted their independence under the
American Federation of Labor and decided to divide the representation turf of the Clifton-Morenci workers. The new Mine-Mill local
was immediately referred to as "the Mexican union" and as a result
of this "divide" strategy, Phelps Dodge avoided a common front in
any effort at contract negotiations.

Phelps Dodge on Trial

The company had a "conquer" strategy for labor as well. In 1941,
Phelps Dodge would make labor history with legal briefs, rather than
with machine guns. Mine-Mill had begun an organizing drive again
in Bisbee in the mid–1930s, one of the first after the 1917 deportations.
To gain official company recognition, union supporters called a strike;
Phelps Dodge responded by firing thirty-five union members. When
the new National Labor Relations Board reinstated them, the company still refused work to two men, identified in court records as
Curtis and Daugherty, on the sole grounds that they were union
troublemakers. The union protested that, when Congress had passed
the National Labor Relations Act, it had established that all workers,
including prospective hires, should be protected from antiunion
discrimination. Could companies like Phelps Dodge wantonly refuse
to hire union activists? This question went all the way to the Supreme Court.

Phelps Dodge did not attempt to hide its view that, as one friend
of the company put it, "labor unions were anathema" to Phelps
Dodge. Company attorney Denison Kitchel argued before the Court,
"It is not an unfair labor practice for an employer to refuse employment because of union membership or activity . . . and the [National
Labor Relations] Board has no authority to order the employment of
or the payment of back pay to such a person."

The junior justice called on to write the opinion deciding Phelps
Dodge's bold claim in *Phelps Dodge v. National Labor Relations Board*
was none other than President Wilson's special envoy to Bisbee
twenty-four years earlier, Felix Frankfurter. Known later in his career

as a proponent of judicial restraint, Frankfurter called here for a strong statement by the court in favor of federally protected labor rights. He responded to Phelps Dodge's claims with history as well as the law. He lambasted the company's reading of federal labor laws as "textual mutilation":

> Discrimination against union labor in the hiring of men is a dam to self-organization . . . . The effect of such discrimination is not confined to the actual denial of employment; it inevitably operates against the whole idea of the legitimacy of organization. In a word, it undermines the principle which, as we have seen, is recognized as basic to the attainment of industrial peace.

The company was eventually required to hire Curtis and Daugherty, and the "Phelps Dodge Rule" became a touchstone in American labor law and history: companies that refuse to hire workers because of their union membership, as Phelps Dodge had refused Curtis and Daugherty, violate the law. Phelps Dodge's antiunion reputation had now been certified by the U.S. Supreme Court.

Mine-Mill Victory, Mine-Mill Troubles

In the early to mid–1940s, wartime price controls and wage agreements brokered through the War Labor Board marked a time of peace and patriotism in the copper industry. Some miners were put under a federal commission for wartime production, and the federal government granted Phelps Dodge $26 million for establishing a new open pit mine in Morenci—more than one-third of the start-up costs. When the war ended, many Mexican-American soldiers returned home to Arizona mining towns proud of their achievement abroad and demanding better treatment as workers at home; in 1946 that momentum was channeled into Mine-Mill Local 616. Phelps Dodge was still resisting a union contract and in the summer of 1946, the union called a strike for health benefits and equal wages for workers of all races. After holding out for 107 days, Mine-Mill finally won an agreement. Thus, five years after Phelps Dodge's embarrassment at the Supreme Court and four years after the founding of the Morenci union, Mine-Mill had its first-ever Morenci contract. The man who negotiated it, David Velasquez, was elected union president. His work was so influential that union members carried a copy of that first contract to future negotiations. Velasquez served for fourteen

years as union president and became known in the copper towns as
el papa de todos—the father of them all.

But part of Velasquez's tenure became a lesson in union futility—
even with Phelps Dodge's antiunion policies for the moment in
abeyance. On the positive side, the union emphasized worker education, aggressive health and safety enforcement, and, most of all,
unity at the bargaining table. Mine-Mill's primary economic goal was
to join all the mining unions in a coalition that could, if necessary,
call an industry-wide strike to raise lagging southwestern wages. But
the Denver-based union's organizing staff and advisers, as well as
some executives, were accused of having ties to the Communist
Party. Maurice Travis, the International Mine-Mill president for one
year in 1946, eventually admitted his party membership. Subsequent
leaders, although they denied any direct ties, steadfastly refused to
sign noncommunist oaths, which were required by the 1947 federal
Taft-Hartley Act. At the same time, the union boycotted federal
labor administration agencies like the National Labor Relations Board
(NLRB), weakening its organizing and bargaining position. When the
leaders finally did sign the oaths in 1949, they were not found to be
credible, even by other unionists. As a result, the CIO—of which
Mine-Mill was a founding member in 1935—put the union on trial in
a series of hearings in San Francisco in 1950. The CIO leadership,
which saw its wider credibility and bargaining strength weakened
whenever companies or politicians raised these charges, concluded
that communists controlled major aspects of the union and expelled
Mine-Mill from the organization. "The union wasn't allowed to
participate in any [NLRB-sponsored certification] elections, so we lost
half our membership nationwide," said Velasquez, who described
the Morenci Mine-Mill leadership as "FDR Democrats." In fact, the
100,000 rank-and-file members of Mine-Mill nationwide were never
viewed as having communist affiliation—labor relations experts called
them "good CIO unionists." They cared about the pay dirt issues of
organizing, education, and winning better contracts.

But in the 1950s those very issues were jeopardized. The CIO
"awarded" the Mine-Mill territory to the United Steelworkers, meaning that the Steelworkers union, which favored mainstream economic
policies over any ideological advocacy, was encouraged to challenge
Mine-Mill for members. Velasquez earned his title *el papa de todos* by
protecting the Morenci Mine-Mill chapter from destructive raiding by
other unions that decimated Mine-Mill unions elsewhere and by

helping to restore a positive picture of rank-and-file leadership to the national union. Craft unions, the Steelworkers, the United Mine-workers, and others attempted to organize or raid operations represented by Mine-Mill in order to enlarge their own membership, Velasquez recalled. Union activities came to include both representation drives and self-protection. "I used to go to different meetings throughout the country," said Velasquez. "We had what you'd call the PD [Phelps Dodge] Council made up of all the Mine-Mill locals in different PD plants—the Laurel Hill, New York, refinery, the El Paso refinery, the fabricating plant in Brunswick, New Jersey. Another in Fort Wayne, Indiana, another in Los Angeles." Those were in addition to the Phelps Dodge Arizona properties. From a 1953 strike, Velasquez helped produce a training film that spread a message of Mine-Mill ethnic diversity and bargaining victories around the country. (The film reappeared in public showings during other strikes, including in 1983, to rededicate unionists to their struggle.)

Locally, Velasquez's Morenci Miners also considered themselves brothers- and sisters-in-arms with a nearby Mine-Mill local in Silver City, New Mexico, whose strike victory against Empire Zinc was enshrined in the 1953 movie *Salt of the Earth*. Clifton and Morenci residents knew the story of that strike against wage and workplace discrimination so well that they referred to it in shorthand as "Salt." Like other blacklisted products of that era, the movie was often banned from theaters—millionaire Howard Hughes even developed a plan to prevent its distribution—but the film drew huge crowds at the union halls where it was shown. At the union hall in Clifton, the film showed round-the-clock when it first came out so that workers of all shifts could see it.

On the whole, Mine-Mill won some important contracts, including one in 1955 in Morenci that provided full medical coverage as well as higher wages. National union leadership also created precedents in bargaining, such as the three-year contract in copper in 1956. Finally, Mine-Mill offered its devoted membership something that unions in other parts of the country often ignored: social activism and an emphasis on member education. Organizers and negotiators like Sylvain Schnaittacher in the Arizona region were legendary for simultaneously maintaining close personal relations with members, cajoling employers at the bargaining table, and, on the side, teaching university courses on labor relations.

Still, the occasional education, organizing, and bargaining successes of Mine-Mill turned out to be a mixed blessing for the miners at Phelps Dodge: they had a union, but it was an outcast. Even without any communists in the local union at Morenci, Mine-Mill often found itself isolated. One reason was the lingering racism of craft union members, who wanted to protect their turf from Mexican-Americans. But Mine-Mill was also quarantined because other unionists spread the word of the national leaders' communist affiliation. Members heard the political smears as a kind of whispering campaign: "The AFL (American Federation of Labor) unions and Phelps Dodge would bring it up and raise a lot of stink over it," said Padilla. "They were always trying to break the CIO." Local unionists were not eager to join a coalition led by outsiders who would bring the word "red" to their towns—this prospect made the entire notion of multi-union bargaining suspect. When Congress passed the 1954 Communist Control Act, national Mine-Mill leaders faced not only the opprobrium of fellow unionists but criminal prosecution by the Justice Department.

"From 1955 on," write copper industry experts George Hildebrand and Garth Mangum,

> the Mine-Mill leadership was under constant legal attack by the federal government, which sapped the union's finances, distracted its officers' attention from union interests and objectives, and discredited and isolated the organization to the point where it became incapable of providing bargaining leadership or even of negotiating effectively on behalf of its members.

Meanwhile, organizing territories became so severely divided among competing unions that companies could easily play the unions off against each other at contract time. Dozens of Mine-Mill locals faced representation challenges and votes from other unions, sapping the Mine-Mill treasury and distracting leadership from day-to-day workplace issues. A significant example of Mine-Mill's failure to win discipline from other unions came in 1959 at Phelps Dodge. The union had called strikes throughout the industry, but was finding it difficult to convince the craft unions to stick with the Mine-Mill position. Even the United Steelworkers, whose wage and benefit goals closely matched Mine-Mill, refused to coordinate its bargaining with its competitor. Phelps Dodge took advantage of that lack of discipline, using replacement workers against one union when another union settled separately. (Richard Moolick, one of the Morenci managers during this 1959 strike, recalled this strike's lessons as the company president in 1983.) Mine-Mill hung on through the mid–1960s at the Phelps Dodge properties in Clifton and Morenci, but its broader organizational goals had been destroyed by anticommunism and union opportunism.

Still, the communitarian ethic of the Mine-Mill years deserves special consideration in light of the later takeover by other unions. If Mine-Mill failed to coordinate the union movement, it succeeded in winning new economic and civil rights for Mexican-Americans and other laborers in the mines, mills, and smelters of Arizona. Many locals, including Morenci Miners Local 616 in Clifton (which led the 1983 strike), stayed loyal to Mine-Mill right through its 1967 merger. The union had fostered community activism and education. The Steelworkers were initially disparaged as outsiders. When, decades later, the hierarchy of the Pittsburgh-based Steelworkers faced its most critical local test in the 1983 Phelps Dodge strike, that insider-outsider tension still had not been entirely resolved.

"Heaven in '67"

During the decades of union formation and struggle, the copper industry itself was reaching maturity. Companies like Kennecott, ASARCO, Anaconda, and Magma had developed significant ore bodies in the western United States and demand for copper had steadily increased: U.S. production of copper went from about 850,000 tons in 1947 to about 1.6 million tons in 1970, and Arizona's share of the production climbed to 60 percent. (Better than one dollar in every ten earned by all workers in Arizona came from the copper industry.) During the same period, employment in the copper industry nationwide rose to a peak of more than seventy-five thousand employees in fabrication and production. The time was ripe for a new union initiative.

On January 18, 1967, after years of belligerent competition and membership raids, Morenci Miners Local 616 and the other Mine-Mill holdouts agreed to a merger with the powerful, million-member United Steelworkers of America. Stridently anticommunist, the Steelworkers had been cautious about any merger lest they, too, suffer the taint of Mine-Mill's alleged links with the Communist Party. They preferred to absorb each Mine-Mill union one by one. But the previous year, the U.S. Supreme Court quashed convictions against

Mine-Mill leaders for allegedly lying on anticommunist oaths. The
path was cleared for a merger and a flexing of new union muscle as
some forty thousand Mine-Mill members came into the Steelworkers.
Steelworkers vice president Joseph Molony, who later took over the
copper unions, said of Mine-Mill, "We used to call them red, and
now we call them red-blooded."

Buoyed by the new membership and its own successes in large-
scale organizing in the steel industry, Steelworkers leadership in
Pittsburgh planned a united front against the non-steel companies—
mostly copper companies like the "Big Four": Phelps Dodge, Kennecott, ASARCO, and Anaconda. Steelworkers leaders felt that the
companies had for decades shortchanged workers in take-home pay,
whipsawing the different unions against each other. (Statistical surveys, although somewhat unreliable, show the 1967 national manufacturing wage at $3 an hour, the average national mining wage at
$3.10 an hour, but the average Arizona mining wage at about $2
an hour.)

The AFL-CIO sponsored an all-unions unity conference in 1966 in
Chicago, where representatives heard for the first time a coherent
call for a strategy called "pattern bargaining." The AFL-CIO felt that
companies of similar size producing similar products should be
pressed into similar contracts. That idea received wide support from
the thirteen unions and more than 320 members attending the Chicago conference. Twenty-five unions sent representatives the following year to Salt Lake City, where the unions established a specific list
of uniform wage, benefit, and health insurance demands. In all, the
demands amounted to an increase of nearly $2 per hour including
wages, pensions, vacations, and other benefits.

Lighthearted unionists called the book of union demands "Heaven
in '67," but company observers dourly called it "the Arizona joke
book." The test of these demands, however, was dead serious: with
their coalition, the unions could sweep the industry with strikes if
the companies failed to agree to demands. In a 1969 study, labor
scholar William Chernish found the new coalition a particularly
intriguing event in American labor relations, bringing on "the charades, strangers and coalition manoevering" of a fully empowered
labor movement. Chernish went so far as to label this effort "the
Great Confrontation" of the decade and predicted that the 1967
negotiations and strikes "may come to be known as the classic case
in the study of coalition bargaining."

The reason the 1967 negotiation was the classic case was because, win or lose, the copper unions were undertaking an immensely complex and risky bargaining program—a program that eventually would have to be mediated by a U.S. president. This challenge was about far more than a "pattern" or even a "coalition"—it was about reordering the entire relationship between labor and management in the copper industry. In steel and autos, industrial unions had managed over the years to win the right to represent virtually all of the industries' workers. In the auto industry, for example, although the companies never physically sat down together with the unions, there was essentially just one union that could press a pattern contract on each company and call a strike if a company refused—the United Autoworkers. These unified structures had never been successfully applied in copper or the other nonferrous metals, because the craft unions there had been so determined to preserve their individual strongholds and because American labor laws encouraged fragmentation by job categories. That's where the "risk" came in: failure to hold together might show corporate America that, in industries with more than one union, companies had only to set the craft and industrial unions against each other to win. The 1966 and 1967 union meetings attempted to make believers out of the craft unions so that the copper companies might gradually be pressed into accepting a unified labor structure, replicating what had been achieved in steel and auto.

Arguments for pattern bargaining became a kind of "party line" stance for American unions. Solidarity in American labor might never mean social action through political parties (that was the inchoate goal of failed unions like Mine-Mill); but solidarity in the "business unionism" sense could mean fighting together for common—and higher—wage and benefit structures. It was, indeed, a powerful idea: when unions with like interests held together in a coalition, they created a kind of labor monopoly. A company that might once have held its competitive advantage in an industry by whipsawing the unions and paying lower wages would now face a united front and thereby be forced to win its cost advantage on other nonlabor issues. The pattern principle was one of justice, but it worked through company balance sheets: if one company held out against the union coalition, it faced the prospect of losing business to competing companies during a strike. The key prerequisite for the pattern strategy was that the unions maintain a heroic discipline against any temptation to settle individually. Any offer by the companies would have to be certified by the unions as a whole, not simply by an individual local's vote. Under this system, union members might realize continuity and predictability in wages and benefits. The unions claimed that companies, too, might benefit from pattern bargaining by receiving stable three-year contracts complete with no-strike clauses. By taking wages out of competition, unions argued that they might also lead the companies to compete on "quality" issues like workplace innovation and technology.

Just as the first confrontations with labor fifty years earlier displayed the might of Phelps Dodge, so too the 1967 union campaign revealed the countervailing strength of the new union culture. Determined to have a grand christening of this new vessel, the Steelworkers (easily the largest of the major represented unions), put Vice President Molony in charge of the new nonferrous conference and the negotiations. Molony successfully convinced the craft unions to stick with the pattern approach through what Chernish called the "highest common denominator"—contract demands broad enough to satisfy any union. (Hence, the union program that miners dubbed "Heaven in '67.") Molony also reassured the crafts by promising them a strong voice at the industry conference and a seat at the bargaining table in each negotiating committee. Cass Alvin, Steelworkers western regional spokesman, recalled that the enthusiasm in 1967 led to a revival of the old universalist Wobbly rhetoric of "One Big Union." Said Alvin, "The 1967 negotiation was a model, a showpiece for the AFL-CIO. We had different union entities, different dues structures, different ratification procedures, different officers. . . . But it was E Pluribus Unum.

"No place, nobody could show as dramatic evidence of solidarity as consolidated bargaining in the copper industry," he said. Years later, when the unions were struggling to hold together during the 1983 Phelps Dodge strike, this ingathering of once-fractured unions would be invoked like a mantra of solidarity: "Remember '67."

The Longest Industrial Strike in U.S. History

When the copper companies learned that the unions were demanding uniform contracts not only at mining properties, but at manufacturing and refining plants as well, they quickly rejected the union proposals. An industry-wide strike, from California to New Jersey, began on July 15, 1967. More than sixty thousand workers walked out at seventy-three locations, virtually shutting down copper, as well as lead, zinc, and silver production throughout the United States. It was an unprecedented show of strength by diverse U.S. unions, and it eventually became the longest industry-wide strike in American history.

All the Phelps Dodge properties closed down. At that time, American companies rarely sought to replace strikers with outside workers, although they had the legal right to do so under a 1938 U.S. Supreme Court decision called *NLRB v. Mackay Radio*. A "gentleman's agreement" guided relations between labor and management—especially big labor and big business like the Steelworkers and Phelps Dodge. Replacing workers was sure to destroy bargaining relationships and might also damage future production. In mining, neglecting a mine could lead to expensive erosion or flooding; a mistake by inexperienced replacements could ruin a furnace and injure workers. In the 1967 strike, only one company, ASARCO, used permanent replacements—and at a refinery rather than a mine or smelter. The appearance of forty replacement workers at the Baltimore facility brought a furious, sometimes violent response from the unions but appeared to have little if any effect on the bargaining. Elsewhere, the strike was remarkable for its civility. Just as there were no replacement workers, there was also no violence at the gate. Pickets peacefully walked their circles and hoped the negotiators would find a way of putting them back to work soon. But there were large gaps between the union and company positions.

The problem initially was not so much the unions' demand for a pattern contract as their attempt to make copper look like the steel industry—the coalition led by the Steelworkers insisted on extending the pattern vertically to each company's manufacturing and refining plants. As much as possible, the Steelworkers wanted to make wages, benefits, and contract expiration dates uniform throughout the industry. In steel, all the major companies had agreed to bargain collectively with the union; the producers could pass wage or benefit increases along to steel consumers. But the copper companies treated such union efforts like poison. One of their concerns was that wages were uneven across the industry and tended to be lowest at the manufacturing facilities. An industry-wide arrangement would put pressure on companies to raise the wage rates in the lower-pay sectors of the industry. As the employers resisted, the strike dragged on through the summer and state economies began to suffer. Another coalition formed—this time of governors appealing to the union and company leaders to find a settlement. Failing in that, the governors called on President Lyndon Johnson to intervene. The president initially authorized Secretary of Labor Willard Wirtz to meet with representatives of each side. Wirtz found "a complete and absolute stalemate," but the strike was allowed to take its course. More than six months after the strike began, President Johnson became concerned about Vietnam War supplies and named a three-man board of inquiry, one that quickly became known as "the three Georges"—George Taylor, a well-known mediator and professor from the University of Pennsylvania Wharton School of Business; Monsignor George Higgins of the National Catholic Welfare Conference; and George Reedy, a former White House press secretary. The three failed to win the confidence of either side but produced a report that recommended limiting the unions' vertical reach by separating copper bargaining from other metals, and separating mining and refining from manufacturing.

The unions worried that what the panel was calling a "neutral" economic compromise might end up being forced upon them. Illustrating the determined rhetoric in the American labor movement in those years, Steelworkers vice president Molony responded to the panel's recommendation, saying that "if our friends in Washington are 'neutral' in the strike, then I'll be 'neutral' next November. Remember, the hottest corner in hell is reserved for those who remain neutral in a crisis."

Amid headlines of U.S. bombing raids on the Vietcong, President Johnson finally summoned the negotiators to the White House on March 1, 1968. As had happened in World Wars I and II as well as the Korean War, union bargaining power was now contending with national security considerations. The president declared, "In my judgment, the national interest requires further and immediate governmental effort to resolve the copper strike." Johnson summoned the core of his cabinet, including Defense Secretary Clark Clifford and Treasury Secretary Henry Fowler, to address the negotiators on concerns about balance of payments as well as the war effort. Phelps Dodge negotiator Pat Scanlon recalled in an interview with the *Arizona Republic* newspaper, "We were called to the White House and jawboned by the president. He instructed us to begin intensive negotiations in the Executive Office Building where he could keep an eye on us." Pointing to "the men who fight for all of us half a world away in Vietnam," the president called on the unions to reverse their opposition to the mediators' division of bargaining proposal. This was a hard call to resist. Steelworkers leaders saw that appeal as their moment of truth. They realized that they might never bring the non-steel producers into the same uniform bargaining structure as steel. The companies didn't want it, and now a president otherwise seen as a friend to labor didn't want it. The unions agreed to soften their demands. But even though the industry successfully resisted common contracts, the unions were determined to have their own unified command center—the so-called "Nonferrous Industry Conference" (NIC)—which could coordinate bargaining and enforce pattern contracts on a local level.

Winning the NIC became the unions' central task. A few days after the presidential jawboning session, Phelps Dodge elicited an agreement from the unions to bargain separately over the company's East Coast manufacturing plants and its southwestern mines. The first serious wage negotiations in months followed. An agreement was reached on the mines, smelters, and refineries, which the Steelworkers-led coalition submitted for approval to the new NIC. With that submission, Phelps Dodge negotiators stopped in their tracks, as if they had seen a ghost. The company was so strongly opposed to linkages with outside unions (even if just through the same contract demands) that its lawyers filed a charge before the NLRB. Phelps Dodge wanted the labor board to declare the copper unions' coalition conference a violation of federal labor laws. Phelps Dodge's complaint was that once a contract had been proposed, the local unions—not a conglomeration of unions from all over the country (and even Canada)—should make the decision about whether or not to accept the contract terms. Phelps Dodge won an initial administrative victory, but then, as was becoming a trend before the courts, lost the war. The NLRB first agreed with the company and ruled that the coalition's preapproval right over contracts was an attack on "the integrity of a bargaining unit," but the unions won a reversal of that decision in the U.S. Court of Appeals. Phelps Dodge appealed to the Supreme Court, but the Court refused to consider the case, letting the appeals court decision stand. The result was that the coalition and pattern, albeit in the mining and refining sector rather than industry-wide, could proceed as proposed by the copper conference. After eight and a half months, at the end of March 1968, Phelps Dodge and the other companies agreed to their first pattern contract.

Though the Phelps Dodge negotiators of 1967–68 might not have recognized it, the ghost that had visited this strike was the Western Federation of Miners from back in 1915. In that earlier era, Phelps Dodge granted higher wages and agreed to bargain with local unionists—but only after an agreement that the miners would forgo national union affiliation. That's what Mother Jones had called selling a birthright for potage. Now the new coalition reclaimed its birthright and a powerful national conference of copper unions was born. From 1968 onward, the company would be required to sit down with a Steelworkers-led coalition in the prime of its power.

Phelps Dodge Acolytes

There was an important additional result from this strike, a quiet footnote that eventually grew into a destructive ideological force against the unions. From his seat as chairman of the Wharton School's industry department, Professor Herbert Northrup, a former manager of labor relations at General Electric, seethed about the strike even as it was settled. He felt that in their effort at industry-wide bargaining the unions had casually skirted labor laws and that the NLRB had refused to protect the companies' rights. Northrup vented his frustration on the *New York Times* editorial page on March 26, 1968, writing, "The source of the danger [to collective bargaining] . . . is massive union power buildup by Government support of union malpractice and by Government maladministration of law." The same year as the strike, Northrup began a program at the Wharton School to reverse that "union power buildup," as he called it, by mustering company labor relations directors in frequent meetings, gathering files on unions (and sometimes individuals), and coordinating corporate attacks on liberal appointees to the NLRB. This program led to a series of Wharton books that provided a formula for weakening unions. One of his loyal partners in this project: Phelps Dodge Corporation.

The Perfection of Pattern Bargaining

From 1968 to 1983, pattern bargaining through the union coalition proved a resounding success at every three-year contract negotiation. Industrial relations scholars George Hildebrand and Garth Mangum have documented the issues for Phelps Dodge in the cycles of contracts. In 1971, the unions demanded and won the first cost-of-living adjustments from all the employers, when Phelps Dodge employees went on strike for about three weeks. In 1974, all the companies resisted a short-lived coalition attempt to win a common job classification system. When that demand was dropped, Phelps Dodge still held out in order to keep the overall wage increase down. The cost-of-living adjustments remained in all the contracts. In 1977 and 1980, according to Hildebrand, Phelps Dodge again resisted cost-of-living increases, taking a ninety-day walkout in 1980 before accepting the unions' demands.

For the most part, the union coalition held together. Sometimes independent-minded union leaders took on the Steelworkers' leadership, such as in the 1976 negotiations at ANAMAX (a smaller copper producer), when a Teamsters leader told workers to defy a strike order. Other small companies like Duval were at times allowed to go their own way as well. But union unity was the rule, with few exceptions. In the fifteen years from 1968 to 1983, starting wages in copper rose at an unprecedented average rate of 14 percent a year. By 1983, the average pay for a union worker at Phelps Dodge was about $12 an hour ($26,000 per year), plus benefits.

In winning these raises, the unions also established with the company a ritual of power. Although the days of deportations at gunpoint and staged "escapes" from town were fading memories, Phelps Dodge maintained a reputation as the hardest, most resistant bargainer. It never continued operations during strikes and never used permanent replacements during these years, but, in fact, deeply embedded within the company culture was a preference for the earlier days of hard-line resistance to labor. Longtime Phelps Dodge counsel John Boland, Jr., said that the company was ever vigilant in looking for ways to cut labor costs. Some officials believed the best approach was to engage the unions in what he described as "overt struggle." After the 1967 strike, said Boland, "the dollar decision was usually to take the settlement and wait for a better time, a more propitious time, or wait for a time that you were so badly hurt that you didn't have any economic choice."

Boland explained that there were several reasons why Phelps Dodge decided to wait, saying, "We were laissez-faire, maybe. Or it was too much trouble. Or the consequences would be too disastrous within the small mining communities to risk it." In the early 1980s, each of these rationalizations began, one by one, to drop away.

 *Chapter 2*

Hard Places

I n the morning light beyond George Munroe's sixteenth floor Park Avenue offices, Manhattan struck a peaceful pose. The dome at St. Bartholomew's Episcopal Church broke a skyline otherwise filled with the city's corporate palaces—the Chrysler Building, Rockefeller Center, the Empire State Building. Beyond "Saint Bart's," as New Yorkers call the Romanesque church, boats and barges moved lazily along the East River. It was the summer of 1982. Munroe had made himself at home here, conquering New York on its own terms. On his bureau stood a display case that contained Munroe's triumph. The luminous bluish-green rock inside had been a gift some years back from the Dodge family, a passing of the "crown jewel" to a man deemed worthy enough to lead the Phelps Dodge Corporation. In the more than 130-year history of this Fortune 500 copper mining and manufacturing firm, other CEOs—Louis Cates and Robert Page before Munroe—had received a similar rock. It contained Phelps Dodge copper from Arizona, the metal that had made billions of dollars in profits for the company since its shift in 1881 from mostly mercantile sales to mining.

On his arrival at Phelps Dodge in the 1950s, Munroe entered America's corporate culture at its heart. Phelps Dodge even had its own quasi-biblical, capitalist Creation myth. Executives learned in their first weeks on the job that, when Anson Phelps incorporated in the 1800s, his firm became the first ever listed on the New York Stock Exchange. The story isn't true, according to Exchange archivists, but within Phelps Dodge the claim persisted as an article of faith.

Munroe wasn't a bad choice for preserving such a corporate mythos. Former Boston Celtics basketball player, Dartmouth and Harvard Law graduate, Rhodes Scholar, Nuremberg judge for the Allied High Commission—Munroe's résumé read like that of some Ivy League superman. After signing on as a vice president and understudy to legendary Phelps Dodge CEO Robert Page, Munroe himself was named CEO in 1969. From there, Munroe's copper star continued to climb. Phelps Dodge consistently had among the highest profits and shareholder returns and the lowest production costs of any American metals producer. In 1980, with the company earning more than $110 million in profit, *American Metal Market* newspaper named Munroe the industry's Man of the Year.

But copper can be a volatile industry, and that summer day in 1982, a year before the copper wars began, Munroe discovered that Wall Street's storm clouds were suddenly hanging over company headquarters. *Business Week* announced on its July 26, 1982, cover: "Management Crisis at Phelps Dodge."

The Crisis

Bad investments, internal dissent, and a worldwide recession had plunged Phelps Dodge into a dangerous spin, the magazine asserted. Worse, the article put the blame squarely on Munroe's shoulders: "Munroe is considered a decent, intelligent man. But he is also known to be extremely cautious and has an aversion to hearing bad news." *Business Week* accused Munroe of failing to make hard decisions, preferring deliberation by basketball team–sized committees instead. Up to 1982, Munroe hadn't even come to a decision on who should be president of the company, opting to hold the title himself for several years while three "vice chairmen" worked under him. Chief company financial officer William Seidman, former top economist to President Gerald Ford, was leaving—reportedly out of frustration with the company's resistance to change. The magazine also noted that other major copper producers had been taken over by oil companies and were somewhat buffered from the present slide in copper prices (Kennecott, for example, had been purchased by SOHIO). Phelps Dodge was independent, in debt, and facing the worst copper prices in nearly half a century.

These, then, were the hard places that made the impending Phelps Dodge–United Steelworkers clash a parable for the 1980s and 1990s: the company faced a triple challenge of stiff international competition, internal resistance to change, and hard-bargaining labor unions. Phelps Dodge came out of the '80s nearly union-less and immensely profitable—one of the richest mining companies in the world. It also emerged as a model for other American companies, particularly in what even conservative publications called its "ruthless" labor relations.

Most labor analysts consider President Ronald Reagan's firing of the professional air traffic controllers (PATCO) in 1981 to be the landmark loss of the decade for labor. But PATCO involved public sector unions in a safety-intensive industry whose workers were legally barred from striking. The Phelps Dodge conflict posed a myriad of challenges immediately relevant to private enterprise in America. With the 1983 strike, a flailing, crisis-driven Phelps Dodge gradually became a model of resolve. Transformation inside the company meant a host of insider battles, sometimes pitting executive against executive. Sharing the labor fight with Munroe was Richard Moolick, who became company president in 1982. Business writers called Moolick "abrasive" and fellow executives thought him sometimes "obsessed" with labor issues. Years later, in interviews for this book, Moolick said with some pride of authorship: "We created a new approach to labor. It was followed all over. Suddenly people realized, hell, you can beat a union. Time was, big unions were considered invincible. We demonstrated that nobody was invincible."

Point Guard

When the swift, ball-handling George Munroe quit the Boston Celtics in 1949 (the founding days of the National Basketball Association), he traded in his green-and-white tank top for an establishment suit. In 1983, still slim but gray-haired, Munroe liked to tell the story about his first nonsports job, at the law firm of Cravath, Swaine, and Moore. "I got $4,000 for playing five months of basketball," he told Tom Fitzpatrick of the *Arizona Republic*. "I thought I was in clover, although people who follow the NBA now laugh about what I was paid. You see, not long after Harvard Law School, I went to work for the highest paying firm on Wall Street and was paid only $3,600 for twelve months." Soon after that move, Munroe won a Rhodes

scholarship and studied at Oxford University. In 1953, at age thirty-
one, Munroe was asked by the Allied High Commission for Germany
in Nuremberg to serve as an appeals judge. Munroe ruled on property
restitution for individuals and businesses persecuted under Nazi
rule. He returned to New York in 1954 to join the pinstripe firm of
Debevoise and Plimpton, which for years had handled Phelps
Dodge's corporate and international legal work. In 1958, Munroe
followed Robert Page, another Debevoise lawyer and a Harvard Law
valedictorian, to Phelps Dodge, where Munroe later succeeded Page
as CEO.

In person, Munroe could be a disarmingly low-key superchief.
Raised in Joliet, Illinois, he had an unimposing, sometimes detached
manner. (During the big strike, Munroe reminded Arizona Governor
Bruce Babbitt of someone "who had just come in from a croquet
game.") A fellow officer at Phelps Dodge described Munroe as "one
of the class acts in American business." Part of that reputation
literally had to do with Munroe's business milieu. He was cut from
the traditional Phelps Dodge Protestant cloth. In New York, Munroe
served as a director of the Metropolitan Museum of Art and the
YMCA. He was a member of the board of trustees of Dartmouth
College and his wife, Elinor, produced films for children. The con-
trast between this elite milieu and Munroe's down-home, Joliet roots
sometimes revealed a kind of split personality. Munroe displayed an
odd mix of social warmth, even grace, and technocratic coolness. He
had lived a storied life, but he was a wooden storyteller: the human
element often came up short.

For example, one might expect a pro basketball career, however
brief, to yield stories of the great cities and the early stars. Instead,
Munroe spoke as a technician—albeit a knowledgeable one—who
followed mostly the angles and arcs of basketball. "There have really
been two technical developments in the game over fifty years since
I've been in," Munroe explained. Basketball, he observed, evolved
"from the two-hand set shots to a one-hand push and then the one-
hand push to the jump shot pioneered by Joe Foltz of the Philadelphia
Warriors." But Munroe considered sports a "crutch" to pay for the
move into a lawyer's life, and he had little to say about the other
players or the towns. (Munroe did mention a college game against
fellow Joliet native George Mikan, one of the first NBA stars—"I
didn't do very well. I think I got only eight points or so.").

Another part of the Munroe lore was the story of his U.S. Navy ship, the *Maryland*, being bombed by a Japanese kamikaze pilot. Describing the scene, Munroe laid out in detail the strategic formation and damage to ship turrets, but he made a passing reference to "gunnery units which were wiped out." When asked directly about the casualties, Munroe responded, "Yeah, I'd forgotten. About twenty-five men on the crew [were killed] manning those guns."

Munroe's relationships with copper miners were characterized by the same combination of technical detail and human detachment. Munroe graduated from college in the years of the Wagner Act, calling himself "very strongly pro-union." Yet he limited his ties to the Arizona mining towns to rare visits from New York, and sometimes other executives wrote his speeches. His athletic prowess alone might have impressed the workers, but, as the coolheaded executive, he never bridged the distance from this team. That distance later haunted Munroe as he struggled to bring the labor unions into his plans for corporate streamlining.

Instead, Munroe focused on the business angles. Munroe shepherded Phelps Dodge through a number of major changes in the mining industry and world copper market. In 1970, Congress passed the first Clean Air Act, clamping down on industrial polluters. At the time, Phelps Dodge was running the largest single polluter of sulphur dioxide in this country—its smelter in Douglas, Arizona. Munroe began pollution control programs there and at other properties that eventually cost more than half a billion dollars and led Munroe to call Phelps Dodge "too good a corporate citizen." Munroe also sought to diversify Phelps Dodge holdings away from copper. The company bought Western Nuclear, a supplier of uranium, and invested in non-copper mining companies elsewhere in the world.

Meanwhile, the World Bank was increasing its loans to countries like Peru, Chile, Zambia, and Zaire to help fund copper mining projects. Many of these countries had recently nationalized their industries and were more concerned with earning foreign currency than with observing laws of supply and demand. With cheap labor and few environmental controls, these copper competitors would soon come knocking (or dumping) on America's doorstep. Imports in the early 1970s represented just 7 percent of all U.S. copper consumption; before the end of the decade, however, foreign copper climbed to nearly a 20 percent share.

In 1977, Munroe made a move to shake up the company with new ideas and increase its political clout in Washington. He lured in former presidential advisor William Seidman as Phelps Dodge's new chief financial officer. Seidman was an old friend from Munroe's Dartmouth days (Seidman negotiated Munroe's first contract with the Boston Celtics). The two men had stayed in touch as Munroe moved from basketball to law to Phelps Dodge, and Seidman, for his part, went from running his family's accounting firm in Michigan to becoming a top advisor to President Ford. Seidman was expected to be the financial man of the hour at Phelps Dodge.

But if Seidman's arrival strengthened Phelps Dodge's voice in Washington, it also exposed a major rift inside the company: managers from mining backgrounds didn't trust New York lawyers or ex-presidential aides to make operational decisions for the mining properties. This tension wasn't new, but in years past it usually had simmered below the surface. For example, when President Johnson had called all the copper company and union officials to Washington to try to settle the 1968 industry-wide strike, the Arizona labor unit flew in and zealously guarded its own issues. To one of Phelps Dodge's eastern labor relations directors, attorney John Coulter, that turf-consciousness was tangible. "They ran their own show in Arizona. It was hands-off. Don't bring in anyone from the East to tell us what to do."

Seidman, who was later assigned by presidents Reagan and Bush to help save the nation's savings and loan institutions as chairman of the Federal Deposit Insurance Corporation, said the divisions within the company became acute during his tenure as chief PD financial officer from 1977 to 1982. For example, not long after arriving at Phelps Dodge, Seidman made his first trip to see the Arizona operations. He expected a warm or at least cordial reception. Instead he got a cool greeting and a crude lesson in the division of labor: "The financial people ran their side and the mining people ran their side and they agreed to keep out of each other's way. As a matter of fact, I had come up with a big new plan for budgets. I went out West to help get the new process started, in which New York was to take much greater control. I can remember a couple old mining types there saying 'It's about even money whether you'll get back or whether you'll be found down a mine shaft.' "

Seidman got back to New York just fine, but western managers successfully resisted his changes for years. The patterns were so ingrained that even the company's controller told a reporter, "Once a year, Western Operations would come in with a project and management would [largely] rubber stamp it." A former director explained that Munroe "definitely delegated a lot of authority to the West . . . because he wasn't an engineer."

But in 1982, the worst recession in the United States since the 1930s sent copper prices plunging. The construction and auto industries—copper's biggest customers after the power companies—were in the doldrums. Furthermore, crushing debt burdens led copper-producing countries like Zaire, Peru, and Chile to keep mining (and pushing down world prices) just when production curtailments were needed most. Finally, Phelps Dodge's diversification efforts had failed on all counts. Investments in uranium had gone sour—a public utility had just breached all of its purchasing contracts when interest in nuclear power dropped. An aluminum investment failed to take off. Oil and natural gas purchases had simply gone nowhere. Seeing losses that eventually mounted to $74 million (nearly half of which came from non-mining operations), Munroe named a crisis management team composed of himself, Seidman, Moolick, and several others. The team decided to shut down all mining operations, avoid some short-term expenditures, and start cutting costs. This would be the first full economic shutdown at the company's flagship Western Operations since the depression.

Phelps Dodge announced salary cuts to management personnel and laid off more than one hundred salaried employees. On April 7, 1982, the company announced the layoff of its entire Arizona and Texas work force, some thirty-four hundred hourly employees engaged in mining, smelting, and refining. Later that month, Munroe decided to take the crisis directly to the workers in what he called "town meetings." (Considering that Phelps Dodge literally owned one of the towns—Morenci—this was a particularly apt description.)

Town Meetings

Munroe knew that the depressed U.S. steel industry was forcing the Steelworkers in Pittsburgh into concessionary talks. Munroe felt that copper, too, needed relief and that Phelps Dodge needed it promptly. By putting pressure on the rank-and-file members of the copper unions, he hoped to convince the international union to reopen negotiations on the current contract and begin to reduce labor costs. The unions had no legal obligation to bargain, but with all the operations idle Munroe felt that they might see the imminent risk to their jobs.

"We just wanted to try to drive home the real world," Munroe said of his visits. "A lot of those people live in remote communities and they've had a pretty easy life—the company had always been a nice comfortable womb. I just wanted to let them know it was not a sure thing."

Munroe arrived in the copper towns looking and sounding more like a copper czar than a negotiator seeking to find common cause with the workers. (The employees, many of whom had worked for years under Phelps Dodge's notorious schedule of twenty-six days on and two days off, might not have agreed with Munroe's description of an "easy life" or a "womb.") Munroe delivered copies of his address to the press and the union locals, although not to the international union. Munroe and his wife then made brief whistle-stops at all the company towns. In the Arizona properties, his first stop was the Mexican-style plaza of Ajo, a town in the Sonoran Desert west of Tucson. Next came Douglas, a border town named at the turn of the century after Phelps Dodge engineer James Douglas. Then Bisbee, the town whose mine had produced Munroe's bluish rock and from which Phelps Dodge decades earlier had deported twelve hundred striking workers at gunpoint. And finally, Munroe visited Morenci, where most of the company's annual output was mined from a two-mile-wide hole in the earth.

"The copper you produce here," he told the miners in his speech at Ajo, "has to compete with copper produced in Canada, South America, Africa, Asia, Europe and Australia. Essentially the price for copper is the same all over the world. And no U.S. producer can continue operating for very long when its cost of producing a pound of copper approaches or exceeds the price for which it can be sold. It's as simple as that." Munroe also asserted that Arizona miners' wages had risen at an annual rate of nearly 15 percent during the 1970s, while the average U.S. manufacturing employee had seen only a 10 percent increase (a statistical difference that the unions countered had simply closed a gap in lower southwestern industrial wages). Then, like a college professor holding class, he displayed a dizzying array of colored line graphs and charts to illustrate his arguments.

"The same eight dollars that Phelps Dodge pays for forty minutes of work," Munroe said, "would buy more than a full shift of work from the average mining employee at a large South American copper operation." (Munroe knew this from the company's own experience, since Phelps Dodge was hedging some of its losses in the United States with investments in operations in Peru.) Finally, Munroe aimed directly at the workers' pocketbooks. "What will we be asking for? Our minds are open, but we know we need a substantial and immediate decrease." Munroe eventually presented himself as an example, taking a 10 percent pay cut in 1982 from his $400,000 salary, although other executives stayed even.

If successful negotiation sometimes demands more of the art of rhetoric than of reality, Munroe had, perhaps unwittingly, taken the wrong tack. By leaving the international union leadership out of his itinerary, he had revived memories of the reflexively antiunion Phelps Dodge. Munroe's officers merely sent the international unions letters asking them to reopen negotiations after his local visits—a posture that Steelworkers International leader Frank McKee would later denounce as the beginning of the company's union-busting effort.

Munroe's Arizona appearances got decidedly poor reviews. Many unionists boycotted the meetings; those who attended tossed barbed questions at the chairman. "The unions objected to my perspective, which they probably shouldn't have," Munroe recalled later. "Even if I thought the devil incarnate was coming and he had information about my job I would go listen to him and evaluate it."

Jack Ladd, the company's soft-spoken Arizona director of labor relations, was angered by the blasé attitude of union leaders. Company officials treated Munroe's rare visits to Arizona like the tour of a head of state, so it angered Ladd that union members "wore their union caps through the entire meeting and they put their legs up on the chairs. . . . I wanted to aim a fire hose at them." At a meeting in California later in the summer, the unions summarily rejected Phelps Dodge's (and, by that time, the rest of the major copper producers') calls for contract concessions. In steel, the unions had also rejected concessions, and that industry was considered far worse off than copper.

Although the unions did not deny that the company was losing money, they argued that labor costs weren't the problem. Instead, they claimed that Phelps Dodge's bad investments and the Reagan administration's international monetary policies had created the crisis; for their part, the labor unions had helped to create the most efficient mines and smelters in the industry. In part substantiating the union claims, *Business Week* noted shortly after Munroe's tour that

Phelps Dodge had the lowest labor costs in the industry. Moreover, the Western Nuclear losses alone were costing the company millions.

On the other hand, the unions could see that some industries were genuinely in distress—and some major unions were cooperating to save businesses and jobs. Most important of these was the agreement between Chrysler and the United Autoworkers. Between 1979 and 1981, the autoworkers agreed to wage cuts in exchange for a slice of the business pie—Chrysler would open its books and provide the unions a position on the board of directors. Then, in 1982, the Steelworkers themselves began concessionary talks with US Steel and other producers. Many of the Steelworkers officers and economists who led copper negotiations had participated in the steel talks. One of those officers was Frank McKee, chairman of the copper union coalition. Faced with the question of whether copper should follow the auto and steel industries into concessionary talks, McKee's answer was "no." The copper industry was in fundamentally better condition than automobiles and steel, something Phelps Dodge officials did not deny.

For most of 1982, copper prices remained stagnant. Even so, Phelps Dodge ended its shutdown, calling more than half the work force back about five months after Munroe's visits. This left union leaders with the impression that much of the activity during the previous months had been aimed at pressuring them—that intimidation rather than cooperation was on the company's agenda. Now the workers were hungry—for jobs and sometimes also for food—and unemployment in the copper towns was still sky-high, at times more than 50 percent.

Munroe has denied that the shutdown was intended to send a message to the unions. But Seidman, seated in his federal office across from the White House, said in an interview that labor was "certainly a part" of the company's reason for the shutdown: "The major part was that [the shutdown] gave us a chance to get rid of our inventories, enhance our cash position, and hopefully have some effect on market price—and hopefully have some effect on the upcoming union problems."

Seidman added, "One of the common problems of unions is that they don't like anybody to talk to their constituents. They might hear something that the union leadership would prefer that they didn't hear. I think it was part of George's basic nature of being a gentleman to tell the people, 'You're in the same boat and if you don't recognize that, we're all going to be out of work. Including me.' "

When the bid for wage concessions failed, the company began to pressure the workers in other ways. Supervisors stopped observing union job classifications and other work rules, and work assignments were summarily changed. The union locals at Morenci were overwhelmed with grievance reports. (Steelworkers local president Angel Rodriguez was accustomed to grievances stacking up annually on a single clipboard; in 1982–83 he ran out of clipboards.) But Phelps Dodge rejected the grievances and dared the union to take them to arbitration, an expensive procedure. In a move that perplexed union leaders, the company also hired a psychologist to train supervisors to change the way they communicated with the work force. One supervisor later recalled that he had been encouraged in these sessions "to bring an end to all this grandfather to father to son stuff. [The workers] are supposed to follow orders from us." One Phelps Dodge executive, future president Richard Moolick, felt that some of the young workers from Clifton and Morenci families were no longer seeking to work hard and advance; he believed that they had come to see work at the mine as an entitlement. When the company hired these workers, Moolick said, it was getting only "generations of sorriness."

Meanwhile, company restructuring architect Seidman announced he was leaving Phelps Dodge to become dean of the Arizona State University Business School. Seidman said that the company's cash squeeze made it difficult for him to justify staying. He had told Munroe in 1977 that he would stay five years to help modernize the company's budgeting and investments strategy; the time was up. But few observers accepted that explanation. One former executive told *Business Week* that Seidman "was having zilch of an impact on the fundamental issues, and at the first opportunity he decided he was getting out." The magazine also reported that "several sources . . . maintain that Seidman fought a futile battle against the corporate culture. As at many minerals companies, the mining engineers who run the primary metals operations have traditionally wielded tremendous power at Phelps. Corporate headquarters rarely challenged them."

Adding to the troubles, internal sniping about Munroe accelerated into hard criticism. *Business Week* asserted that Munroe was failing the leadership test and that there was doubt "whether the company can implement—or even find—a way to survive in its present form." Other top talent besides Seidman was leaving. As one former employee put it, "George [Munroe] is a hellishly nice, bright guy, but he cannot grapple with a decision. He only makes a decision when it is forced on him." The magazine concluded, "Independent thinking or dissent has never been popular at the company."

It took a new combination of leadership qualities to turn Phelps Dodge around—an officer with the intelligence to manage in New York and the strength of personality to drag the resistant Western Operations officials into new financial times. And that's exactly what Phelps Dodge got when the board of directors elected vice chairman and longtime mining engineer Richard Moolick president in July 1982. Two of the three company vice chairmen had departed in 1982, leaving Moolick the company's senior homegrown executive. A thirty-year Phelps Dodge man, he had earned the promotion. Yet, Moolick's arrival went largely unnoticed except in the bland business press releases. He was unlikely to have been found at the top of anyone's list of essential early decision makers in the Phelps Dodge strike. In fact, during his entire presidency, not a single newspaper feature in Arizona—or anywhere else—ever profiled Moolick and what he brought to this top spot. Moolick was a firm believer in executing his will by proxy while staying out of the limelight. If (as many company officials treated him) George Munroe was the czar over Phelps Dodge, Richard Moolick became his Rasputin.

President Moolick

From his earliest memories, Richard Moolick was fascinated with minerals and aggressively determined to get at them. Recalling his upbringing in Southern California, Moolick said, "When I was a kid I used to take the old rock specimens that were around the house that my grandfather had given my mother. I'd be out there as a preschooler, pounding the hell out of that, trying to get some gold out of pyrite. I never got any of course." Later, he ranged across the southern Sierras in California and Nevada and showed a knack for recognizing mineral formations. "I felt I was damn good. By the time I had fine-tuned myself, I could go out and look at a district, maybe spend six hours there and draw my conclusions. Then I would get the reports and find out that I was right on."

When World War II began, Moolick enlisted in the Navy and flew bombing missions in the Marshall Islands. Moolick explained that he chose to become a pilot because that's "where you can do the most damage."

After the war, Moolick's eye for rock led him to the University of Arizona School of the Mines. Graduating in 1949, he was hired by Phelps Dodge as a junior geologist and gradually worked his way up to chief mining engineer. He became something of a company legend for spotting rich ore bodies. Assignments took Moolick to mineral deposits around the world, from Peru to Turkey to South Africa. He returned to Arizona as mine manager at what he called Phelps Dodge's "gem"—Morenci. Altogether, Moolick spent more than twenty years at the company's Arizona and New Mexico properties.

That was enough time, he said, to develop an eye for labor relations as well as copper. Moolick quickly became frustrated with the conciliatory attitudes of Arizona officers toward labor. In 1982, when he was offered the presidency of Phelps Dodge, he elicited a novel promise from CEO Munroe. As New York–based president, Moolick would have primary authority over Western Operations' labor issues. Traditionally, the Phelps Dodge president made technical and financial decisions dealing with the properties and carried out general oversight. As Seidman had discovered, the firm's Western Operations managers called their own shots. But Moolick was planning "a whole new ball game" based on what he called "the Moolick treatise."

Moolick's portfolio adjustment (unknown to the unions) radically altered the company's approach to bargaining in the 1983 contract rounds. The Moolick treatise laid out two primary arguments. First, the copper market was not going to recover as quickly as some experts (and many in the company) were predicting. "I was always a free thinker and looked at everything and drew my own conclusions. I'd been hearing the forecasts for some time. I concluded in late 1981 that this [turnaround] wasn't going to happen that way. And it didn't." Second, Moolick decided that labor unions had become the primary obstacle to the company's survival in hard times. Part of Moolick's stand against the unions grew out of his opposition to the cost-of-living increase in the union contracts. On paper, Moolick saw inflation and, therefore, wages rising. But copper prices were dropping. "One line was heading off into the sky and one line was heading into the earth," he said. Moolick believed that, because copper prices depended primarily on world economic growth and inventory levels, copper companies were foolish to peg wages to inflation—a provision that all the U.S. copper producers, including Phelps Dodge, had accepted since 1971. Moolick felt that the company had "caved in" to the unions in 1980 during a ninety-day strike in which Phelps Dodge had resisted continuing the cost-of-living increases. Still, Moolick's prior history and statements in interviews strongly hinted that the president had something else on his mind as well.

Moolick had long been a union fighter. Taking college jobs in California, he came to see unions as impediments to a person's free choice of work and union members as dissenters from proper American political values. Working as a part-time printer, Moolick recalled, "We weren't above helping out on strikes at some of the newspapers." By "helping out," Moolick definitely did not mean picketing. "I was born with the thought that you walk through a picket line. Nobody can keep you out. You walk through. You've got a right to. . . . That was my gut feeling.

"You're naive if you think it's good to operate with a union. It's no way to work for a company, for the employees, or for anyone." As for Phelps Dodge, "Mine-Mill [the original Morenci union] was an old and militant union. The first time I sat at a bargaining table there were some card-carrying commies on their side. To me it was an affront to sit across from a goddamned commie. And those people remained in the Steelworkers, too, you know. It was the same crowd."

In 1959, Moolick made his first management move against the unions. The transportation union in Morenci called a strike after the miners and other unions settled a contract with the company. The union was confident that no one else could perform the skilled work. Moolick recalled, "We trained a guy in three or four hours. There was one glass-eyed accountant driving a locomotive. One guy had pneumonia and was in the hospital one day, the next he was running a bulldozer." Claiming that the strike was illegal, Moolick fired the striking transportation workers and put in new hires.

As superintendent of a Phelps Dodge New Mexico branch in the 1960s, Moolick again moved against unions. "I precipitated a strike," he recalled. The unions there argued that nonunion construction work violated their contract with Phelps Dodge. Moolick had an itch to take them on. "It puts them in a bad light" with the public, he said. Moolick had calculated that New Mexico political leaders would be sympathetic to the company when they learned that most of the nonunion workers there were Mexican-Americans. Organized labor had no particularly strong base in New Mexico. Moolick won that battle and increased the number of nonunion contracts at the mine. Moolick made one other move that echoed years later in Morenci: "There were lots of threats and so forth. . . . So I'd gotten an ex-FBI man in the guise of a peddler to stay at a hotel. He would tell me about telephone conversations [of union leaders]. I never asked him how he got them. But he'd tell them to me."

Battle Plans

By February 1983, as the Steelworkers were holding their bargaining coalition conference in Phoenix, Moolick, too, was formulating his next attack plan. He worked several fronts at once. At one point, he began lobbying the other companies "to take the unions on," he said. He framed his bargaining strategy around one essential demand—abolishing the cost-of-living adjustment (COLA), in which the companies raised wages across the board by about nine cents per hour for every 1 percent increase in the consumer price index. This part of Moolick's agenda initially drew strong interest from the other companies' presidents. Twice the company leaders met in New York. On another occasion, they retreated to the posh White Sulphur Springs resort in West Virginia. The participating presidents included Frank Joklik of Kennecott, Ralph Hennebach of ASARCO, James Marvin of Anaconda, and Wayne Burt of Newmont. Said Moolick, "My position was there's no time like the present to go after the unions on a united basis." Moolick was most interested in swaying Joklik of Kennecott, the leading copper producer and the usual union pattern-setter for the industry. But Moolick was disappointed to find Joklik "talking in parables" instead of agreeing to hang tough. "They ended up of course caving in [to the unions]. We were the only ones who went after them."

On a second front, Moolick sought to apply a new legal strategy. Moolick wanted to use the labor laws to replace union members in the event that his bargaining plan precipitated a strike. The order to begin this research was delivered to the company's Arizona lawyers on Valentine's Day 1983.

Phelps Dodge and the Wharton School

The background to these orders, however, may be traced to events years earlier and far away from Arizona. For nearly a decade, Phelps

Dodge had participated in an elite East Coast business colloquium comprising up to ninety of the largest U.S. companies across a range of industries. Meeting three times a year at Philadelphia's Hilton Hotel or the New York Harvard Club, the group was sponsored by the University of Pennsylvania business school, known worldwide as the Wharton School. Professor Herbert Northrup, a prolific academic writer and former labor relations specialist for General Electric, had established the Research Advisory Group (RAG) in 1967 to get a picture of companies' management and labor concerns—and to help fund some of his own projects. The RAG was an offshoot of the school's Industrial Research Unit, which brought Wharton industrial relations specialists into one cluster of offices. Northrup's graduate students and selected faculty members, in turn, participated in the planning, execution, and follow-up consultations of RAG activities. The meetings were informal, friendly affairs in which Northrup wore many hats at once—scholar, organizer, and industry guru. Northrup often voiced the opinion that the 1967–68 industry-wide copper strike, which brought about multiunion coalition bargaining, was a threat to American management's right to control its future. In this view he had no stronger ally than Phelps Dodge. The company was one of the earliest members of RAG, and top Phelps Dodge management had been attending the Wharton meetings for years.

In 1982, just at the time that Moolick took over as president at Phelps Dodge, Northrup's group published an analysis and guide for companies that wanted to continue operations during strikes. Called simply *Operating during Strikes*, the book was conceived by Northrup, written by Wharton professor Charles Perry and two private lawyers, and funded by Phelps Dodge and the other RAG participants, as well as by conservative think tanks like the John Olin Foundation. Northrup carefully cultivated the alignment of interests between the companies and the RAG in regular newsletters sent on official University of Pennsylvania/Wharton School stationery. In a 1983 newsletter, Northrup made a pitch for raising membership fees to each RAG member, noting that the companies' funds had helped make the school the largest academic publisher in the industrial relations field:

> Your support is deeply appreciated and every effort will be made to make you proud of it. We have turned the literature around so that the liberal union bloc no longer dominates it and we shall continue, with your help,

to outdistance them with a realistic approach to problems. To all of you,
my heartfelt thanks.

What Northrup meant by a "realistic approach" to problems was
explained within the pages of *Operating during Strikes*. No ordinary
academic analysis, the book was effectively a how-to guide for companies contemplating replacing their union workers. Its chapters
included discussions of the legal issues of permanent replacement,
as well as practical advice about having enough food and beds for
replacement workers forced to sleep at the plant site, installing extra
telephones, and even checking the local liquor laws to ensure that
beer could be served on the plant site to calm nervous replacement
workers. The guide pointed out that "Ping-Pong, pool, darts, and air
hockey may also prove to be a good investment" and that "consideration may be given to scheduling 'happy hours' after each shift
change."

Phelps Dodge not only ordered a box of *Operating during Strikes* in
1983, but distributed the book, according to one company official, as
the strike "bible." Throughout the strike, Phelps Dodge officials
made presentations about events to the Wharton group in the quarterly meetings in Philadelphia and New York. With this kind of
advance work and academic attention, the Phelps Dodge–union
conflict may have been something of a demonstration project, a kind
of business school experiment. In his memoranda, Wharton Professor
Northrup himself referred to Phelps Dodge as a "case study."

An academic study with these kinds of real-world ambitions would
not have surprised Northrup's business school colleagues: a Wharton
School centennial publication issued in 1981 noted that, under
Northrup, the Industrial Research Unit "ventured into controversial
waters, and financial support from the federal government and the
mainstream foundations fell sharply. Northrup's consistently pro-
management studies, however, found new funding with corporations
and politically conservative philanthropies."

The centennial book (which, for an internal publication, was surprisingly critical of Northrup's activities) noted that Northrup had
quit as chairman of the industry department and taken a year off
after faculty criticism of his bias toward business. Northrup's philosophy was, according to some of his associates, modeled after that of
his famous mentor at General Electric (GE), Lemuel R. Boulware,
whom Northrup had served in the late 1950s. The philosophy held

that companies should approach bargaining with the same techniques with which they approached the marketplace—secure the best information, aggressively advertise the product, and don't back down. (The term "Boulwarism" became notorious to labor unions when GE used the technique in a 1960 strike that turned violent; the NLRB eventually declared Boulwarism an unfair labor practice because it excessively restricts a company's willingness to bargain on issues raised by unions.) Northrup later published a strong defense of Boulware. With the RAG's meetings, publications, and practical bargaining lessons, "Northrupism" takes a place beside Boulwarism, as a tested, scientific strategy for operating during strikes and replacing unions.

In an interview, Northrup acknowledged that the book was his idea but said that it merely coincided with, rather than caused, the upswing in permanent replacement activity by Phelps Dodge and others. "I know that [Phelps Dodge] ordered a number of copies of the book and I gather that they used it quite a bit in setting up their policies," said Northrup. "[But] I wasn't thinking of permanent replacements when I suggested that book. We were dealing with companies operating during strikes," Northrup said, meaning that the companies might hire temporary replacement workers. "What people use the book for you can't control."

Many of the examples in the book, however, involve early instances of companies using permanent replacements, and Northrup's newsletters are replete with invitations to companies to consult with faculty members. (Northrup's public view of the use of permanent replacements emerged later; after his retirement in the early 1990s, when permanent replacement had become a virtual policy of American companies, he said of a strike at Caterpillar tractor, "The only way to beat a strike like this is to threaten to replace the workers." Companies that did not do this "lost every time, badly and expensively.")

Moolick's Assault

With the Wharton School's labor brain trust in reserve, Phelps Dodge launched its antiunion crusade from New York. Richard Moolick's special arrangement with CEO Munroe gave him complete authority over Phelps Dodge's Western Operations. This left some other company officers embittered, but, if they disagreed or attempted to limit his actions, Moolick kept a close eye on them. When it came to miners, Moolick used video cameras for surveillance. During strikes, protesters around the plant were videotaped so that the company had evidence available for arbitration hearings after a discharge. "A camera," Moolick said, "is better than a cannon."

Through a different medium, Moolick also watched his own fellow executives, concerned that they might, as he put it using one of his favorite verbs, "cave in." Moolick's right-hand man was ex–FBI agent and company vice president John Coulter. Plain manners and mono-tone voice aside, Coulter was one of the company's most colorful characters. He joined Phelps Dodge after nine years as a counterespi-onage agent in New York. In the 1950s, Coulter helped bag the most important Russian spy ever captured in this country, Colonel Rudolph Abel. ("A newsboy flipped a nickel on the ground, breaking it in two pieces," Coulter recalled of the FBI's big break in the case. "There was a piece of microfilm in it.") Coulter became Moolick's point man. "I sent Jack Coulter out there to be my eyes and ears," Moolick said of Coulter's move to Arizona after the start of negotia-tions in 1983. "I wanted to and intended to make this a cold, hard run." Moolick added that "The whole show was me using Coulter. . . . Anybody else, they were on the periphery."

That strategy to limit input into the negotiation and strike plan excluded George Munroe as well, of whom Moolick said: "Strong men gave him trouble." Moolick ridiculed Munroe's whistle-stop tour the previous year as "dumb—a very embarrassing thing. Why make yourself appear weak in front of the labor force?" Moolick resented that Munroe had ventured into what Moolick saw as "his own" labor territory, but the trip had taken place while Moolick was overseas examining prospective properties in Australia. "It burned me up because it wouldn't have happened if I had been in New York," Moolick said. In fact, Moolick attempted to keep Munroe at a distance from the labor negotiations process whenever possible; he knew that Munroe sometimes expressed concern about the status of the company's reputation or "citizenship" and was concerned that Mun-roe might yield under pressure to appeals by the unions or Arizona Governor Bruce Babbitt. "There was a period where Jack Coulter and I, one or the other, would stay in New York City so that no one in the labor area could get to Munroe. We figured he was very weak." On the other hand, Moolick owed his leadership to Munroe and could not have pursued his goals without at least Munroe's tacit support.

Moolick also feared that the independent-minded general superintendent of operations, Arthur Kinneberg, or even the local mine managers might give in during hard negotiations with the unions. Moolick suspected that Kinneberg had asked Munroe to make the town meeting tour while Moolick was gone as a direct challenge to his authority over Western Operations. So, along with Coulter, Moolick sent out "envoys" (resentful company officers at Western Operations referred to them as "spies") like company attorney and current mining division president Steven Whisler to keep an eye on local operations. The envoys regularly reported back to Moolick or Coulter on whether his approach to the strike had the backing it needed.

Prelude to Negotiations: The Union View

As Moolick set the rules for his new "ball game," Steelworkers treasurer Frank McKee put forward the unions' contract position. A deliberative union assembly, the Nonferrous Industry Conference (NIC), set the priorities for negotiating what the unions now routinely called the "pattern contract." That NIC congress, which met in Phoenix in February 1983, was intended to create a kind of representative democracy, though it was well known that McKee set the agenda. The NIC was comprised of the Steelworkers and more than twenty other international unions from machinists to electricians to transportation workers. This was what Cass Alvin, the editor of the publication *Steelabor* and western region spokesman for the Steelworkers, had called "E Pluribus Unum"—a showcase of the many unions united.

Representing more than half of the twelve thousand Arizona copper workers, the Steelworkers were by far the largest member of the NIC. With the AFL-CIO Industrial Union Department, the Steelworkers had spearheaded the union coalition movement in 1967. Since that time, a Steelworkers leader had always been at the NIC helm. By all accounts, McKee had already made the lead economic decisions before the NIC congress opened, mirroring Richard Moolick's approach at Phelps Dodge. McKee's goal was now, as it had been since the first pattern, to draw one company into the NIC's proposed contract and create a master agreement for all the other companies to follow.

Frank McKee

Sixty-two years old and known as a "hard-line, bread-and-butter unionist," McKee was the picture of international steel union authority. He had been raised amid the western steel mills of Seattle in the early part of the century. McKee remembered standing outside the Bethlehem Steel gates as a boy during the depression "while my daddy begged for a job." He had become a union grievance man, local president, district director, and, finally (though he hoped to go still higher), international treasurer. McKee was of the Irish stock that historically ran the Pittsburgh-based union—indeed, one of his longtime friends was Steelworkers president Lloyd McBride. McKee looked and sounded the part of a steel union chieftain. He spoke with a voice of authority, and a swath of fair hair stood out from his rumpled face. The third-highest international official from the top, he sometimes ruled with an imperious snap of the fingers; he was used to getting his way.

At the NIC congress in Phoenix, all the unions sent high-level representatives. McKee delivered the conference keynote address, "Mucking Out Some Myths." (A "mucker" is the clean-up laborer in the pit). More than any other union document from this period, McKee's speech set the tone for upcoming negotiations—and in many ways, for the entire Reagan decade for labor:

> We in labor learned our economics the hard way—not from curves and graphs but from standing in long soup lines, seeing padlocked factory gates, "*No* Help Wanted" signs, and from just being too broke to buy a beer. We know the cruelties of theories that say that the poor can be helped only if the rich get richer. . . . What is needed, therefore, is some people economics, value economics, demand-side economics, which must be in place if supply-side is to follow. That's what we in labor have been saying right along and that's what collective bargaining is all about—making demand-side economics work.

McKee rejected the idea of making major economic concessions to the copper producers in the upcoming contract talks, pointing out,

> In a special session last May in Los Angeles the solid bloc of unions . . . concluded it was the lack of market for copper caused by the faulty economic policies of multinational corporations and the Reagan Administration and not labor costs that were at the root of the industry's problems.

On the issue of cost-of-living adjustments (COLA), McKee pursued the same tone:

> The mining companies continue to point out that their problems began when unions forced them to accept the COLA provision in labor contracts. . . . We were forced to strike to obtain and later to protect COLA in 1971, again in 1974, 1977 and to some degree in 1980. It remains the hook on which industry hangs its case . . . claiming that in no way can the COLA costs be recouped in a depressed market. Still another myth. They are not telling the whole story. All we want from the COLA provision is to keep the wages from being eroded by inflation. . . . Without COLA, the general wage increase certainly would have been much higher than the modest 3 percent annual rate we negotiated in primary copper in our settlements since COLA.

If McKee's speech, with its references to union events of 1967, 1971, 1974, and 1977, sounded like a recitation of the generations of Israel, there was a reason. As McKee's toughest challenge approached, he wanted to get the workers thinking again about that most sacred of labor values—solidarity. Solidarity meant reminding the companies that union members stood (and if necessary, would fall) united. The past fifteen years showed an almost unblemished record of victories and tangible economic improvements for the unions. Only on rare occasions, such as when the Teamsters insisted on going their own way in 1976 with a minor company (ANAMAX), had the pattern broken down. What politician could claim to have delivered the goods so consistently to his constituents? And who wanted to back off a proven union product? Certainly not Frank McKee.

At this conference session, the mood was mostly upbeat. There was one behind-the-scenes lobbying campaign by union members at Anaconda for wage relief (the company was headed for almost certain bankruptcy, partly the result of Chile's expropriation of Anaconda mines in the 1970s). But the dominant union view was that, if one producer failed, others who were more efficient would pick up their production—and their jobs. The wage structure of the industry should depend on the companies that flourish; copper as an industry was not threatened. Advancing the no-concessions argument for the craft unions, International Machinists president William Winpisinger attended the conference and vigorously encouraged the other leaders to stand united with the Steelworkers. He was especially vigilant in urging the representatives not to back down on the cost-of-living issue, a benefit that had been hard to win in 1971 and would be all the more difficult to get back if it were ever dropped.

The Kennecott "Bombshell"

Two months after McKee's speech and well before negotiations usually began, the Steelworkers announced what George Hildebrand, a labor scholar and arbitrator in the industry for thirty years, calls the "bombshell." In early April, McKee and his lieutenant, district director Robert Petris, conducted secret negotiations with Kennecott Corporation's chief negotiator, Judd Cool. Nearly a month before Phelps Dodge and the unions sat down to talk, McKee and Cool announced that Kennecott and the union coalition had reached agreement on a new three-year contract. The plan was beautifully simple: the unions conceded to industry troubles by offering a wage freeze and reductions in a job security program; the company responded to that offer by continuing cost-of-living increases for inflation. This was precisely the contract McKee had envisioned at the NIC meeting, and now he had it signed and sealed.

McKee called Kennecott the "Cadillac" of the industry for its generous contract provisions and positive, take-charge role as the industry leader. As a past Steelworkers district director, McKee personally had conducted the Kennecott negotiations through the 1970s. Later, as NIC chairman, McKee again worked directly with his old bargaining adversary. Each had something the other wanted: McKee could assure Kennecott a stable run of operations with a no-strike contract; Kennecott in return provided the Steelworkers with a lead contract that could be used to pressure the other companies to sign. The 1980 three-year contract had worked just that way. Kennecott had set the pattern of a wage increase and continued COLA, forcing the other companies into the mold.

But Kennecott's management approach to labor was different from other companies, especially Phelps Dodge. For one, Kennecott had always been more congenial to the entire notion of the union coalition. Kennecott directors actually preferred the bargaining discipline of settling all the contracts with the unions at once, at one table. Phelps Dodge had long resisted such a bargaining process, preferring to whipsaw the unions against each other and cut costs wherever it could.

Moreover, Kennecott had been taken over by a cash-rich oil company, SOHIO, in 1981. When SOHIO examined the company books, it decided that more, not less, high-level cooperation was needed between labor and management in copper. In 1981, Kennecott president Frank Joklik ordered labor negotiator Cool to begin regular meetings with Steelworkers International and local representatives in an attempt to avoid a strike in 1983. The program was dubbed "Strike Free in '83." The early agreement with the Steelworkers gave Cool the result that management said it wanted.

But such an agreement was not at all what Phelps Dodge wanted, and McKee already knew as much. In 1980, Phelps Dodge had resisted the Kennecott-led pattern contract (a strike lasted ninety days) before finally falling into line with the rest of the industry. The central issue in 1980 was cost-of-living adjustments, and the 1983 fight looked like it was shaping up the same way. McKee said in an interview that the NIC had set its priorities through a democratic debate (albeit guided by Steelworkers economists and aides) and a final vote. His mandate was to seek a contract with a wage freeze but continued cost-of-living adjustments—the same contract that he had won from Kennecott.

As with Moolick and his intention to "take on the unions," McKee's apparent willingness to "take on" Phelps Dodge rested on a range of motives. In February 1983, at nearly the same time the copper unions in Phoenix decided to reject any reductions, negotiators in Pittsburgh agreed to a concessionary contract in the steel industry—a temporary freeze of the cost-of-living increase. McKee said that he had opposed give-backs in the steel industry. "I used to tell [Steelworkers president] Lloyd McBride every Sunday on the golf course that he had made a big mistake," McKee said. Moreover, Steelworkers president McBride became ill in early 1983, leading to speculation about who might succeed him. Some observers felt that McKee was positioning himself as the radical Steelworker, an alternative to pragmatists like Canadian-born steel leader Lynn Williams. Whatever the source of his combativeness, McKee was not one to shy away from a fight. He was even less likely to avoid a fight when Phelps Dodge reverted to its old habits of ignoring the international union.

McKee's early Kennecott settlement not only established the 1983 copper pattern, it ended any possibility that the leading companies could unite (as Phelps Dodge had hoped) in the kind of economic front that had brought concessions in Pittsburgh.

Holding the pattern in copper would require the rest of the "Big

Five" producers—Magma, Inspiration, ASARCO, and Phelps Dodge—to sign onto the same basic terms as the Kennecott contract. As the June 30, 1983, contract expiration deadline neared, Magma, Inspiration, and ASARCO, one by one, came into the pattern. The theory was proving itself yet again, and McKee was pleased. When one company settled, it created pressure on the holdout company to do the same or lose money during a strike. The holdout had to make a difficult calculation: would taking a strike win more union concessions—and cost less in the long run—than a settlement? From inside the halls of Phelps Dodge, however, a new guard was preparing to apply the harshest cost-benefit calculus possible. A strike could not only break the pattern contract but end union representation altogether.

The Negotiations: Day One

The Phelps Dodge negotiations began at the Phoenix Ramada Inn on May 4, 1983, with a familiar cast of characters and an invitation to negotiate that, in light of later events, stood out as pure wishful thinking. Standing in the hotel's Coronado Room, Phelps Dodge labor relations director Jack Ladd announced: "I hope we can get through these negotiations without bitterness and acrimonious statements by either side." A down-home character in manners but a sharp strategist, Ladd was well respected by the unions. He had been attending or leading these negotiations every three years since the 1970s. A career Phelps Dodge employee (as many of the top officials were), Ladd owned a ranch in southern Arizona where he raised cattle and built his own windmills. Alongside Ladd sat the other eight members of the company negotiations committee, including representatives from each mining property and legal counsel John Boland, Jr.

For the unions, the lead negotiator was Alex Lopez, director of a Steelworkers subdistrict that included Phelps Dodge's New Mexico and Morenci, Arizona, properties. A former brick mason at Kennecott, Lopez was as big as a bear and had the kind of fist-pounding temper that quickly reminded corporate officials of the meaning of "labor muscle." Unions were made for this: a bright Mexican-American smelterman with years in the fires becomes union grievance man, local union president, regional international representative, and now, chief negotiator for the Phelps Dodge negotiations.

Lopez's New Mexico assignment carried a special cachet in the labor community. Under the banner of the Mine-Mill union, the largely Mexican-American locals had won the famous strike against Empire Zinc enshrined in the 1953 movie *Salt of the Earth*. The radical heritage of southwestern U.S. labor was rooted in Lopez's district, and Lopez had won praise for his modern-day leadership there. Still, if Lopez was respected for his union know-how, he was also considered somewhat green; this was his first assignment as chair of a Steelworkers bargaining committee. With Lopez sat Morenci union local president Angel Rodriguez and officers from twelve other unions.

Phelps Dodge had already broadcast its contract demands through newspaper ads, direct letters to employees, and media interviews. The company referred frequently to its 1982 losses of $74 million and called for wage cuts of up to $2 an hour, the end of the cost-of-living adjustments, and concessions on benefits and medical care. Ironically, only three days before the start of these contract talks, Phelps Dodge vice president Richard Pendleton had told the *Washington Post* that the copper recession was over and that Phelps Dodge was "in reasonably good shape. We're upbeat, but I think we're realistically upbeat." What did the company expect to hear from the unions after they saw the concessionary contract proposal? "There was room for compromise," said the company's absentee mastermind, Moolick, "but that would have required them giving in on COLA. . . . They were locked in because the union mentality will not allow later negotiations that give one company a better deal." Moolick understood that when a company insisted on certain concessions, it got a strike.

Phelps Dodge also handed out a detailed list of proposals on work rules, pensions, and other matters, which became the "PD" list. Although the list was long, the union leaders had seen many of the demands before. But there were two rather alarming surprises as well. First, the company was unilaterally terminating all "side agreements." These were accords dating back as far as the 1950s that covered gaps in the contracts (for example, who paid for fireproof hairnets in the smelter) and had been understood as agreements in perpetuity by the union locals. Second, the company was insisting on the managerial prerogative to return to the notorious "26 and 2" work schedule, literally twenty-six consecutive days on the job followed by two days off. If that wasn't enough, McKee assistant Carl

Morris informed the negotiating committee members that Phelps Dodge chief negotiator Jack Ladd had approached him before the meeting and pulled him behind a big plant in the corner of the room. "New York is serious," Ladd said. "We're not going to back down." Ladd seemed to Morris to be communicating both a confidence and a threat: the old Western Operations deal—the one that gave Arizona negotiators the power to compromise without New York's interference—was gone. Morris wasn't sure what to make of it. Truth or dare? If what Ladd said was true, then the unions had their job cut out for them.

For their part, the unions came to the bargaining table with a list consisting of the NIC proposal, which had been formulated in the February meetings, the Kennecott settlement, and their own special issues list called "AW," for Arizona-wide. The first thing the company would see was the preamble to the NIC report, which echoed McKee's February "Mucking Out Some Myths" speech:

> The industry is literally in the eye of an economic storm that rages across the industrial world. While companies report loss of earnings, our members and their families suffer far more. Company fortunes lost are recoupable. Workers' losses are not. . . . They are the victims, not the culprits in these economic circumstances.

On cost of living, the proposal emphasized, "We have had COLA protection for more than a decade. We must maintain the integrity of that protection against the rise in consumer prices."

From the first words offered by both sides, set down in meticulously detailed minutes by Morenci Miners local president Angel Rodriguez, the points of tension were clear. Frank McKee stood up at the first session and said that he didn't want to get into "a shouting match," but "PD [has been] very vocal in the press and that may be of concern to our members." (The Steelworkers union provided its complete minutes for this book. Phelps Dodge declined to provide its minutes, saying that they included ad hominem observations that the company did not want to share.) Robert Petris, Steelworkers district director, followed McKee with a terse statement of purpose: "What I have to say I can say in two words: 'Kennecott Settlement.' Meet it and we're home free."

Ladd countered for Phelps Dodge, "It's a strange situation when we bargain in the shadow of the Kennecott settlement. . . . I dislike saying 'I told you so,' but we sat here three years ago and I said ninety-cent copper is not staying. Steel and autos will go down." The price of copper had dropped to less than $.80 a pound, which Ladd said justified special relief for Phelps Dodge. Ladd vented his frustrations in a pointed attack on the whole notion of pattern bargaining:

> These copper companies are [all] different other than the fact that we produce copper. All we hear are stories that all copper companies are the same and all wages and benefits should be the same. A particularly frustrating problem is paying a wage that we can't afford to pay when our profitability is going down and wages are going up. When we get into a position where the company is running for the employees, that's not right. We have to have the right to run our business. We have a lot of problems facing PD. We intend to do our best to convince you that we've got to do something else.

To complete this first meeting, the Steelworkers called on Edward Ghearing, their cherubic, chain-smoking economist, to reply to Ladd and justify the Kennecott pattern. "I don't share your views that copper companies are different," Ghearing said. "You make copper, you sell it for the same price within fractions of a cent. . . . You compete in the same markets. Demand in areas served by copper is picking up. Housing—firm revival. As far as copper imports, we can work together in that area although it won't be easy." Ghearing's was the first and only offer of cooperation by either side in the entire six-week period of prestrike negotiations.

Ray Isner of the Operating Engineers recalled later that, before discussion of economic issues began, "It took days if not weeks to settle on one issue—Portajohns!" Isner said that the company's answer to any request or issue raised by the union was a blanket "No." That inflexibility struck the union leadership as an intentional provocation. Negotiation theorists sometimes describe bargaining table challenges as steps in "Getting to Yes," as the title of a widely read 1981 book from the Harvard Negotiation Project called them. Even with the threat of a strike, negotiators expect to find some common ground stemming from the long-term bargaining relationship. Hard positions can be massaged into general, more flexible interests. The Phelps Dodge round of negotiations, however, had very early displayed an approach to bargaining that might better have been labeled "Getting to No."

When the second day opened, the company's pressure tactic that had nettled the union leaders in the past—juggled job assignments—became a contract demand. The unions launched a chorus of complaints:

> *Unions:* I'm talking about using a Steelworker as a boilermaker, a boilermaker as an insulator.
>
> *Ladd:* You have other examples?
>
> *Unions:* Mechanics running locomotives. Locomotive engineers working as panel builders. . . . At Ajo, in the crusher, giving our work to a laborer.

To the uninitiated observer, it might have appeared that Phelps Dodge had everyone doing everyone else's job.

> *Ladd:* I think I understand the demand. In response, this isn't temporary. We have to reorganize to operate more efficiently. We don't want to restrict a certain job to a certain occupation.

This appeal by Ladd, although delivered in his usual low-key manner as just another management demand, signaled a revolution in work assignments throughout the United States. In the traditional science of production, perfected early in the century by Ford Motor Company and Frederick Taylor, companies matched their workers with machines; the right part always fit in the right place. Unions later utilized this system to help define relative wage rates and sometimes to protect jobs. But in the 1980s, new technologies, new workplace designs, and new management philosophies began to render the old order obsolete. Sometimes even the worker was rendered obsolete. Skilled craftspeople were no longer needed to do some of the complex jobs; fewer unskilled workers were needed to do basic labor. More machines, larger shovels, bigger trucks, conveyors instead of trains—mining operations, in particular, benefited from technology and redesign. Productivity in the copper industry, measured by tons of copper per man-hour, was on the rise even as total employment by copper companies was declining. After Phelps Dodge's 1982–83 layoffs, the company reduced its Arizona work force by more than two hundred jobs—in part because it had the capacity to do more with less—and redesigned assignments in many of the positions that remained. In past contract negotiations between Phelps Dodge and the Steelworkers, job assignment issues had come to light one by one. In these 1983 negotiations, Phelps Dodge's position on assignments revealed that the company intended to cut as wide a swath in the bargaining as it possibly could.

No More "High Roller"

Distribution of detailed economic proposals began in earnest on June 10, 1983—less than three weeks before the contract's expiration date. Minutes from the June 10 negotiation session show Phelps Dodge and the unions still battling in rhetorical language. "The days of being a high roller are over with," said Ladd, as he announced an "offer" of a complex wage-price bonus to replace COLA. "Copper is very sensitive to price," Ladd said. "That's what hurts us—and we're faced with millions and millions of dollars in environmental costs. We have waste disposal problems—these problems are bad enough, but so are the costs. We're proposing to relate COLA to the price of copper." From a perspective of economic logic, Ladd's point was reasonable enough, but the company was being deceptive in calling the wage-price bonus "COLA." In its somewhat dizzying details, the proposal was really profit-sharing dressed as a cost-of-living increase. The current price of copper was $.70 a pound. Only if copper prices reached $1.20 per pound—$.50 a pound higher than their present level and $.40 a pound over Phelps Dodge's profit line—would workers get any increase at all, even to match the inflation rate. Aside from the problem of meeting the Kennecott pattern contract, such a bonus system had long ago been rejected by the unions because it punished and rewarded workers directly by the often harsh bumps of the copper markets. Back in the 1930s, the price-based wage was known as the "Miami Scale" (after the mines at Miami, Arizona) and it was one of the first provisions that resurgent unions later that decade had worked to eliminate. Perhaps an executive with a fat base salary could afford to ride this scale, the unions argued, but hourly workers could not.

The unions offered their own economic proposal instead—a request for a $.25 an hour wage increase, continued cost-of-living adjustments, no medical copayments, and unchanged vacation benefits. In short, a proposal that completely ignored the company's appeal for relief.

If the two sides were speaking a different language, their prospects of hearing each other were jolted again when, on June 12, eighteen days before the contract expiration date, chief company negotiator

Ladd was injured in an accident and had to withdraw from the talks. (He had been working on one of his homemade windmills with a crowbar when he slipped and fell more than twenty feet, breaking several vertebrae.) Pat Scanlon, a vice president and former director of labor relations for Western Operations, was called from his daughter's Stanford graduation ceremonies to replace Ladd.

Inspiration Copper had now joined Kennecott in the pattern, making the union contract tally two (out of five) top copper companies that had agreed to the wage freeze, assorted cost containment efforts, and continued cost-of-living adjustments. Hearing that there was progress at Magma as well, union leaders were increasingly optimistic about getting all the agreements settled before the expiration deadline of June 30, ten days away. At the same time, another headquarters-based Phelps Dodge official appeared in Arizona—the ex–FBI man, John Coulter. Coulter was a new face to union members, but a familiar one to Western Operations officials. He had once been in charge of labor at the company's fabrication plants in Connecticut. His presence infuriated the western company officials because they were accustomed to staffing the negotiations without intervention from New York. Coulter's arrival amounted to a vote of no confidence. Years later, Moolick explained that, with negotiations moving into serious discussion of wages, he was concerned that Scanlon or General Superintendent Arthur Kinneberg might reassert Western Operations' independence and offer a settlement. Coulter was to be, as Moolick said, his "eyes and ears."

"Tight as a Fist"

On June 22, 1983, a little more than a week before the contract was to expire, the Steelworkers-led bargaining committee met privately to decide what to do about the company's tough stand. The meeting took place in the Arcade Room at the Ramada, and, for a time, the room resonated like its name. Minutes of that meeting show a rare (and wrenching) volley of dissent within the union committee. One of the dissenters was Frank Krznovich, a dour boilermaker, described by Steelworkers local president Angel Rodriguez as "a voice in the wilderness"—that is, the only union leader openly expressing doubt over the union's bargaining position. At this meeting, Krznovich insisted that, although coordinated bargaining had brought a lot of gains, "we're placing too much emphasis on the Kennecott settlement." Krznovich dared to suggest a compromise on COLA, a proposal that would have broken the pattern.

The minutes continue: "Brother Russ McConnell jumped up and said that he was appalled at what he was hearing. . . . 'We're all supposed to be leaders and we should be generating some optimism. We're going to be getting a settlement without a strike. But we as a committee have to go in to talk to the company tight as a fist.' "

Apparently the rest of the union committee agreed with McConnell. At the next negotiations session two days later, on June 24, the exchange went as follows:

Scanlon [Phelps Dodge]: We gave you a (COLA) proposal the other day—You have anything to say?

Lopez [Steelworkers]: We do, but not to be printed.

A brief discussion on COLA, which amounted to rejection of the company's proposal, followed. The exchange continued:

Scanlon: How about the remainder of the proposal?

Lopez: We have indicated a "No"—gave you a counter which you have rejected.

Scanlon: Do you have any more to say on economics?

Lopez: No, we have less than a week. We're going to have to start moving.

The week that remained was no more productive. Phelps Dodge withdrew its "price-based COLA" proposal. Scanlon said that the company's substitute offer would be to freeze wages for current hires and reduce them for new hires—but COLA would have to be abolished altogether.

"Don't Fuck with Our COLA"

Now the Moolick position had been offered in full. When the unions summarily rejected the proposal, Scanlon said Phelps Dodge would impose its terms in lieu of a contract: "We're planning to communicate contents to employees early next week." He also notified the union that the company was bringing in a private security force in case of trouble. A union representative responded, "The presence of an outside security force could provoke problems." Why, the union leaders asked, would the company bring in security if it wasn't planning something that the miners would find explosive?

Two more days of frantic discussions produced lines like these:

Scanlon: It's sort of an immovable object–irresistible force type thing.

Lopez: COLA is mandated not only by the conference, but by the people. The guys are saying 'don't fuck with our COLA, pension, wages . . .'

Scanlon: We look at economics different from you.

Lopez: We took our best shot.

Scanlon: You're not taking your best shot when you refuse to talk on COLA and wages. That's not your best shot.

Lopez: Let me assure you, we carefully polled our committee. It's not there.

Meanwhile, Magma, the third largest producer after Kennecott and Phelps Dodge, fell into line on June 29, agreeing to the pattern contract. ASARCO came in at 11:30 P.M. on the night of the strike deadline. Phelps Dodge was now the only holdout. In many negotiations, a last-minute meeting cuts through the fog of company-union rhetoric; deals get struck. No such thing happened this time. The talks ended in a staid last-minute meeting between Steelworkers McKee and Petris and the Phelps Dodge negotiators—with Richard Moolick, as always, far out of anyone's view (but Coulter quietly scribbling notes). The union representatives emerged from the meeting telling the press that Phelps Dodge was resorting to "bullet bargaining," a term that had special local meaning. It referred to the 1917 Bisbee deportation by Phelps Dodge. Sixty-six years later, the clock again ticked down to midnight and neither side blinked. "We were between a rock and a hard spot," said Steelworker coalition chief McKee. "It was playing out like a Greek tragedy," said Phelps Dodge's Scanlon. Scanlon certainly knew that the conclusions of such tragedies were preordained.

Angel's Inheritance

In the late afternoon before the strike deadline, Morenci Steelworkers local president Angel Rodriguez and the union coalition's chief negotiator, Alex Lopez, sat in a booth at the Ramada restaurant waiting for "the call." Despite the titles "president" and "chief negotiator," Rodriguez and Lopez carried no executive powers. Instead, the Nonferrous Industry Conference chairman, Frank McKee, carried the real authority. He would make the call.

Rodriguez understood this. It was all part of an old compromise shaped in 1967, the year before he began work at PD: local leaders gave up some of their power to the larger coalition so that the companies would know they were bargaining with "One Big Union," as the IWW had coined the expression decades ago. Industrial relations expert William Chernish wrote of that earlier negotiation, "The local union officials . . . quickly found out that they were no longer the spokesmen for their respective unions, but that representatives assigned by the coalition leaders were in charge of the negotiations."

For the past five years, Rodriguez had been president of Morenci Miners Local 616, the largest of all the individual copper union locals at Phelps Dodge. In a community where tradition and family counted for plenty, Rodriguez had the right lineage. His father-in-law, David Velasquez, was something of a legend—the first laborers' union leader to negotiate a contract at Morenci.

Rodriguez's own father had been one of Velasquez's first union troops. "Daddy was a smelterman," said Rodriguez. "He worked several different jobs—a puncher in the converters, in the reverbs as a furnaceman, then a skimmer. But all his career as I remember it was in the smelter. So when I went to work in the smelter, everybody knew 'Coffee.' He drank a lot of coffee, so everybody called him that.

"A lot of the old-timers had worked with my dad and helped build the union. They had helped integrate the showers and fought for better housing for Hispanics and the Indians and other minorities in the community. So we had a lot of help in organizing new workers. The old-timers would remind them what they had to struggle for.

"When I was growing up, Mine-Mill was the union in Morenci. Those were also the days of the McCarthy red-baiting and Mine Mill was accused of being communist-dominated. I used to overhear the conversations at home. My dad was a very strong union man, and he defended the union."

Rodriguez was known as a low-key union leader. Management and his own union members praised him as a good negotiator and a gentleman. Although he was also chairman of the local Democratic Party (in the only Arizona county to oppose Ronald Reagan in 1980), he was in other ways the model of a 1980s conservative: a hardworking, born-again Protestant, married, and the father of nine children.

As the negotiations began with Phelps Dodge, running the union became an increasingly heavy load for Angel Rodriguez. Membership was down because some workers couldn't afford dues; many others had been laid off. Everyone had been out for nearly six months during the 1982 recession; barely two-thirds of the Morenci work force had been called back. Moreover, Arizona was a right-to-work state, which meant no one had to join the union, but everyone got the contract benefits. The number of free riders seemed to have climbed with the recession. Although the Morenci Miners had kept membership rates high, some said that membership in other unions had fallen to as low as 60 percent. Even Rodriguez's father-in-law, now long retired from his union leadership role, was sounding restrained and cautious about the strike.

But at meetings and in private conversations, Rodriguez heard that the overall community of union members was as strong as ever. He kept in touch with the other smaller unions, from trainmen to machinists to electricians—the so-called "PD Unity Council." Members were strong and ready to strike, their leaders said. Despite the bad economy, Rodriguez expected them all to show up at the midnight strike deadline. How could it be otherwise, Rodriguez reasoned? "Union was a way of life," Rodriguez said, "something that you grow up with." Of the holdouts, some would rejoin the union when they saw it was threatened. Rodriguez believed that the unions had become what Mother Jones envisioned in her speech in Clifton some seventy years earlier—not just laborers working together, but a united political community. Clifton and Morenci—and Bisbee, Douglas and Ajo—would again raise the flag of union solidarity, a heritage that had won them not only their good wages, but basic human rights.

Because of the Steelworkers' strict hierarchy, it was Frank McKee, the old-school "steel" Steelworker, who raised his hand over his head at the Ramada on June 30, 1983, and snapped his fingers. Negotiations chairman Lopez knew he was being summoned. McKee had reached a decision. (Steelworker procedure authorized the walkout without a vote on the company's last offer.) "Alex, tell your people we're not getting anywhere," said McKee. "PD wants to try and bust us. Can you get your troops together?" Lopez looked over at Rodriguez. Of course they could get the troops together. Of course they could whip Phelps Dodge.

 *Chapter 3*

Midnight at Morenci

We're not going to lose.
                    —Ray Aguilar

Shortly after 11:30 P.M., on June 30, 1983, smelter crane operator Ralph Martinez hopped into his Ford pickup and drove the five minutes from his rented Phelps Dodge house in Morenci to the mine gate. So did trainman Tito Carillo, pit laborer Mike Abrams, and picket captain Jim Krass. So did dozens of others. They came almost instinctively and in such numbers that they caused a mile-long traffic jam on Route 666 by the mine entrance. They were there to usher in the strike. To the public as well as to the union workers, a strike can be as abstract as the very notion of "economic warfare"—wage and benefit disputes, picketing, bursts of temper, newspaper articles full of claims and counterclaims, phlegmatic editorials. But not at the deadline. Especially not with a business whose fires run nonstop. Now the strike was imminent, unavoidable.

At the gate, those most committed to the strike resolved to be the first gatekeepers, the first pickets. Being first was a badge of honor and an element of local history. At the Open Pit Bar just down from the Morenci gate, the old-timers began their strike stories: "I was up at the first picket line at midnight . . ." and then the saga of '46 or '59 or '67 followed. "Hey, it's your livelihood at stake here," said crane operator Martinez, a union man at Phelps Dodge for fifteen years. And it was also your community. So you came to the gate, he said, "the way you come to see the Morenci Christmas tree lights go on." Midnight on June 30, 1983, in Morenci marked the birth of a new strike.

Smelterwomen, Vietnam Vets, and Union Mystics

When the strike began, Lydia Gonzales Roybal was a mill "mainte-nanceman," as she described it. Hired originally in 1978, she applied for the skilled job "on a dare" by men who said a woman couldn't do it. "I had three kids and no child support because my husband had left me," she recalled. She took the apprenticeship at the mill and quickly proved the men wrong. Yet, at the time of the strike, she was still the only woman in her division. She and her mother went up to the gate at 3:00 A.M. "for the memory of my Dad," she said. "He was very union-oriented, and so we all were."

Three Vietnam veterans, transportation worker Mike Cranford, machinist Joe Sorrelman, and miner LeRoy Cisneros, also went out. Behind their unionism dwelt a Vietnam tragedy. *Time* magazine had published a two-page feature about the trio in 1970, headlined "Semper Fidelis: The Marines of Morenci." The article described Morenci as the small town that suffered more than any other in America during the war. Nine buddies from Morenci High School had enlisted in the Marines and gone through training together, the article said. Six of the nine were killed in action, leaving only Cran-ford, Sorrelman, and Cisneros. Their photographs appeared side by side. *Time* concluded that an "unquestioning patriotism persists among most of Morenci's tough-minded mining families, despite the town's heavy loss." When Cranford, Sorrelman, and Cisneros came home from the war, they were side by side again, working for Phelps Dodge. At midnight some ten years later, all three honored the picket lines.

Copper unions offered some of the same discipline and support that the three men had experienced as Marines. "I couldn't betray the other people in the union," said Sorrelman, a Navajo Indian whose father had been recruited by Phelps Dodge during World War II from the town of Lukachukai on the Navajo reservation. The elder Sorrelman arrived in Morenci in the back of a flatbed truck. Added Cranford: "We wouldn't let one of the group fall out [in Vietnam]. And that's where it all starts. That's where your unionism goes back to."

Also at midnight, Leo Aguilar met his brother Ray at Ray's package store, Clifton Liquors. Leo was a boilermaker on layoff. Ray was a Steelworkers picket captain. Both supported the strike, but Leo told Ray that many others on layoff weren't so sure. Some were in debt to

Valley National Bank for their cars and to the Phelps Dodge Mercantile Store for their groceries. "Too many souls owed to the company store," Leo said. His voice resonated deeply in the closed quarters of the store: "Ray, we're going to lose this one. The best thing is if the union accepts what they can so they can hold the union here and keep us together." Ray scolded his brother, "No, we're not going to lose."

Faith in Union

Ralph Martinez drove past the gate and headed toward the Open Pit for a beer. He spotted a familiar face in the crowd as he neared the Morenci ice house. Ralph's son Mike, then nineteen years old, stood in the ice house parking lot with some friends and waved his father over. Mike was in his second year of theological training at a Catholic seminary in Ohio. He came home during the summers to visit with his old high school friends and help in the parish. He knew why his father was around this late and he recalled the tautness in his father's face—a look that every three years meant "strike."

Growing up in Morenci, Mike had learned children's lessons about the meaning of the union. He used to see his father come home from the mine coated in soot. "He was completely black and I used to ask him 'Where do you eat lunch, Dad? Doesn't your food get all black?' He told me that they used to have to eat their lunch with their ventilators on, taking a bite between breaths. Then, with the union, they won a lunchroom." But on this night, Mike learned an adult's lesson about the union. He sensed something heavier and brooding in his father. Everyone knew about Phelps Dodge's threat to continue operating without the strikers. That had never happened before. And they all had read the mine manager's letters threatening that workers who honored the strike might lose their jobs.

But in spite of what seminary student Mike Martinez thought he saw on his father's face, in spite of the company's threats, in spite of Leo Aguilar's midnight doubts, few of the rank-and-file union members really believed that this strike would end differently from successful strikes in past years. Ralph believed the union would prevail. The workers had heard other claims in previous years and they responded in kind: "PD will flex its muscles. We'll flex ours. PD'll make a few claims, crunch a few numbers, cut a few deals, and then we'll settle. Everyone will be back at work in a few weeks. Maybe a few months. It'll all work out. Meantime, Viva la Huelga!" Union member Abel Peralta put his lunch box on a shelf and told his wife, "Honey, this one will be over in a couple months, like always." Boilermaker Pete Castañeda and his wife didn't take the time to worry; they went hunting on the day the strike began. As always, the Steelworkers had taken their strike vote well before the negotiations. As always, the membership agreed. Strike if the company won't meet the pattern. That membership vote was the end of direct union democracy in the negotiation process; a contract signed by the union presidents had turned decision-making powers over to the copper conference representatives. Come hell or high water (or both), the rank and file put its faith in the union leadership. If the stakes of the battle were high, the methods of warfare seemed time-proven and reliable.

There was, after all, an old, almost family relationship between Phelps Dodge and the unions, one forged in machismo. "It's always been kind of a battle with them," said Ralph. "PD symbolized power. They were the ones who gave you your jobs. They were the ones you bought your food from. They were the ones who sent you your power bill. This was not like working for IBM or ATT. PD was a lot more than a copper company.

"If somebody threw a rock and broke a light bulb, they were the ones to investigate. If your kids were trouble makers, they would come to your house in that white Phelps Dodge security truck and ask you about it."

So when the chance came to give a little push back, union members relished it. But in the cycles of strikes prior to this one, life had gone on behind the scenes. No replacement workers were contemplated; the company simply shut down. Union members knew their jobs would be waiting for them when they came back. Phelps Dodge factored strikes into its maintenance schedule and used the time off to make repairs. Meanwhile, the company offered credit in its mercantile store and delayed collection of rent payments. Health benefits at the PD hospital were extended. To be sure, union members picketed—but some were also authorized to continue working in order to help update or maintain equipment. The union issued special cards to those workers. Many union members became so accustomed to the strikes that, like the Castañedas, they saved a little money in order to take extended vacations every three years during the strike. A virtual picket-line pool was created so that members could get some time off and drive the ten hours across the Arizona and California deserts to take their kids to Disneyland.

Though the past niceties were absent this time—no credit, no special union cards, no rent delays—Ralph Martinez heard the consensus at the Open Pit that PD's threats to take the union on weren't serious. And if they were, why, the union was strong enough to resist. But if the union members were confident of union loyalty, they did not yet know about the new Phelps Dodge discipline that had taken hold inside headquarters on Park Avenue in New York City.

Angel's Burden

Angel Rodriguez wanted to be at the gate with his troops, but hearing those last "No's" from the company (and, to be sure, helping his Steelworkers deliver a few of their own) had kept him all day at meetings in Phoenix. He telephoned the union office in Clifton and told picket captains Jim Krass and Mike Espinoza that they needed to get the men out in big numbers, to let the company know right away that the union could show its muscle. Rodriguez was exhausted from the day's events, but a few hours after the call from McKee he drove back to Clifton and Morenci.

· Rodriguez arrived at the picket line after 2:00 A.M. and shuttled back and forth between the line and the union office until dawn. Later that morning he led a mass meeting in Clifton. The turnout was huge and support for the strike was enthusiastic. But there was a sober note: for the first time in anyone's memory of PD strikes, the smelter stacks still chugged out a full plume of smoke. Supervisors and other management workers were making copper.

Phelps Dodge now put Moolick's strategy to work. The company immediately began a newspaper and letter war against the union, explaining in detail the rights of permanent replacement workers to take union jobs—and keep them even in the event of a settlement—and alternately coaxing and threatening strikers. In a series of newspaper ads published locally, the company argued that Phelps Dodge wages were higher than just about anywhere else and urged employees not to squander a good thing. Company officials even began to contact some of the senior union members to warn them about losing pension increases if replacement workers took their jobs. Phelps Dodge lawyers asked for (and got) injunctions from judges to limit pickets to five per gate. The company also tried to win an injunction against unruly language (words like "scab") but here the judges refused. Finally, Morenci mine manager John Bolles sent out a series of letters with threatening messages like this one: "Too many people for too few jobs is like a game of musical chairs. Have you thought about what it means to you and your family if *you* don't have a chair when the music stops?"

All current and furloughed employees were invited to take the jobs left vacant by strikers. In the first days of the strike, despite the pickets, several dozen did. The unions responded with appeals to members reminding them of their legal right to strike, weekly $40 strike payments, and a call to honor the picket line. As part of its public relations campaign, Phelps Dodge continued to tell reporters that "union-represented" workers were coming across the line—a legal truth, but little more. (This approach was deceptive because many of the initial strikebreakers had never been union members or had dropped dues payments when they were laid off. But all hourly workers at Phelps Dodge, including nonunion replacement workers, were "union-represented" because National Labor Relations Board rules held that the unions legally represented everyone.)

As the first days passed, the pickets marched in their circles and shouted epithets. Those who crossed the picket line tried to lie low. The company helped them by following the suggestions of the Wharton book, *Operating during Strikes*: tour buses were hired to transport workers en masse, and reimbursement was offered for any extra costs resulting from the strike.

Reporters like Don Harris of the *Arizona Republic* did their best to explain to the Arizona public what was happening. He wrote:

> So complex and unclear is the conflict that it has left some in the copper industry wondering what Phelps Dodge is trying to accomplish. All other major copper producers settled with a group of more than twenty unions, agreeing to freeze basic wages for three years while continuing to pay cost-of-living raises. Phelps Dodge balked at the cost-of-living provision, and killed it and any chance for labor peace.

Steelworkers local president Rodriguez declared, "We are preaching non-violence," but a copper firefight gradually escalated. In the first three weeks, violence mounted against strikebreakers, strikers, families, and mine properties. On July 2, newspapers reported the first punch: a strikebreaker was knocked in the face after work. There were no arrests. On July 10, a railroad trestle was burned; on July 12, eight windows at the smelter were shattered by rocks.

Soon, reporters were calling the copper towns "a burning fuse." Negotiators for both sides retreated to their own camps as the raw language of corporate and union power took hold. Rallies of as many as sixteen hundred strikers and supporters shook the Clifton football stadium. There, the strikers learned that their work in the fiscal quarter just before the strike had produced a profit for Phelps Dodge—a better performance than any of the other copper companies that had already agreed to the pattern contract. There were also low times for the strikers. A union chalkboard registered the small but growing list of line-crossers, and, on the same day as the big rally, a bolt of lightning struck a utility pole at the mine gate, scattering the union pickets. Shaken strikers wondered whether Nature, too, was taking sides.

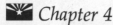 Chapter 4

Copper Wars

The bullet that pierced Chandra Tallant's skull early
Wednesday also shattered a fragile peace in this small
Arizona mining town.
                    —*Arizona Republic*, July 28, 1983

To this day no one has established who fired the weapon. No one could even be fully certain of the motive. But the shot was fired in the heat of the strike, four weeks after the first pickets, and the bullet tore into the house of the man known as Ajo's first strike-breaker, Keith Tallant. It crashed through a bedroom wall, through a pink pillow, and into the head of Tallant's sleeping three-year-old daughter, Chandra. The little girl was rushed by helicopter to a Phoenix hospital for surgery, and, miraculously, survived. But the incident drew accusations in the media against the unions and an immediate offer of a $100,000 reward from Phelps Dodge.

Keith and Marla Tallant had lived for four years in the boxy, copper-roofed company house in Ajo, at the edge of Arizona's organ pipe cactus forests. A burly shovel operator, Tallant had been laid off his job for nearly a year during the 1982 recession. He had never been a union member, believing more in his right to work than in any debt to labor unions for his $15-an-hour job. When Phelps Dodge announced it would continue mining operations during the strike, Tallant declared to his wife and anyone else who wanted to know that he, too, would continue to work. Although union friends warned him that once he crossed the line he would be their enemy, neither Tallant nor anyone else in Ajo believed that serious violence would hit this town. The Phelps Dodge mine and smelter in Ajo employed fewer than six hundred miners, a third the number at the flagship mine in Morenci, and Ajo had none of Morenci's reputation for union radicalism. But if this could happen in Ajo, what might be next? The bullet that struck Chandra Tallant was a startling salvo—to the town, the company, the unions, and the state.

Mystery over the bullet's origin only drew more attention to the strike. In addition to the human tragedy, the shooting was a public relations nightmare for the unions. If a striker was responsible, whatever public sympathy might have existed for the unions in this right-to-work state could evaporate. If a striker was not responsible, then the unions needed to establish that quickly. Instead, the unions got the worst of both worlds. Pima County sheriff Clarence Dupnik arrested a striker, keeping the case in the news—but then let him go, citing a lack of evidence. No one else was ever charged. With a headline announcing, "A Child Lies Wounded," the *Arizona Republic*, the only statewide newspaper, held the shooting up as an example of the inhumanity of unions, declaring, "What did the child do to deserve a bullet? She has a father working to support her while other Ajo kids' dads are on strike against the copper mines."

In an effort to immediately show that he was not letting the strike dissolve into anarchy, Arizona governor Bruce Babbitt entered the picture. In his fifth year as governor, the forty-four-year-old Babbitt had received increasing attention from what Washington insiders call "the Great Mentioners," influential writers and fundraisers in national politics. Babbitt was a surprising chief executive for a state that produced (and elected) conservatives like Barry Goldwater. A Democrat and ex–poverty warrior, Babbitt believed in a strong role by government to improve equality, reduce poverty, and save the environment. At the same time, he was a prototype of the Bill Clinton "neoliberal" (Babbitt was a founding member with Clinton of the Democratic Leadership Council) and he held that states should aim to solve their problems with a minimum of federal intervention. In 1982, Babbitt had been elected to a second term as governor by a comfortable margin (with the strong support of copper unions and the AFL-CIO), and there was speculation that he might run next for the U.S. Senate or eventually even for president. Of course, pundits and voters interested in Babbitt's future would want to know one thing in particular: how well he responded to a crisis.

Whatever the political consequences, Babbitt said the Chandra Tallant shooting focused him on one fundamental priority in the strike—avoiding loss of life. He visited Chandra in a Phoenix hospital after her surgery. The surgeons removed life-threatening blood clots but had to leave the bullet where it rested. "Here's this kid sitting on her bed, playing with a teddy bear, and she has a scar right there in the middle of her forehead," Babbitt said. "Mrs. Tallant just looked at me and asked, 'What are you doing to make sure this doesn't happen to someone else's kid?' "

Babbitt knew that strikes—especially mine strikes—bring with them picket-line violence and acts of intimidation. That was to be expected, perhaps even tolerated to some extent. But, he said, "This was a galvanizing point. This incident said to me, you've got to think about how to handle violence when it gets beyond the routine sort of scuffling on the picket line." So as Babbitt pondered, the unions scurried to put on their best face, and Phelps Dodge moved into a new phase of its strike plan. The shot fired in Ajo was only the first of many explosions to come.

※

Seven days after the Chandra Tallant shooting, the strike tensions heated up to match the stifling Phoenix temperatures. It was an August day that defied the mantra Arizonans swear by: "Hot, but dry." The day was hot, humid, and miserable. A stagnant brown cloud of desert dust and car exhaust covered the city. The negotiations were again stalled. Phelps Dodge was operating a limited production schedule with several hundred management workers and about three hundred employees who had crossed the line (many of whom previously had been on lay-off rather than active work status). Now, Phelps Dodge's New York brass had flown into Phoenix. Chairman George Munroe arrived "for something he couldn't do over the telephone," Steelworkers publicist Cass Alvin predicted. "This isn't such a good time of the year to be in Arizona." In fact, company officials were so nervous about potential union response to their actions that, instead of meeting at the copper-ornamented western headquarters building on Central Avenue in Phoenix, they secretly reserved an upstairs suite at the Doubletree Hotel a mile away. Vice President John Coulter, the former FBI man, had each executive drive to the meeting separately and along a different route—an old antiterrorism tactic. In this delicate phase of operations, said Coulter, "We wanted to shake anybody that was following us."

Advance press statements about the meeting sidestepped any

details. Chief Phelps Dodge negotiator Pat Scanlon said of Munroe's visit, "He's coming in strictly to be updated on how things are going. As far as I can tell, the meeting does not indicate any change." A reporter asked Scanlon whether the company intended to begin hiring outside permanent replacements, the single most likely event to turn a strike into a full-fledged brawl. Scanlon replied, "Not yet." But Scanlon was playing word games with the reporter. Replacing the union was exactly why the executive officers had come to town. A better word choice for Scanlon would have been that replacement actions were imminent—and even that would have been an understatement. For as of this August 1983 meeting, said company president Richard Moolick, "I had decided to break the unions."

Though CEO Munroe had always been the media's lightning rod during the strike, no one attending this meeting doubted who was in charge now. "Dick Moolick was the guy that made it all happen," said Jack Ladd, who had been chief negotiator until his windmill accident. Moolick had taken three critical steps toward this moment. First, he had broadcast his intentions of "taking on the unions" to the other company presidents, putting his own reputation on the line as the 1983 negotiations approached. Next, he had maintained a harder line than all the other copper producers by refusing to continue quarterly cost-of-living increases, which had been a part of union contracts since the early 1970s. Finally, he had decided for the first time in the company's modern history to continue all operations during a strike, creating an immediate need for replacement workers. On the balance sheet, there was little to be gained by such a move— the company had shut down the year before when copper prices were eighty cents a pound, ten cents a pound higher than they were in August 1983. None of the other companies were then operating at anything near full production for Phelps Dodge. In fact, the company's private legal counsel and adviser, John Boland, Jr., and various Phelps Dodge officials proposed a partial shutdown to Moolick. But Moolick refused in order to deliver the knockout blow to the unions.

All of these decisions, of course, required CEO Munroe's approval. But that's where the 150-year-old firm behaved, literally, as an empire. Munroe, the czar, directed the financial side of the company's vast world holdings and, with his golden résumé, boosted the company's standing on Wall Street. Moolick, the gritty, creative, unstoppable (and sometimes insufferable) engineer, had received the power of Rasputin; the strike decisions were his to call.

Privately, Moolick doubted Munroe's will to make the hard decisions, like breaking the union. But if there had ever been any doubt in either Moolick or Munroe about who would make the Arizona labor decisions, that doubt had evaporated in the solemn meeting in Munroe's office in 1982. There Munroe had promised Moolick the Arizona labor portfolio as part of Moolick's powers as company president. According to Moolick, neither Munroe nor the board of directors ever raised a question about the use of permanent replacements. Now Munroe's promise was bearing its prickly fruit.

Negotiating in bad faith violates labor laws as defined under the National Labor Relations Act. Despite Moolick's assertion of "room for compromise," had his intent to break the unions been publicly revealed, the company might well have been charged with breaching provisions that require good faith bargaining and forbid discrimination against unions. The federal labor board and courts might then have preserved the union jobs for the duration of the strike. But Moolick had the protection of experience: after years in the business (and with the Wharton School's legal and practical guide) he knew what kind of public acts or statements could be held against the company. In addition, Moolick could rely on a regional director of the NLRB in Phoenix who was widely considered a friend of management (see chapter 8). After inviting current and former employees to cross the line (fewer than five hundred out of a total of twenty-four hundred did), Moolick decided to permanently replace the work force with strikebreakers.

Moolick stood ready to give the orders from New York, but Munroe felt that some executive diplomacy was now in order. That's why the great powers of Phelps Dodge assembled for the secretive August 4 meeting. Doubletree Hotel employees might well have wondered at the succession of men in dark suits heading to the same luxury bedroom suite. Room service provided extra chairs. CEO Munroe welcomed everyone. Next to him sat Moolick; next, Vice President and Director of Western Operations Arthur Kinneberg; Vice President John Coulter; chief negotiator Scanlon; and labor relations director Jack Ladd (bandaged and in a wheelchair from his injury). There was no vote. Moolick praised the management team effort at continuing operations and announced the next phase—that the company would begin hiring permanent replacements on the following Monday.

"Any comments?" he asked. One of the group blurted out excitedly, "We're home free." Moolick cautioned: "You ain't seen nothin' yet."

As the former Morenci manager, Moolick knew something about the charge that would go off in the hearts of workers when they saw outsiders taking their jobs. Unions generally maintain at least a veneer of control over a strike when the replacements are crossovers and furloughed employees. Strikers can look their ex-colleagues in the eye and cuss them out; they can impose a measure of shame. These are neighbors, friends, family. But outside replacements are a declaration of war on unionism. They have just one role—to take union jobs—and they are virtually immune to pressure from the unions. After the executive meeting, Phelps Dodge called a press conference. With Coulter's twisting route through town and Scanlon's savvy spin doctoring, the company had preserved an element of surprise. But the evening news reports of Friday, August 5, 1983, announced the declaration of war: the Morenci, Tucson, and Phoenix employment offices would begin hiring outside replacements on the following Monday.

The Day That Everything Stopped

With Phelps Dodge's announced plan to hire permanent replacements, word went out in Clifton and Morenci that Monday would be "the day that everything stops." This was not a union message. It was a community siren, conveyed from house to house and telephone to telephone. Mine manager John Bolles, whose home overlooked the town centers and whose office was just down from the plant gate, heard it coming. On the Sunday after the Phoenix meetings and the day before the employment office was to open, he awoke to headlines in the August 7 *Arizona Daily Star*: "Windows Smashed in Morenci; Tension Builds on Picket Lines." The story quoted Ernie Valenzuela, a five-year employee: "There's going to have to be some violence here—you just can't let people take over your job, your home. It's just going to be one hell of a mess if they bring in people off the street. It's going to be a battle." Union spokesman Cass Alvin told reporters that, by bringing in outside hires, the company was "inviting trouble. . . . It would take an army to protect the mines."

Friendly and well liked by the union members, mine manager Bolles felt a heavy burden of responsibility to Morenci, the company town. A Montana native, Bolles had worked with the union and clergy to help break down the old barriers of racial and ethnic discrimination against Mexican-Americans in Morenci. He had also tried to get away from "Papa Dodge"—the old-fashioned paternalism of Phelps Dodge. But now there was really nothing he could do. New York was exerting its full prerogative again as land and business owner. No one had invited him to the Phoenix meeting. Bolles didn't know it then, but Moolick had decided that he was an obstacle to winning. ("Morenci was the gem of Phelps Dodge," Moolick later explained. "John wasn't strong enough to handle the gem." Bolles was later transferred to Ajo.) Anticipating a bloody Monday, Bolles headed to his ranch across the New Mexico border in Silver City for a Sunday horseback ride into the desert.

Where a festive, mile-long chain of cars had ushered in the strike at midnight five weeks earlier, Monday, August 8, arrived with an angry crowd that by midday swelled to two thousand men and women—a third of the population of Clifton and Morenci combined. Leading the way from Clifton to Morenci was Frank Andazola, Jr., known to his friends as "Beaver." A career electrician, he was one of many who stood to be permanently replaced. His father, Francisco, an electrician and plumber, was about to retire—forgoing his fortieth year (and company recognition) because he couldn't afford to wait out the strike. Beaver's brother, the ex-rock crusher Bobby Andazola, phoned in his support from Phoenix where he was working a job in construction. (Bobby's famous highway stand would come some months later, at the strike's first anniversary.)

Some demonstrators, like crane operator Ralph Martinez, arrived thinking of resistance rather than aggression—they believed they might still move a mountain by chanting "Union," screaming "Scab," and demanding a contract. Others felt that it was time to show muscle, to carry out the prophecies of the Sunday paper. At about 8:00 A.M., two permanent replacement applicants wheeled their motorcycles into the employment office parking lot near the Open Pit bar on Route 666. They were greeted by two hundred furious unionists. The two men, one a Morenci native with a reputation as a renegade, had never worked at Phelps Dodge, but now they brashly moved through the gauntlet of union protesters in order to apply for the union jobs. The crowd wrapped itself around the office like a snake and demanded that employment director Dick Boland close it down.

Boland, a short man with a halting voice, rushed over to the employment office from the central administration building down the road. He never made it in the door. State troopers had arrived and were escorting the two men out of the building. Strikers promptly kicked the motorcycles to the ground. Machinist Conrad Gomez watched the gasoline ooze from the motorcycles and asked a friend for a cigarette—"and I don't smoke," Gomez recalled later. Instead of setting the fire (and igniting the mob), Gomez and the others began to demand that the office shut down. As the two strikebreakers departed, several in the crowd warned Boland that the replacements had better not go in to work or the crowd would follow them in. Boland promised that they wouldn't and agreed to close the Morenci employment office. But within minutes, a rumor spread that the men had been allowed in a back entrance of the Phelps Dodge mine. As the clock ticked down toward the 3:00 P.M. shift change, protesters surged toward the gate, making a half-mile human chain along U.S. 666.

A chilling chant went up from the crowd at the gate for mine manager Bolles to "Close it down!" Seeing that sixty state troopers would not be able to control the crowd, state Department of Public Safety (DPS) commander Ernie Johnson cautiously approached and picked out the first union member who looked like he might have some authority, six-foot six-inch operating engineer, Rick Melton. "I'll make you a deal and talk to John Bolles and ask him to come down," Johnson told Melton—if Melton would keep the crowd from attacking strikebreakers who were leaving or attempting to come in on the shift change.

The scene had all the markings of an Old West showdown. Two Phelps Dodge officials—Bolles and company attorney Jim Speer—appeared from behind the mine gate, smelter smokestacks in the background. They walked down the highway, away from the mine entrance. Two union members—Melton and boilermaker Angel Peralta—walked slowly up the highway to join them. (Knowing that any violence could legally be attributed to the union, elected union leaders stayed away from the rally.) Wearing the copper star of Arizona's DPS on his shoulder, Johnson came over to mediate. The five men gathered directly in the center of U.S. 666. Hundreds in the crowd followed and formed a cordon behind this nervous convocation. Peralta opened by telling Bolles that "something has to be done, and it has to be done right now, or you're going to see something you've never seen before." Peralta asked him for "a ray of hope" that the mine would cease operations. Melton added, "Whatever you do Mr. Bolles, don't lie to me. A thousand people can get pretty upset, and I can't negotiate for them. I can only tell them what you tell me."

For the first time in his thirty-plus years in mining, including the years down a shaft, John Bolles felt a shiver of fear for his life. He told the two men that he could not close down the mine but that he would cancel the shift changes for twenty-four hours. He wanted a promise that the crowd would lay down their sticks, clubs, and baseball bats. He also informed the two men that Governor Babbitt and top union and company negotiators were flying in to Clifton for emergency meetings. Peralta and Melton passed along word of the shift cancellations and the Babbitt visit. Hoping that this would be enough to calm the crowd for the moment, Bolles waved one of the company transports out the gate, but protesters surrounded the bus full of strikebreakers and yelled at the occupants to get out. When the strikers began to rock the bus back and forth, union spokesman Melton rushed over and begged the protesters to register their grievances later at the Clifton courthouse. In the end, Melton had to board the bus himself and escort it through the jeering masses.

Much of the crowd finally dispersed, murmuring on the way out that operations still had to shut down. Bolles, meanwhile, returned to the mine and told the three hundred or so remaining workers that they had the option of staying the night or going home. Fearing the wrath of the protesters, most decided to spend the night on cots inside the mine.

Rain began to fall over the yawning pit. A scattering of strikers kept a vigil at the gate, most just watching smelter smoke rise into the late afternoon mist.

Bruce Babbitt's Peace Shuttle

On the evening of Monday, August 8, 1983, Governor Babbitt left Phoenix for Clifton on a bumpy, storm-blown flight in the state's twin-engine airplane. He had taken this same flight just two and a half months earlier to deliver the graduation address at Clifton High School. On that day, he warned students that times were changing, that the copper industry might not be able to provide them jobs as it had to their parents. They needed to look to the future. Babbitt remembers thinking during his crisis return to Clifton that perhaps these were the death throes of copper.

From his window seat, Babbitt watched the lightning, listened to the strategies of his chief of staff, Andrew Hurwitz, and mulled the odd twists of Arizona history. Scion of a pioneer family and himself an expert geophysicist (as well as a Harvard-trained lawyer), Babbitt understood equally well Arizona's geologic and social fault lines. From an early age, Babbitt was a rock hound, exploring the dried river beds and abandoned mines around the Grand Canyon. His was the kind of childhood that spurred western novels, not just presidential ambitions. As a grade-schooler, he often hiked to the edge of the Mogollon Rim where, looking south, he could see the copper smelters outside the town of Jerome. When the mines there were still active in the 1950s, "you could see the slag piles glowing at night," Babbitt recalled. With buddies, he climbed down lost shafts, tramped through tunnels with carbide lamps, and knocked hunks of rock off the wall to put in a collection.

Babbitt's rock hunting led naturally to studies in the sciences. After taking his undergraduate degree at Notre Dame University, he won a Marshall fellowship and completed a master's degree in geophysics at Newcastle upon Tyne, England. His thesis was titled, "A Paleo-Magnetic Chronology of the San Francisco Volcano Fields." Years later, Babbitt changed directions, attending Harvard law school and heading South to march with Martin Luther King, Jr.

As he bounced through the stormy night in the state airplane, Babbitt recalled how Arizona's first-ever chief executive had made the same trip by train during the famous 1915 Clifton-Morenci strike. On that trip, Governor George Hunt had expressed his support for the strikers' cause and then called in the National Guard to keep scabs out of town. Babbitt thought of his trip as the return of Governor Hunt—but with an unfortunate historical twist. "I thought, you know, I'm going to disappoint them. Whether or not a governor ever had the power to unilaterally shut a company down, I don't. My options are pretty limited. I am operating with a [Republican] attorney general who will at every turn be waiting to do the opposite of everything that I want to do. And there's a legislature sitting in Phoenix ready to have hearings at the request of Phelps Dodge the minute they can get away with it in public opinion."

Chief of Staff Hurwitz reported to Babbitt that the union would ask him to shut the mine down and the company would ask him to call in the National Guard. Arizona laws "gave Phelps Dodge all of the cards," Babbitt said. "There was nothing suggesting I had any jurisdiction to be there at all. And a lot of union people didn't understand that.

"On the flight over, I was listening to Andy spin out a million theories about what it was all about and watching the lightning out the window. I knew that theories and analyses don't really have much to do with this. You just gotta walk straight in and assess the situation. My essential political problem was that I had virtually no leverage." After a harrowing hour of circling due to the storms, the plane set down on the rough Clifton runway. DPS cars, their lights flashing the emergency, rushed Babbitt and staff the six miles north along U.S. 666 to the courthouse.

Flashbulbs, halogen lights, television cameras, and several hundred strikers greeted Babbitt at the mid-evening gathering. The union brought in chief negotiator Alex Lopez and local Steelworkers president Angel Rodriguez. The company sent chief negotiator Pat Scanlon and the duo of mine manager Bolles and attorney Speer, who had defused the highway crowd earlier in the day. The groups settled into separate rooms at the courthouse. Flyers pasted to the walls told of upcoming construction work and warned of the building's instability, a curious parallel to the talks that were beginning.

As expected, the unions asked Babbitt to order Phelps Dodge to close down. Phelps Dodge asked Babbitt to order the unions off the highway and to protect the strikebreakers with troops. Babbitt met separately with each group, shuttling between rooms like a peace negotiator. He spent much of the time sharing "war stories" with his staff as he awaited offers of compromise. One of the clearest messages Babbitt heard from the company officials was that they had no new authority to negotiate. Phelps Dodge, said Babbitt, "stayed as far away from the issues as they possibly could. They took a sort of hyper-correct view: 'We've made an offer. We're waiting for a counteroffer. And we have nothing to say in the meantime.' Their labor negotiating strategy was carefully planned and they stuck to their script." Still, negotiator Scanlon (who had originally denied that a permanent replacements plan was in place) now had received an okay from Moolick to offer a ten-day moratorium on hiring replacements. By midnight, Scanlon had offered the moratorium and both sides had agreed that a federal mediator would be called in for the negotiations in Phoenix. That was all. During the ten-day moratorium, Phelps Dodge planned to keep operating its mines, and, meanwhile, push the legislature and governor for protection of outside workers. (According to Rodriguez, most historical accounts of this strike err by reporting that Babbitt arranged a mine shutdown.) The union leaders grudgingly accepted the moratorium. Babbitt flew with his staff back into the night.

∿⁂

The reaction to the midnight agreement was even more explosive than earlier. The smelter stacks were still belching sulphur, and the community had reached the end of its own collective patience. In as great a number as the day before, the protesters returned to the gate that next morning, August 9. The crowd was angry, waving bats and demanding a shutdown by noon. A little before 10:30 A.M., Scanlon, Bolles, and Boland could see through the administrative office windows about three hundred yards south of the gate that the crowd was eyeing the central offices. "We had been told that many of them had been up all night drinking at the gate," said Scanlon. "You could see them moving up to the gate with softball bats, lengths of pipe, chains." Administrators monitored CB radios, and Bolles claimed that he heard reports of strikers driving through Morenci waiting for an order to torch the Phelps Dodge houses. (The state police said later that they never had any evidence of this.) A fear of armed attack also hung over the company officials—most miners as well as managers owned hunting rifles.

With a knock on the office door, solemn Steelworkers local president Angel Rodriguez and negotiations committee member Ray Isner, an engineer, entered the Phelps Dodge mine office. The company and union reps had stayed in separate rooms the night before. Now they told Scanlon face-to-face that the union had completely lost control. "The people at the gate say if the company does not agree by twelve noon to shut down production, they will rush the gate and the DPS officers," Rodriguez told Scanlon. "They say they will go inside the plant and drag everyone out. If that means killing them, they say they will kill them." The sight of bats waving in the crowd outside drove home the imminence of the threat. "We concluded they were serious," said Scanlon, a wiry, soft-spoken executive.

Word of the possible invasion passed through the mine as well. Workers there started to fashion what one company official described as "the weirdest assortment of weapons you've ever seen—clubs, boards with nails sticking out." A blacksmith area was converted into a workshop for shields and metal weapons. Workers in the smelter turned around a huge lead pellet cannon usually used to blast deposits off the interior of furnaces. They were preparing for a copper war.

State DPS officer Dave Boyd, an expert marksman and rodeo rider, was one of sixty officers assigned to the gate that day. When Boyd heard about the crowd's threats, he started to calculate his options. "I began to count the baseball bats, and then I counted my rounds of ammunition. I don't know why you think about things like that, but that's what I was thinking." He could see that DPS was outnumbered but calculated that each officer could take out several men. If the crowd stormed the gate, that might be necessary, he thought.

Prior to the mass rallies at the gate, DPS had moved more freely among the strikers. "We could talk to them, see what they felt," said Boyd. "Now a line was drawn, and they were on one side and we were on the other."

It was an hour and a half before the noon deadline. "We're working against the clock," Scanlon nervously told union leaders Rodriguez and Isner. They could offer no extension. Scanlon attempted to reach company president Moolick, who was supposed to be responsible for such critical strike decisions as shutting down the mine. Scanlon reached Munroe instead: "George said, 'You're on the scene. Do whatever you think is proper.' " Scanlon turned the copper bracelet on his wrist a few times, took another look out the windows, and then wrote up a brief statement agreeing to meet the mob's demands. "I signed it on behalf of the company and ran off two or three hundred copies," Scanlon said. "When we got it out there, I guess it was about ten minutes before twelve."

Union president Rodriguez read the statement over a bullhorn to the crowd: "The company agrees to stop copper production at its Morenci branch immediately. The company also agrees to stop hiring new employees for the Morenci branch immediately." Scanlon, however had not made any promises of a shutdown at the other company properties in Ajo, Bisbee, Douglas, or El Paso, Texas. Any concerns that the crowd might include these sites in its list of demands were eased when Rodriguez followed his reading of the company's statement about the ten-day shutdown with a few calming words of his own. "We've got a victory here," Rodriguez declared. "Let's don't blow it. You've got it in writing. [The strikebreakers] are going to come out peacefully. Don't punch the cars—don't throw anything. Just watch 'em." A mass march followed along the highway, with some of the strikers waving their bats and chains in victory. Now the chant was "Union! Union! Union!"

As the union crowd moved past the administrative offices, an office employee videotaped the raucous departure. The company would later use these scenes to forever ban many of the strikers—Frank Andazola, Jr., for one—from work at Phelps Dodge. Also watching the strikers from a hill overlooking the gate was a plainclothes special intelligence officer named Steve Kuykendall. Greenlee County sheriff Bobby Gomez was not eager to turn his county over to DPS (state troopers were often regarded by local law enforcement as arrogant and capable of making a sheriff look helpless), so he had called Kuykendall to see if the state organization known as the Arizona Criminal Intelligence Systems Agency (ACISA) could give him a hand. As Kuykendall watched the gate drama unfold, he made a note to himself to recommend to his boss in Tucson that they assist Sheriff Gomez. This strike might call for some undercover work. For the next several weeks, through informants and high-tech spying equipment, Kuykendall and two other ACISA agents "attended" more union meetings than most of the members.

A third set of eyes on the strikers were those of DPS trooper Dave Boyd. For the first time that day, Boyd could drop the idea of having to take aim at a striker. He relaxed his hands and set down his rifle. "It's a wonder no one was killed," he said later. "You know why nothing happened? I can only think of one reason. Because they didn't have a leader telling them to go in [to the mine]." Still, raw force had accomplished what five weeks of negotiations could not—an agreement to shut down the mine and stop hiring permanent replacements.

Moolick's Fury

When CEO Munroe informed president Richard Moolick about the ten-day shutdown later that afternoon, Moolick quietly burned. He had worried all along that someone would back off his "game plan." And now someone—in fact, George Munroe himself—had done just that. Though at least one of the Western Operations managers insisted that he had spoken with Moolick before the shutdown, Moolick said he wasn't consulted—and that if he had been, he would have responded, "No way." "They were buying the Steelworkers rhetoric," Moolick said of the gate confrontation. To get the full story and castigate his troops, Moolick flew back into Phoenix from New York—just five days after flying in for the permanent replacement announcement. "I was prepared to fire Scanlon, Bolles, and [general superintendent] Kinneberg," Moolick said.

Scanlon arrived at about the same time as Moolick did and met with him in the Sky Harbor Airport coffee shop. Moolick had never seen anyone so shaken—"I was a combat pilot in the Marshall Islands and there's only one guy I've seen terrified like that. He'd gotten hit with flak. Pat's lips were trembling, his voice was trembling, and this was eight or ten hours after the incident."

After hearing from the ex–FBI man, Coulter, who agreed with Scanlon's decision to shut down, Moolick backed off from firing anyone. Instead, he called a meeting at Phelps Dodge headquarters in downtown Phoenix. He closed the curtains in the glassed-in conference room and, under the portraits of the Phelps Dodge founders, admonished the group for backing down. He informed them that, to keep all the hourly workers who had crossed the line on the company's side, each one would continue to be paid for a forty-hour week during the shutdown. Then he announced a new plan for avoiding a repeat when the mine reopened, something that shocked several of those present. "I had twenty shotguns smuggled in [to the mine] with a bunch of ammunition," Moolick explained later. "The big argument was—I was going for double-aught shot and another guy was going for number seven [pellets]." The latter was birdshot, while Moolick's choice was buckshot—about four times as deadly. "They won that one," Moolick said. The guns were sent in with number seven shot.

Another threat to Moolick's "game plan" arrived in the person of Phelps Dodge counsel and negotiator John Boland. Boland had been doing Phelps Dodge's legal work for thirty years and was considered one of the most authoritative voices in the company's Western Operations. He also had a feel for the common worker. In the 1940s, in an effort to save his asthmatic son's life, Boland had moved his family from New York to Tucson. While awaiting his license to practice law, Boland ran a Tucson gas station. (Boland sometimes played the iconoclast: he drove a Chevrolet Corvair with a vanity license plate that said "NADER," mocking the consumer advocate who had labeled those cars unsafe at any speed.)

Boland and his son Dick, the Morenci personnel manager, arrived together at headquarters for the emergency meetings. They sat quietly through Moolick's criticism, and afterward told Moolick privately that they felt Morenci should be shut down for the longer run. The Ajo property, which was easier to manage during the strike because the Tucson-based sheriff's department had taken charge of law enforcement, could pick up some of the production. On why he made this pitch, John Boland said later, "The events going on around us were so traumatic that men of goodwill . . . had to have thought that night about whether we were doing the right thing by the company and by the community. Those are the kinds of thoughts one gets at night—not the kinds of thoughts that appear in public."

Already seething at Munroe and Scanlon's ten-day shutdown, Moolick was infuriated by this proposal, seeing it as a sign of weakness. He reconvened the executive meeting after lunch to ask other officers what they thought of the shutdown alternative. Other than the Bolands, no one spoke up for it. Although there was some sympathy for the shutdown position among Phelps Dodge's other Arizona managers, those officials knew that Moolick could not be turned back. Morenci would reopen at the end of ten days. The Bolands, like mine manager Bolles, were eventually demoted by Moolick—in part because of their expression of community concern.

Copper Towns Come to Phoenix

As originally agreed at the emergency meeting with Babbitt, a federal mediator entered the negotiations in Phoenix to try and bring the parties to a contract agreement. But the more significant action occurred on a political plane. Strikebreakers, strikers, company officers, and union leaders flowed into the copper-domed state capitol to sway their governor. Many of these people had worked to elect Babbitt and had known him long enough to call him "Bruce." Strikers explained their position and asked Babbitt to keep the National Guard away. Strikebreakers asked for protection. Babbitt and Chief of Staff Andrew Hurwitz met almost daily with union and company officials.

During this ceasefire, Phelps Dodge aggressively moved into the legislature. The company accused Babbitt of having withheld law enforcement protection during the gate incident by assigning only sixty officers. Arizona Republican Party chairman John Munger rushed to this political opportunity, declaring, "Governor Babbitt is grossly negligent in his inexcusable failure to act decisively. The governor's weak-kneed response and the shutdown of the Morenci mine . . . has, so far, cost Arizona's economy $8 million in lost copper production."

Reminiscent of Phelps Dodge's glory years early in the century, the company called on Arizona's top lobbyists to do its bidding. A well-known local powerbroker, lawyer Jim Bush, pressed the Republican majority in the legislature to pass laws showing that "right to work" in Arizona meant more than the technical right not to join a union. "There's no right to work if you can't get there without having your life endangered," he asserted, urging the legislature to take the law enforcement powers away from Babbitt. Phelps Dodge Western Operations director Kinneberg echoed that view, declaring to the newspapers that the only reason Phelps Dodge had closed down was because "the company had a gun to its head."

Top Republicans, including the legislature's judiciary committee chair, proposed a bill to tighten Arizona's right-to-work law to help the strikebreakers. The bill would shift law enforcement controls from the governor to the attorney general (a Republican), who could then order DPS or police agencies to the copper towns. With this barrage, the Republicans were on the verge of launching a coup d'état on behalf of Phelps Dodge.

On August 11, two days after the shutdown, federal mediator Sam Franklin reopened the negotiations at a new site, the Desert Hills Hotel near downtown Phoenix. The union minutes note rather dryly, "Mr. Franklin stated that the activities of the past week had not led to a resolution of the dispute. 'Rhetoric does not settle disputes—full discussion does lead to a settlement,' he said."

After hearing separately from each side, Franklin met the press. Reporters asked whether he saw any basis for a settlement. Franklin, a grizzled, retired Steelworker with an arm etched in tattoos, responded that he could think of "only one strike in human history that ended without a settlement." An uncomfortable silence settled on the room, and finally one reporter asked, "Which strike was that?" Franklin responded: "When the Israelites fled Egypt, crossing the Red Sea." That remark brought howls from the gallery—but these were reporters, not union members, laughing.

At the Table

Back in the negotiating room, Phelps Dodge again demanded major reductions, including an end to cost-of-living adjustments. The company also proposed changes in its medical coverage on a piece-meal basis, which the unions considered an attempt at delaying or avoiding consideration of the union package. The company's approach put the unions' hard-won wage structure in danger. If one company broke away from the pattern, then all the others could also start demanding wage reductions. Outside the hearing of the mediator and company, union spokesman Cass Alvin drilled the union committee at these August 11 meetings. "We have a commitment to thousands of people—we've come in bare-assed, asking for nothing more than what we had before. Make it clear that nothing is settled until everything is settled."

In somewhat more diplomatic language, when federal mediator Franklin entered the room, Steelworkers district director Robert Petris made a pitch to Franklin for first principles: "One, the pattern has been set. PD has chosen not to go with it, but the pattern still has to be met. Two, we will not bargain one issue at a time. Three, in other settlements there were accommodations to meet those particular problem areas in each company. We will talk to PD's problems in particular." Franklin responded that this list was not enough, that it gave the company an excuse to back out. He asked if the union had a position that would be the basis for an "unofficial settlement." Petris responded only by saying that the unions refused to "sell our souls"—meaning abandon the pattern—to Phelps Dodge. Petris's rare appearance showed how the pattern itself had risen to the level of principle.

At the next day's negotiation session, Franklin, frustrated by the gridlock, called for innovation and some collective brainstorming. He got only the storms. Phelps Dodge's Scanlon told the unions that "the company wants to be innovative, so I suggest that the unions take what PD has offered"—wage cuts for new hires, reduced medical and vacation benefits across-the-board, and termination of cost-of-living increases. Petris replied sarcastically that "accepting PD's offer is not my idea of innovative." Scanlon waved his arms and declared that he had dined the night before with company president Moolick and "Moolick stuck his finger on my chest and said 'You give away one million dollars and that's all the concessions we will give.' There's no more money in the pot." So Scanlon offered to leave the old medical care package intact. With that, the table fell silent.

A few days later, on August 15, union leaders caught up with Franklin out of earshot of the company negotiators. The previous negotiations session had been the first time they heard Moolick's name brought up at the table. They asked Franklin if he thought the Phelps Dodge negotiators had any real authority to act. Showing some insight into the Phelps Dodge hierarchy and the tight plays called for by the company's game plan, Franklin responded cryptically, "They have the authority within their framework." Franklin suggested that it was time to bring the true decision makers from both sides together—Moolick of Phelps Dodge and McKee of the Steelworkers.

When Franklin left that brief meeting, Petris, the Steelworkers district director, criticized the members who were beginning to push for a settlement. Petris reminded the bargaining committee that the dispute with Phelps Dodge was not simply about cost-of-living adjustments or medical care but about an entire union platform of coordinated bargaining that had been constructed over a period of fifteen years or more. "Any deviation," Petris warned, "would set us back to prior to 1967."

As the ten-day cooling-off clock ticked down, mediator Franklin brought Moolick and Steelworkers coalition chairman McKee together for the first time on August 16. Moolick described the meeting as a kind of gathering of the godfathers (even down to the solemn voices) but one of the leaders was clearly in a better position than the other to hold onto his power. According to Moolick, "I said 'Frank, I don't have any give in me. Do you have any give in you?' " The response, Moolick said, was no. "We talked about golf mostly." McKee told reporters after the meeting, "I wish I could say 'Yes, it's going to get things going,' but it wasn't this type of meeting." Moolick and McKee met privately on two other occasions at a New York restaurant, but they never found any common ground. Moolick said that bright prospects for operating the mines with replacement workers led him to the conclusion that "there wasn't any reason for me to talk."

On August 20, the last day of the shutdown, the negotiations dragged along like a death march. The company argued that it could save $25 million over three years by terminating cost-of-living adjustments. The unions repeated their position that they could not back off the contracts signed earlier with other copper producers

(Kennecott, ASARCO, Inspiration, and Magma) but would scour work rules and other local conditions to come up with some savings. That wasn't enough for Phelps Dodge. The parties began bickering over minor matters such as how much money could be saved by reducing the number of company janitors. In almost absurd attention to detail that day, Scanlon told the unions, "We want to stop furnishing gloves except in abnormal wear."

Days of Decision

As the two sides again stalled, Governor Babbitt faced perhaps the most difficult decision of his career. Should he call in the troops when the mine reopened? Organized labor regarded such an action as a politician's deadliest sin. Union memory ran back to a time in history when American common law regarded strikes as criminal conspiracies against companies; police force was justified to stop the conspiracy, and if the troops didn't outright open fire against strikers, they were usually a symbol of strikebreaking. Governors had sent the National Guard to places like the coal mines of Ludlow, Colorado, where, near the turn of the century, Guardsmen gunned down strikers and children sleeping in tents. Before 1983, the most memorable recent use of the Guard had been the governor of Ohio's attempt to break up a student protest against the war in Vietnam. When the Guard fired into the crowd, killing four students, this action became known as the Kent State massacre.

Babbitt already had on his desk a plea from Greenlee County sheriff Bobby Gomez. Gomez had been "chased out of town" by the crowds, said Babbitt aides. Gomez's fifteen-man force, even with DPS, didn't have much bargaining power against two thousand strikers. Hovering over any of Babbitt's decisions was his own political future. Arizona's conservative majority might approve of National Guard intervention but liberal Democrats certainly would not. Labor might never forgive him. Babbitt played poker-faced in public, telling reporters, "In the immediate crisis there are lives at stake and you just simply check the politics and do what business has to be done. You let the future take care of itself."

Inside the governor's office, Babbitt called an emergency meeting to chart a plan. This was vintage Babbitt: bring a half-dozen top aides to the executive conference room and offer them a complex problem; then, poised at a table under the state seal, challenge their answers with the Socratic method. Called in on this day were chief of staff Andrew Hurwitz, executive assistant George Britton, and top aides Chris Hamel, Fred DuVal, and Ronnie Lopez. They were joined later by DPS director Colonel Ralph Milstead. "What are our values? What are we trying to accomplish?" Babbitt asked the group. Executive assistant George Britton, regarded as the dispassionate "Mr. Spock" of the governor's office, answered, "We're going to have little effect on the negotiations. The company has chosen to break the union, and our ability to have leverage on that is minimal." Britton had been sent by Babbitt to take a close look at the problems in Morenci. He reported back at this meeting, warning, "Everybody has a gun up there—I mean everybody. The company has a gun. The strikers have a gun. The kids have guns. This is a hunting community and the sheriff has really lost control. The traditional bounds of civil law obviously aren't being enforced very much." Though he didn't provide details, Britton also referred to "intelligence" on the strike that suggested trouble.

From the community angle, Babbitt also asked to hear from aide Ronnie Lopez, who had once worked in a copper smelter and had risen from community leader to justice of the peace to governor's aide. A handsome, stocky man with jet-black hair, Lopez was Babbitt's only Mexican-American aide and a former leader of the influential Phoenix activist organization "Chicanos por la Causa." Lopez had grown up in Miami-Globe, a mining community near Phoenix. At the time of the strike, his mother was a miner for one of the companies that had agreed to the pattern contract. Still, Lopez said that the governor's choice was "between law and order or civil disorder." He had spoken with friends in the copper towns who indicated that, after the ten-day cooling-off period, there might be thousands of people back at the gate in Morenci. Lopez felt that the governor should be ready for the worst. Speaking several years after the strike, Lopez explained, "We needed back-up support for the Department of Public Safety. At that time, I didn't view calling out the Guard [in Morenci] like calling out the Guard at Kent State. It wasn't to break down the labor dispute. It was a support system for the DPS front line. . . . [But] if I knew then what I know now, we would never have done it." Aside from the fire Babbitt took from labor unions, Lopez's union mother refused to speak to him for years after the Guard went in.

Executive assistant Britton said of the day's conclusions: "We played off each other. How should the Department of Public Safety respond and could it respond in a manner which didn't provoke additional violence? The conclusion drawn not by governor's staff but by [DPS's Milstead] was that they just didn't have enough people."

At the end of the meeting, Babbitt outlined what he called "the paradigm." "We protect life first, human values second, and property third. Anything that minimizes the possibility of somebody getting killed or injured—that's the choice option." No one said anything out loud, but the Socratic outcome was clear: the Guard was going in.

Higher Intelligence

What was the "intelligence" that had informed Britton's and perhaps other officials' thinking? In late August, a sketchy *Arizona Republic* article indicated that state agents were "blending" into the protest crowds to make videotapes and take photographs of union members in Clifton, Morenci, and Ajo. Governor Babbitt's chief of staff Andrew Hurwitz told a reporter, "I don't believe there were investigations of strikers." Hurwitz may not have been intentionally misleading the reporter—the state DPS was not involved, and Hurwitz may have had no reason to inquire into other law enforcement techniques. But, in fact, there was much more than a mere investigation of strikers going on in the copper towns—there was ongoing infiltration.

After intelligence agent Steve Kuykendall's preliminary visit to Morenci before the shutdown at the gate, three agents for the independent state organization known as ACISA were assigned to provide intelligence for the Greenlee County sheriff's department and assist DPS, which up to that time had not sent in its own intelligence officers. ACISA was Arizona's own CIA, complete with disguises, fake IDs, a truck licensed to a fictitious cattle company, and a wad of money for informants. On one occasion, the agents put together $20,000 in "flash money" to attempt to entrap arms sellers. (The latter operation never produced more than an empty hand grenade box.) Three agents—Kuykendall, George Graham, and R.(who could not be reached for agreement to be identified)—were authorized by ACISA Director Frank Navarrete, a former Phoenix police captain, to hire union informants, bug union meetings, and create a computer data base on anyone suspected by the agents of being a "troublemaker," according to Graham.

ACISA was originally the brainchild of Arizona Senator Dennis DeConcini, who wanted to boost drug investigations on the Arizona-Mexico border. When Arizona's Republican-dominated legislature challenged ACISA's usefulness in 1982 (funding for ACISA came through federal and state coffers), director Navarrete responded that he was improving the agency's work in what he called a "metamorphic transformation." The Phelps Dodge strike gave Navarrete an opportunity to show off the organization's strengths. Still, there was something missing from the decision to launch this intelligence operation against the copper strikers: a claim of organized crime or drug trafficking. Although news reporters failed to report the extent of the operation, they did quote Navarrete defending ACISA's presence in the towns. He explained, "What happened during the strike doesn't fall within the definition of organized crime, but from my perspective, it's organized labor." Navarrete added that there was potential for criminal activity in the strike and that such activity fell within his responsibility. Certainly the Chandra Tallant shooting or the company railroad trestle burnings invited aggressive investigation. But much of the bugging was done to stay a step ahead of the union rather than investigate suspected wrongdoing. ACISA was authorized to carry out the buggings without judicial approval on the basis of a curious state law that allowed unconsented tapings when one person present was aware and agreed.

ACISA's strategy was to attempt to isolate what Graham called "the big mouths—the ones talking about trouble." The agents developed a network of informants and met with them out of town. "Then we wired some union members or we would meet with them and they would brief us," Graham said. None of the informants was told about any other informants. "We were using about five [informants] at any given moment. And as many as eight or nine moved on and off [assignments]," said Graham.

The eavesdropping units—"body bugs" in the business—"were taped generally in the waistband or at the ankle under socks." They were expensive, state-of-the-art bugs, with miniature tape machines as well as transmitters. The agents could listen live or tape and listen later, depending on the location and the agents' level of concern about the informants "getting burned," Graham said. No strike informant was ever discovered, apparently because the unions never chose to search their members. Morenci union president Angel Rodriguez said later that he had more faith in his members than to order them searched, and he expressed shock that these meetings had been wired. Graham declined to identify any of the union members who took part as informants, but he did say that many of them had been informants on criminal matters to the sheriff's department at other times in their lives.

One of the reasons ACISA was able to keep its presence secret was that it also was coordinating visits to Morenci by sheriff's department deputies from throughout the state to bolster Sheriff Gomez's staff; the towns were already swimming in new faces.

The infiltration operation worked this way: a union leader would pass around word of a special meeting or send out flyers. The members often assembled in an area that had been the meeting ground for the first union organizers forty years earlier, an area known as Potter's Ranch. "They drove their four-wheelers on dirt roads off the highways," said Graham. "It was very hilly and rocky and full of cactus and brush." Members sat on rocks or on their cars. In another area, "We were thinking of putting bugging devices in trash cans," said Graham, but that turned out to be unnecessary because the informants were willing to do the job instead.

Graham himself usually listened to the union meetings, either through tapes brought in by the informants or directly through the transmitters. When the meetings were too far out of town for transmitters, the informants were on their own. "We would give [the informants] good advice, and hope they'd come out with their heads clean. Of course they were there to listen and gather, not to solicit attention." Graham said that ACISA's payments were "fairly benevolent—a couple hundred bucks right off the bat" when informants were being tested for their reliability and productivity. Payments later varied.

"We probably didn't make every meeting—but then we would have our people go into the union halls, too. When nothing was going on, union members would meet there, talk, and blow off steam."

Agent Kuykendall made occasional journal entries during his time in Morenci:

> When I arrived [in Morenci] . . . there were around 3,000 strikers armed with baseball bats and many with concealed weapons rioting at the main gate of PD's plant. They had broken the windows out of many cars and were threatening to blow up the plant with dynamite because the mine was running with strike breakers from outside of the area in an attempt to destroy the union. . . .

With the assistance of the company and the Greenlee County Sheriff's Office we began to identify around twenty to thirty of the most violent of the strikers. . . .

Agent R . . . was sent up to work with me on August 10 and we began to develop informants . . . R is an active "born again Christian" (that's the way he describes it) and had a very good idea—that we try to contact all local ministers and look for non-violent union members that would be willing to help us identify those that were breaking the law. We began to do that immediately with some success. Also we got some good names from deputies that were working and living in the area. Within a few days we were in the middle of everything. . . .

We put electronic monitoring devices on informants and sent them to "rallies" in an attempt to stay ahead of the plans.

On Aug. 17 I was scheduled to meet with the Governor on a briefing the following day. On that same day, while rushing out of the sheriff's office to meet a group of informants, my revolver . . . accidentally engaged [and] my right thigh exploded with the impact of a .357 magnum hollow point.

Of Kuykendall's comment about "the assistance" of Phelps Dodge, Agent Graham said: "I know for a fact that we gathered information from the company . . . and we briefed them." Graham himself went into mine manager John Bolles's office and briefed the chief of company security. Kuykendall was the first to brief the company, starting his own undercover work in the towns several weeks before Graham. (The full record of the visits and of the agents' other activity is impossible to gather because ACISA's files were dispersed or destroyed at the time the agency was disbanded in 1984, just one year after the strike investigation.)

"I remember once telling [the company] about our concern that their rear gate was going to be compromised," said Graham. The company's assistance to the agents included basic data on current and former employees, psychological profiles, and photographs. In addition, on several occasions, Graham and other agents took a telephoto lens behind the company gates to photograph picket members as part of the growing face book on likely "troublemakers."

Agent Graham said that to his knowledge, neither union strike strategies nor strike strength information was ever communicated to the company. "We were on the side of the law rather than on one or the other side," said Graham. "Although there was probably more congeniality between Phelps Dodge and us, we didn't go in there and get in bed with them." Still, intelligence on the strengths or weaknesses of the other party is one of the highest valued commodities during a strike; good information feeds confidence. Whether Phelps Dodge was getting detailed reports or just police reports from ACISA, one of the remarkable features about the early phase of the strike was just how confident Phelps Dodge was of winning.

※

As for the National Guard, Graham and the other agents said that Navarrete asked for their view, presumably to be communicated to DPS and Governor Babbitt. No agent ever directly met with Babbitt—that idea was proposed and then dropped after Kuykendall's injury. But agents did communicate to DPS and to Navarrete "freeflowing information . . . so the person who's receiving it has all the flavor," said Graham. That meant including rumors and other unfounded claims in the information; Graham said that it was sometimes as important to know what was being said as what actually happened. "Our recommendation was that the Guard should be sent for safety, to secure the area." Graham said that ACISA was getting "a lot of big talk" about the union keeping the company closed down and even repulsing the state police. "They'd say, 'We'll show them who owns us.' " ACISA director Navarrete himself delivered "memos" with the intelligence evaluations to Babbitt, but Navarrete said that it was possible no one in the governor's office, including Babbitt, ever knew the extent of the investigation.

Cooling-Off Winds Down

As tensions mounted toward the end of the cooling-off period, there was an occasional moment of relief—or at least of laughable absurdity. Early in the week of August 15, when no commitment either way about the Guard had been announced, one belligerent group of strikebreakers drove the four hours from Morenci to Phoenix and demanded a meeting with the governor. Chief of Staff Hurwitz explained that Babbitt was momentarily away in San Diego, but arranged a meeting with the acting governor. That was the colorful Secretary of State Rose Mofford, whose beehive hairdo was recognized as a virtual state historical site. Mofford was born in Globe, Arizona, a mining town, and was said to sympathize with the strikers. The strikebreakers relentlessly demanded that the National Guard be sent to Clifton and Morenci. Mofford explained that the decision was not up to her, a response that upset one of the delegation leaders. The frustrated spokesperson burst out, "You know what the problem is with you government people? You don't have any balls!"

Mofford, momentarily startled, fired back: "Why, I should think that would be self-evident."

⚜

State records show that the National Guard was activated on August 10—just one day after the miners forced the shutdown. Fixing the exact date is of more than mere historical interest. Part of the continuing union anger against Babbitt (right through his 1988 run for the Democratic Party's presidential nomination) stemmed from members' belief that Babbitt deceived them. As late as August 15, Babbitt was quoted in the *Arizona Republic* telling the unions, "I will call out the Guard only as a last resort." Babbitt conceded later that he "anticipated" using the Guard if the cooling-off period failed to progress towards a settlement, but he didn't want to broadcast it. His public reticence was in the unions' interest, Babbitt said—the company would have been even less willing to bargain had it known that the Guard was likely to come in.

Babbitt also defended his decision to call in the Guard by pointing to his obligation to enforce the law: "Having had ten days to prepare for things, it would be the height of deceit to have ten police out there and say I've been caught by surprise. . . . It would be irresponsible to do it. And the crowd having gotten its way once sort of ups the ante. I really very early on—probably after that second day—said look, a repeat performance at the end of ten days will serve no one. The drama has a preordained ending at the end of ten days.

"When you do make the judgement that it's going to get out of hand you really have to be very precise and very unequivocal. By taking a few steps back you build up expectations and create bigger problems. When you do draw the line, you have to draw it sharply."

A later claim by members that they had no knowledge that the Guard would be dispatched is belied by a special set of minutes prepared by Angel Rodriguez after a meeting with the governor on August 17, two days before the cooling-off period was to end. The minutes state that Babbitt told a group of at least seventeen union members that he was under pressure to enforce the law, and that "It was his duty to do so and this was his justification for calling in the DPS and the National Guard. . . . It was obvious that Babbitt intends to use them to keep the gates open at the properties."

According to executive assistant Britton, DPS could get enough men to handle law enforcement at the reopening of the mine if it didn't have to worry about logistics. "The Guard would pre-position equipment in case things really went to hell," said Britton. "That was the history of the armored cars, the armored personnel carriers, which never carried guns on them."

One thing Babbitt insisted on: this would be no Kent State and no Ludlow. Babbitt found another historic analogy more appropriate; he alluded somewhat obscurely to the "Whiskey Rebellion"—President George Washington's suppression of revolting Pennsylvania farmers in 1794. Washington's successful peacekeeping maneuver (and now Babbitt's) was a sudden, unexpected show of massive force. Washington's was the largest assemblage of troops since the Revolutionary War. Babbitt's was the largest mobilization of military power in state history.

 *Chapter 5*

Hard Times

We are afraid. We are fired. We are having to move. Our whole world is falling apart. Please help us.

—Letter from a striker's wife to Angel Rodriguez, August 26, 1983

At 5:00 A.M. on August 19, 1983, the several-miles-long National Guard convoy dubbed "Operation Copper Nugget" rumbled onto the winding last legs from Safford to Clifton to Morenci. As the first light of dawn hit Route 666, eastern Arizona's native roadside attractions glowed in polychrome reds, greens, and golds—first the rolling cumulus clouds, then the prickly pear cactus, the dry hills, the precipitous canyons. At this hour, the yellow highway lines themselves could have been streams of copper tracing a path from the city to the once-fuming Morenci smelter.

About fifteen miles south of Clifton, near the Gila River, the terrain drops steeply. From on high, the lead officers in the convoy could already make out a sandy stretch of earth and shimmering man-made lake that would be their beachhead. Those were the giant slag heaps and tailings ponds of the Phelps Dodge–Morenci mine. But first the Guard would pass through sleepy-eyed Clifton. A solitary brick smokestack surrounded by burnt black hills—last remnant of the early-century smelters—marked the entry to town. Continuing along 666, the trucks crossed a bridge over the San Francisco River, a creek usually, except during the fall rains when the river swelled into a full-fledged current. Here, giant cliffs rose abruptly behind a jumble of matchbox and brick houses.

The convoy continued past Clifton High School; P.J.'s Big Dipper Restaurant; the Rode Inn motel (the only lodgings not owned by Phelps Dodge); a Sears Roebuck catalog store; Town Hall, whose town seal displayed the Spanish explorer Coronado with a modern smelter rising behind him; a claustrophobic town jail, built right into the cliffs, with the inscription, "The first inmate in 1881 was the miner who built this jail"; and Sacred Heart Church, built by parishioners at the turn of the century from rocks chosen one by one from the surrounding hills. Bolted to the belfry of the church, a statue of Jesus looked out over the canyon and the highway.

It was well known that in Morenci all bowed to Phelps Dodge—one no-nonsense miner told an anthropologist doing research there, "You can't take a piss without PD's okay." Clifton's 4,250 inhabitants, on the other hand, cultivated their independence from Phelps Dodge and Morenci. The two towns had separate high schools, separate business districts, and, most obvious, separate town leadership. Even country ballads noted the difference: journeyman D. T. Gentry sold his song "Open Pit Mine" to the country singer George Jones in the early 1960s, and radio stations throughout the country broadcast a tale of Clifton and Morenci:

> From Morenci, Arizona, where the copper mines glow,
> I could see Clifton in the canyon below
> In Clifton lived Rosie, we danced and we dined,
> On the money I made in the open pit mine.
>
> I loved my sweet Rosie and she loved me too.
> There was nothing for Rosie that I wouldn't do
> Her hugs and her kisses they were something divine.
> Gave me reason for working the open pit mine.
>
> While I was out walking with my Rosie one day,
> We passed a store window with rings on display.
> I bought the 'un she wanted, they really did shine.
> Spent the money I slaved from that open pit mine.

Life took a dismal turn in the song when "Rosie would go dancin' and drink the red wine, while I worked like a slave in that open pit mine." The unnamed miner shot Rosie while she was on a date with someone else, threw her body into the Morenci mine, and then shot himself, too. The recording climbed the country "Top Twenty" in 1962 and became popular again a few years later in a full band version by Johnny Gray. Something about the 1983 strike—its harshness perhaps, or the divide between Clifton and Morenci—brought the song back to the jukeboxes at both the Open Pit bar in Morenci and the El Rey lounge in Clifton on the day the Guard came to town.

⚜

A different twist on life in Clifton was presented in a dissertation by Pennsylvania State University graduate student Victor Ciuccio. In the early 1970s, Ciuccio came to the area to do research on poverty among minorities in the United States. He singled out Clifton as an example of a Mexican-American community that defied the then-prominent "culture of poverty" theories. Despite its remoteness, Clifton provided wages that were on the whole above average. Ciuccio concluded that although Phelps Dodge may have brought in the jobs, the miners' unions had been essential in bringing economic justice to all the town residents. The union provided a counterbalance to what Ciuccio called Phelps Dodge's oligarchy. When the miners' union was founded in 1942, the number of Mexican-Americans on the town council suddenly shot up from zero (where it had been since the turn of the century) to an average of three and sometimes as many as five or six by 1964. "The general attitude of union members is that their local organization of workers is the only group which will 'fight' the company," Ciuccio writes. By August 1983, Tommy Aguilar and Edward Marquez, both Mexican-Americans, former Phelps Dodge employees, and founding members of the miners' unions, were mayor and vice mayor, respectively.

But there were limits to Clifton's countervailing political power. When Ciuccio wrote in 1975 about the unions' (and Clifton's) successes in fighting Phelps Dodge, he certainly had not envisioned a company supported by hundreds of soldiers, one hundred military vehicles, SWAT teams, undercover agents, Huey helicopters, and a general.

"It was like a war"

At about 6:00 A.M., early-riser Josephine Rivas stepped onto her porch overlooking Sacred Heart Church and Route 666 for a breath of air. "First the DPS cars came, one after another with their lights flashing. Then all these trucks. Then the tanks came through on platforms. It was like a war."

She fetched her bird-watching glasses. "I looked through my binoculars and I saw a man up on the cliffs above the highway. Then I saw he had binoculars and a rifle and he seemed to be looking across at me. We just stood there looking at each other. Then I guess he changed his mind [about the potential threat] and he hid behind a mesquite tree.

"So I went over to the other side and looked across and saw some other men up in the hill, and all of them were carrying these big rifles."

Josephine and her husband Antonio were lifelong Clifton residents, now retired. Antonio had made local history back in the late 1950s when he broke Phelps Dodge's race barrier in the locker rooms—a Mexican-American, he rinsed himself in the Anglo showers. Now the couple watched that union history sink into an abyss. The first wave of the mobilization seemed to be directed right at them. "We decided on purpose to move early in the morning," explained Babbitt executive assistant George Britton. "We knew everyone would be out looking onto the street. We wanted this to be a show of strength." He said that such a display would prevent another mass protest at the gate, as well as foreclose any preemptive strike against the Guard. "We had intelligence that someone might try to blow up a bridge," Britton said, a reference to the state intelligence agency ACISA's work. Britton and General John Smith, head of the Guard, rode in the first vehicle as the convoy continued from Clifton to Morenci.

In all, more than 750 law enforcement personnel arrived that morning in Morenci, including 426 state troopers and 325 National Guardsmen. Roy Gann, one of just a few union pickets at the gate, looked overwhelmed as he told a television interviewer, "I guess General Babbitt has done his job." Others said they felt downright deceived. "He flat-out lied to us," said Grace Carroll, staff representative for the AFL-CIO in Tucson. "The governor had told me 'I will never call out the National Guard to face the strikers in the streets.' After we saw the Guard, I finally got him on the phone. I said, 'They're right here.' He said 'Well, they are there. But they're there to put up soup kitchens and dig latrines and that's all.' "

"We were tricked," said one member of the Morenci Miners Women's Auxiliary. "They sent us home from the gate so Governor Scabbitt could bring in the National Guard."

Along with the Rivases, much of Clifton and Morenci turned out to witness the parade of power. The shoulder of Route 666 in Clifton became a kind of reviewing area as residents (many of them decorated veterans of World War II, the Korean War, or Vietnam) watched the hardware roll by. Suddenly the highway had become a thoroughfare for vehicles with names like "gamma goats" and "APCs." The troops were armed with M-16s.

Among the startled onlookers were Army Corporal Tony Tellez and his father Chito, a retired thirty-three-year trainman for Phelps Dodge. Tony Tellez was on leave from the 148th Infantry in Germany, a mechanized unit that in 1983 patrolled the Berlin Wall. Now the same military vehicles Tony drove to create a cordon against communists were being used in his hometown. "It's like when you want to psyche out or intimidate a person," he said. "You might show him this and say, 'Hey, this is what we have. So don't try anything.' "

Tony pointed out the vehicles and explained their various functions to his father, who stood alongside. The Guard convoy began with jeeps, followed in intervals by two-and-a-half-ton and five-ton trucks. One for supplies, one for troops, he explained. Then came the "gamma goats," bizarre-looking six-wheel amphibious carriers. Next, even heavier vehicles that Tony said must have been meant for pure intimidation. Neighbors thought they were tanks, but Tony corrected them. "I counted at least five APCs—armored personnel carriers," he said. "Those have infantry uses. You can be mobile for combat in different types of terrain. You don't have to worry about whether you're on a road. If there's a tree, knock it down." Then a fleet of Huey combat helicopters flew over. In all, "It was an awesome sight to see," said Tony, not intending a compliment. "Maybe they thought DPS couldn't control [the strikers]. But this stuff would."

Tony found the eventual siting of the troops at the Number 10 Phelps Dodge dump in Morenci especially troublesome. "They were protecting the copper mine, rather than staying outside of the fence and protecting common people. They should have put them in a neutral area."

In an effort to make the National Guard show of strength look like overkill, the union sent a total of nine pickets to the gate, one less than the court injunctions allowed. Later that morning, as company buses cruised slowly past the picket stand (Phelps Dodge ordered the drivers to drive at 5 mph at the picket stand), one strikebreaker looked out at the lines of troops and the SWAT team and told a reporter, "It looks like they called a war and nobody came." Union spokesman Cass Alvin accused Babbitt of being "in Phelps Dodge's back pocket," to which the governor sharply responded, "I'm in the back pocket of the American judicial system." Union picket captain Krass, who had watched the scene at the gate degenerate from a union celebration ten days earlier to this depressing invasion, sounded a gloomy prophecy: "On this day, PD has ripped the knife right down to the bone."

Daily Tally, Permanent Loss

As the Guard settled in for what would be a six-day stay near the gate, Phelps Dodge started looking for skilled craftsmen to run the big machines, as well as other outside hires to eliminate the remainder of the union positions. The company advertised and recruited among jobless engineers in Utah and throughout Arizona. An ominous count began in the newspapers: the company claimed to be moving toward full operation and the union alleged that Phelps Dodge was lying about the numbers to make the unions look weak.

But the union claim looked less and less credible as newspaper and television reports showed the new hires crossing the line and the smelter moving back up to capacity. The presence of the National Guard offered a kind of insurance to anyone who had been afraid to cross the picket line before. Unemployed miners, neighboring farmers, Tucson engineers, jobless journeymen—hundreds of people entered Morenci applying for work at $7 an hour or better (skilled jobs were advertised at $11 an hour and up). Twenty-four-year-old bulldozer operator Scott Jackson had been laid off for most of the year, and the unemployment checks that helped support his wife and two young daughters were about to run out, he said. Arlene Boling and Gloria Arána had been low-paid farmworkers nearby and wanted a bigger paycheck. Skilled engineers Art Pritchard and Joe Epperson, who had been working at Phelps Dodge before the strike, came from a large nearby Mormon community, and said they didn't want to fall behind on credit payments. "I have the same right to work as they have to strike," Pritchard said.

With each replacement worker, one more union slot disappeared. Phelps Dodge made certain of that by having each new hire sign an unusual contract—in later strikes elsewhere such contracts became standard—promising that they would not be terminated in case of a strike settlement. The company well knew that, when unions do make concessions, they want an agreement that strikers get their jobs back. With the backing of Reagan-era labor law changes, Phelps Dodge now could just say "No."

Back at the Table

During the weeks after Phelps Dodge restarted the mine and smelter, Governor Babbitt, federal mediator Franklin, and other community officials continued to try to bring the parties to a settlement. But Phelps Dodge smelled victory, and Frank McKee stood firm on a union tradition that rejected going back to work without a contract. More than that, McKee still believed he was right: Phelps Dodge could afford a contract that included cost-of-living adjustments. That claim still had some outside support. For example, Governor Babbitt, in his visit to the negotiations on August 24, pointed out to Phelps Dodge that of the six companies that had settled, "each . . . feels that they got concessions which in their eyes were more important than COLA." Babbitt also reminded the parties that this was not just a local crisis. National attention was now focused on the state (and, though Babbitt didn't say it, on his political reputation as well). "There's got to be a way to settle the differences. There's an enormous public stake in this process," he said.

To boost morale and solicit a new union vote of confidence, Steelworkers leader Frank McKee called for a meeting of the Nonferrous Industry Conference in Tucson on August 27. This conference was made up of union leaders from across the country who set wage policy for all the copper unions and had originally established the goals of a wage freeze for three years. But, as McKee soon understood, confidence was a commodity in short supply.

Before that gathering, McKee convened a smaller group of leaders in Phoenix, on August 26, to get an update on the Phelps Dodge negotiations and prepare for the Tucson meeting. The Phoenix meeting was attended by regional chief Petris and top representatives from each of the international unions (although notably absent were local leaders like Morenci Steelworkers president Rodriguez). Detroit lawyer Duane Ice, one of the Steelworkers' top legal consultants, also provided a briefing on the legal status of the negotiations. This union meeting was the most solemn—and suddenly stormy—union meeting to date.

Ice, a rural Michigan native, explained in his flat midwestern accent the depressing details of a new Supreme Court decision, *Belknap v. Hale*, which not only allowed Phelps Dodge to permanently replace strikers (a company right on paper since the 1930s), but authorized the new hires to sue if they were laid off to make room for returning strikers. This court decision, the unions believed, had led to the company's issuance of contracts promising the replacement workers that they would not be replaced. (Later, at the negotiations table, Phelps Dodge's Scanlon made explicit the link between the court case and the contracts, explaining that the company could not lay off the permanent replacements without facing legal liability as a result of the Supreme Court decision. From the start, the company could have named temporary replacements, but that would have gone against Moolick's larger plan.)

Ice pointed out that if the replacement strategy worked, the company could not only continue operating but decertify the unions within a year. Ice then described a list of options available to the unions, but he was interrupted by McKee, who insisted, "There is no option except what we're doing." At that point, Petris, McKee's lieutenant and one of his oldest friends from the Seattle steel local days, took a deep breath and stepped over the ancient union protocol of deference to the chairman. "Frank," he said, "I'd like to hear the options and I think the others here ought to hear them, too." McKee was incensed at what he correctly perceived as a crack in union unity. And the crack quickly widened further.

A representative from the International Association of Machinists, whose president, William Winpisinger, had been unwavering in his support of the pattern contract, took this moment to speak. "You can't win 'em all Frank. Let's cut our losses and fight another day," said George Bowles. The Machinists, the second largest union in the coalition with some four hundred members, might limit strike payments, Bowles said. If skilled machinists went back to work, the company would have many of its top positions filled. McKee responded with astonishment, "You tell Wimpy [Winpisinger] that's not good enough. You tell him to put some more money in the pot." McKee repeated his declaration that the Kennecott pattern was still the only option, and then he dramatically exited the room.

Petris recalled that the discussion ended there. No one challenged McKee—he was standing on his record, which, they all knew, was unblemished by a loss. What's more, with the ill health of Steelworkers president Lloyd McBride, McKee stood a chance to be the next Steelworkers International president, so he carried more than his own weight in authority. Winpisinger would have to come through with more strike support payments (and he did). As for Petris, his interruption, though he didn't realize it until later, had placed a forty–year friendship on the line with the strike.

Whether or not there might have been any chance for other union leaders or the rank and file to express their dissent at the conference, fate and Phelps Dodge blocked the way.

On the same day that participants in the plenary nonferrous meeting arrived in Tucson, a law enforcement assault began on union members in Ajo, the town where, a month earlier, Chandra Tallant had been shot. The Pima County sheriff's department, in concert with Phelps Dodge security officers, reported that a day after the shutdown in Morenci, union members had marched on the Ajo mine gate, attacking cars and strikebreakers and violating an injunction. Now, on August 27, seven armed deputies surrounded the house of striker Antonio Santiago, Jr.; they handcuffed him and charged him with rioting. Three deputies also entered striker Art Vega's house and arrested his wife, Diana Vega, handcuffing her in front of her four-year-old son. The scene was repeated at the homes of eight other strikers. The strikers were all charged with felony rioting and their bail was set at $15,000 or more each—$175,000 for the group of ten.

The unions protested angrily, arguing that when strikebreakers had been charged with criminal assaults, they had been released on their own recognizance. But Justice of the Peace Helen Gilmartin, a Phelps Dodge security guard on furlough (she had won the judicial position after a nomination by Phelps Dodge and her car still sported the license plates "PD AJO") refused to reduce the bail.

The Steelworkers moved quickly to get their people out of jail, but the town of Ajo didn't have bondsmen who could cover so much bail. So McKee and Steelworkers lawyer Ice had to drive from one desert town to another to find a bondsman. "The bond had been designed to be prohibitive," said Ice. On that August 27 afternoon, as the temperature rose to over one hundred degrees, the ten suspects were hauled from the Ajo jail to Tucson in the back of a van with no air conditioning.

What galled the unions (and later impressed the federal courts) was the alleged role of Phelps Dodge at every step, from gathering evidence for the Ajo arrests to encouraging the sheriff's department to press for high bonds. Ajo was a small property with a work force of less than six hundred. Phelps Dodge closed the mine down for ten days in Morenci, but in Ajo the company merely canceled two shifts. Ajo mine manager Carl Forstrom was determined to clamp down hard and rapidly on the strikers who caused the August 10 gate disruption that shortened the Ajo shifts. (Indeed, Phelps Dodge president Richard Moolick later promoted Forstrom to Morenci mine manager as a reward for his toughness.)

According to court records, on August 11, the day after the Ajo gate incident, three Phelps Dodge officials had met with the county attorney, sheriff's department, and state police, reviewing a list of suspects. One unnamed company representative told the sheriff firmly that Phelps Dodge "wanted those people off the street." The company representative then pushed for the arrests and high bonds. (Once summoned to court, Phelps Dodge failed to locate its time logs showing where its security police officers were on the day that the arrest warrants were issued, leaving the impression that these officers were working in tandem with the justice of the peace and local law enforcement.) Phelps Dodge had also established a charge account for sheriff's deputies at the company store.

A federal appeals court that reviewed Phelps Dodge's actions concluded in 1989 that there was enough evidence of a company conspiracy against the unions for a jury trial. Evidence about the company's actions, the court said, "may be viewed as Phelps Dodge's own confession of its intent. . . . [The evidence] . . . goes to the most critical issue in the case: whether Phelps Dodge intended to violate the strikers' civil rights. . . . Based on this direct evidence, a jury could infer that Phelps Dodge was a participant in the conspiracy."

Although the unions won that decision in 1989, the immediate effect of the arrests was to raise further cries of injustice. Union supporters—including the Machinists, who had felt that some concessions might have been in order—protested vigorously. A Tucson rally drew the largest crowd yet, more than thirty-five hundred union members and supporters who jeered Phelps Dodge and called for the strike to go on. McKee entered a tumultuous, cheering union hall after getting the ten strikers out on bail. "By the time I led those poor people from Ajo [into the rally]," McKee said, "there was nobody that dared stand up and complain about anything. The union was standing behind them and that's all they cared about."

Attention turned instead to the town-to-town picket line effort and to launching legal action against the company. The unions filed unfair labor practice charges against Phelps Dodge before the National Labor Relations Board, their last chance of stopping the company's permanent replacement plan. If the company was found to have broken certain labor laws during the strike, the courts could have required it to hire back striking workers. But unless the NLRB ruled that the company had broken the law, the union jobs were now gone for good.

Profiles in Pain

As the flow of defecting union members and outside hires increased, the union effort looked increasingly futile. A series of family breakdowns and tragedies began.

While based in Phoenix for the negotiations, local Steelworkers president Angel Rodriguez received an urgent letter from the wife of a striker:

> *Dear Angel,*
> *. . . I feel very scared that you guys don't know what is going on here. Our kids are very frightened. My one little girl will not go out of the house without an adult. . . . I had surgery in May and as a result I still have a knob in my stomach as big as a fist. I went to the [Phelps Dodge] doctor today . . . who told me that I could not see a doctor without $26, which I did not have. I asked him who said so and he said it was orders from the General Office. . . . Then I went to the Emergency Room to get the dressing and supplies but [the doctor] had called the E.R. and told them not to give me anything. Now I ask you, what am I going to do? . . . Can't you come home and help us?*
> *We are afraid. We are fired. We are having to move. Our whole world is falling apart. Please help us, Angel, we desperately need it.*
>
> *Beverly Cole*

My Brother the Strikebreaker

No one in Clifton will soon forget the afternoon that Chase Creek shook with the Torrez brothers' crashing blows. If neighbors didn't see it for themselves on the square, then they heard about it that night at dinner or at the Clifton social club or at the union hall. Descriptions of the Phelps Dodge strike as a civil war suddenly became much more than metaphor. The battle between brothers was over a way of life—union or no union. After the fight, Fred Torrez told friends over and over, "You just don't expect your own brother to help break the strike."

The Torrez family had literally built Phelps Dodge's Morenci operations. Grandpa Luis arrived from Chihuahua, Mexico, at the turn of the century and labored in the Morenci mines for more than twenty years. He and Conchita, his wife, raised a substantial labor force. Torrezes built the Morenci smelter, blasted the first holes in the new pit, and breathed in the first silicate and arsenic. Phelps Dodge's glossy company-wide periodical had twice featured the family on its cover—the second time just a year before the strike. In the color photograph, some sixteen Torrezes, young and old, gaze out at the camera from the steps of a train engine with the Phelps Dodge logo—more than 150 years of PD labor by one family. Peering ahead stoically are brothers Fred and Roy (Luis's grandsons), already with fifteen years of seniority apiece.

Fred, the union man, worked as a welder all around the mine. Roy coordinated blasting at the open pit. As a supervisor, Roy was a manager, nonunion, and obliged to keep working during the strike. But just as Phelps Dodge work was a family tradition, so was honoring the picket line.

"Dad had been a strong union man," said Fred, who asked that the names of family members be changed. "Back in those years there used to be a lot of racial discrimination. I used to see him on strike and sometimes I would man the picket lines for him." In the 1983 strike, Fred's brother Roy was initially spared the harassment aimed at scabs. Fred explained, "Everyone knew my brother was a foreman" and that he had to cross the picket line.

Soon after the National Guard had come to town, Fred ran into Roy's son and daughter-in-law in the Clifton auto parts store. "They had been living in Utah, but this was September," said Fred. September was no time for a vacation, so Fred knew that Roy had encouraged them to come. "He told them these were good jobs and the strikers were fools not to hold on to them." Roy's son, José, crossed the picket line and took a job as a train engineer.

Pressures between the two brothers continued to build in quiet ways—more encounters at the store, a family conversation, the talk (less restrained) of children. Then Fred's nineteen-year-old daughter ran into the strikebreaker's wife at the local Circle K convenience store. Fred's daughter called the other woman a "scab-lover." They exchanged words all the way to the Chase Creek laundry, where the threats became louder. By the time Fred and Roy had been summoned, the two young women had challenged each other to a fight.

At this point, Chito Tellez, a retired trainman who also lived on Chase Creek, had come out onto the balcony of a nearby building, along with several others, to see what the commotion was about. He recalled, "We had a ringside seat." Instead of breaking up the fight and leading the women home, the two brothers stared each other down and started hurling enraged epithets—and then blows. "They charged like bulls," Tellez said of the two brothers, who both stood better than six feet tall and two hundred pounds. "They were yelling 'my mother such and such.' One of them was yelling 'I was born a scab'—that's what he was saying. Then they swung like they meant it." Father Steven Stencil came out of Sacred Heart Church a block away to try to stop the fight, but the blood was already flowing. As more and more neighbors gathered, the canyon resonated with the fighting brothers' accusations and blows. They swung and wrestled, connecting hard with their punches. Finally the Clifton police arrived and pulled them apart, clawing and cussing.

The brothers' feud "divided all the family," said Fred. "When my dad ended up in the hospital, there we were—two sons in the same room—but we didn't talk to each other. At Christmas we would see my mom and stay on separate sides of the room. We were like strangers." One rainy afternoon more than a year later, an unbalanced load of rain-soaked ore caused a Phelps Dodge railroad car to dump its contents the wrong way on the job. The supervisor watching over the car was Roy's son, José. He had advanced quickly to that position because the senior union people were out on strike. The load of smelter-bound rock crushed him.

Only at the wake did the two brothers again squeeze each other's hands. "That's when I made my mind up that this was too much," Fred said. "It's a sad thing that it has to come to a death to get the family together, to get out of something like this. One of my brothers never did come down to the funeral. A lot of bitter feelings would not go away."

Faith

The door of Chito and Livia Tellez's pastel-blue matchbox house opened into a world of ceramic statues, acrylic wall hangings, and unbending faith. The house contained just three rooms, and the visitor saw all at once: a bright living room full of tabletop statues, especially collies; a simple kitchen; and the bedroom, an open hub between the living room and the kitchen. A broad blue-and-orange sports pennant hung above the queen-sized bed, an incongruous suggestion of loyalty. "Father Joe gave us some tickets," said Livia Tellez. "There were so many people you couldn't even get close. But it was worth it just being there." The pennant, it turns out, celebrated a visit to Phoenix by Pope John Paul II.

Chito Tellez had been a converter puncher and a trainman for 33½ years at Phelps Dodge, Livia said proudly. A puncher's job was to convey air into a 2,000-degree molten copper tank (the "converter") to purify the copper. Chito's switch to trainman was a break from the smelter's noxious sulphur and arsenic gasses. In 1982, a year before the strike, Chito retired altogether from the company "on account of two runaways," Livia said. "The first one hurt him. The last one put him out. The brakes gave out at Shannon Hill the second time bringing the cars down. So the children got together and they told him, 'Dad, get out before you lose your life. You've been working there long enough.' "

References to family—they had four daughters and two sons—came out in virtually every sentence from Livia Tellez. A son and four sons-in-law were working for Phelps Dodge in July 1983 when the strike began, and they all went out on strike. But in August, when the company began to hire permanent replacements, one son-in-law suddenly went back in. Livia thought it was because of her daughter's pressure: "She said she might divorce him because they were in a bind. They had a sick little girl and another boy who had some medical problems. So my daughter told him he had to keep his job.

"After our son-in-law went into work we never saw our daughter, never saw our grandkids, never saw our son-in-law. This is a very close-knit place. If we would see them in the Phelps Dodge store or maybe J. C. Penney, they would run off. If I was in the meat department and she saw me, she would go to the vegetables so she wouldn't have to face me eye to eye."

Usually it was their daughter turning away, but Chito and Livia, too, would avert their gazes. "There are a lot of aisles in that PD store," Chito added.

Why was their response was so harsh? "Blood is sacred," Chito said. By that, he meant that the Tellezes had union blood. He felt it was wrong for the son-in-law to go in despite the sick child. Striking family members could find other work, albeit out of town. "I could see right from wrong," he said. "I was a grievance man for fifteen years."

Livia didn't attempt to reconcile with her daughter. "My faith held me apart from her on this point. I would say, 'Well, one of these days she'll come back to us one way or another.' "

Strikebreaker

Mary Beager, pointing to the street outside the Clifton house she rented, said, "I called this Vietnam Road. It was a battlefield." Five feet four inches tall, bowlegged, and a bundle of muscle, she began work in the Phelps Dodge rock crusher in 1977, one of several women Phelps Dodge hired after the industry was accused of gender discrimination. "Of course I went out on strike," Beager said. "My dad had been a union man. He told me that a woman, especially, needs the union behind her." Beager did picket duty initially and then worked twelve-hour days at the union hall, sending out strike payments and paying out overdue bills.

"I enjoyed it. I got to make sure the checks went out, July through August. Everything was going fine, except when they started hiring and people went in. I had worked hard to get to [the position of] crusher operator. I kept in contact with people. A whole bunch of people I knew were going in. I got upset when I could see that my position was going to be gone."

Beager said that she was also getting frustrated by the way scarce union funds were getting doled out. "I did not like people coming in and wanting checks for utilities when these were bills that had been past due even before the strike. They were expecting a payment for that too. And some of them got it. I kept hearing all kinds of things—people getting car payments.

"Some of the other girls [at the union office] had decided to go in. I said I don't know. I tried to drop a hint at the office that I was having doubts, that I was thinking about going in. Nobody said anything. So I made sure they were all caught up, that everything was in order. I wanted to leave work in order." The next day she met three other women at a bus stop where the Phelps Dodge transport picked up workers.

"This was a bad time for a strike," she said. "The economy was bad all over. . . . I also hated not to see a union there. Once the union was gone the company could do anything it wanted." Still, her ambivalence didn't stop her. She took the bus through the gate and went back to her job at the crusher.

When she crossed the picket line, Beager's biggest concern was how people would treat her fourteen-year-old daughter, Morella. Union members put the mark of Cain on strikebreakers—and passed it along to their children. "When I got off work, I had to go through the lines [of picketers]. There was yelling and screaming." That was when union members first learned that Mary Beager had crossed the line. On the way home from school, the children also had to go through the lines because the road crossed one of the Women's Auxiliary picket areas. Not long after Beager crossed, several strikers followed her daughter to a friend's house where she was visiting. "They called her a scab"—and worse.

"My friend said to them that my daughter had nothing to do with the strike. Then the crowd threw rocks at the house. My friend called the cops and she got a gun to protect herself. I called Morella and said don't come home. They'll kill you."

"Doris [one of the picketers] was one of the worst ones. Doris said, 'Get that scab out of your house.' Then the cops came and arrested my friend Sally because she had a weapon. It was the longest night I ever went through. Finally I picked up my daughter but she couldn't stand it anymore."

A few days later, Morella ran away from home. "You hear about broken families here?" Beager asked. "That's mine."

Brother Mike

In Ignazio Silone's labor novel from the 1930s, *Bread and Wine*, a workers' activist disguises himself as a priest, Father Paulo, in an effort to save Italy from its spreading fascism. Silone writes of this ruse, "The habit doesn't make the monk." In besieged Morenci, Arizona, in July 1983, Brother Mike Martinez was asked to take the monk out of the habit to help save the unions from Phelps Dodge. His father, striking crane operator Ralph Martinez, put the question to him at breakfast during the first weeks of the strike: "Would you put on your street clothes and march the picket line?"

In the summer of 1983, Mike was well into his undergraduate training for the priesthood in Ohio, with a concentration in Latin American studies. Among his readings had been a history of the Chicano struggle, called *Occupied America*. It described a failed 1903 strike by Mexican *mutualistas* (mutual aid societies) in his hometown area, the Clifton-Morenci mining district. Several strike leaders were arrested, tried on conspiracy charges, and deported to Mexico to break that early strike against Phelps Dodge. Mike had brought the book back from Ohio during summer break and given it to his father. "I told him that the company had become more sophisticated but basically there could be the same type of occurrence, there could still be lives that are destroyed. My dad would say, 'That was then and this is now. You can't blame the company.' "

But then Ralph Martinez began to see his son's dark warning take shape. A few weeks after the strike began, Ralph asked Mike if he would walk the picket line so that Ralph could search for other work and continue to receive the union's $40-a-week strike allowance. Mike honored his father's request, though he was surprised to find that he had not fully made up his mind about the morality of crossing the picket line. People had been out of work and children were hungry. His initial reaction on seeing people he knew cross the line was, "I didn't favor people who did it, I just didn't understand everything about it. . . . I didn't throw rocks or cuss or flip the bird. But I'd hold the sign. Some of my friends from high school [had crossed]. They knew I was studying to be a priest and when they passed they would turn their heads. They couldn't look me in the eye."

Soon Mike was asked to take a firmer stand. Ralph Martinez's union friends knew about Mike's studies and asked him about the church's view of strikes. On the picket line he gave his first sermons. "Strikers would ask me, 'Hey you're going to be a priest, what do you know?' " Mike formed his response by reading biblical passages, Vatican writings like Pope Leo XIII's Labor Letter, and more down-to-earth works like one called *Christ in a Poncho.* "First of all, I applied the Golden Rule—we forget about that because it seems so simple. In a strike situation, it means we have to ask about the morality behind the law. Saying that somebody has a right to work, they ignore the fact that by crossing the line they're stealing the food off someone else's table who's in a struggle. I thought it was so ignorant to use the phrase—'the right to work.' That's why you get these labels like 'scab'—Your neighbor's down in the dirt and you're kicking him instead of helping him out of the mud.

"I told them the church was very clear. People have the right to form a union. People have the right to protect themselves. And if you have that right, then it's undermined by right-to-work laws. In fact, that nullifies the right to strike, to negotiate. It's a very immoral situation when it occurs."

Strikers asked Mike why the Phoenix church leaders weren't more outspoken on the strike, and he responded, "Well, I wish I knew the same." He wrote Bishop Manuel Moreno. "Here's this wild-eyed seminarian who's trying to tell the bishop something. I wrote the letter to Bishop Moreno with great respect but I also said what I felt. Other priests who heard I wrote a letter asked me who am I to do that? And my response was, who do I have to be to do that?"

As Mike delivered his sermons, the battle between strikers and nonstrikers began to tear at the soul of the town. "I was at my friend's house one time and his mom and dad were outside in front. They told us to come outside. We were there twenty minutes, then all of sudden we saw a house catch on fire up on a hill. It was an empty PD house and they knew it was going to happen and they went outside and took us with them. Then there were what people called 'rock parties.' Just throw rocks at scabs' houses. I didn't participate in any of this and I don't condone violence . . . but when people are backed up into a wall, they fight. They couldn't see any other recourse."

Finally, the strike came to the church itself. At Holy Cross Church, a modern, Phelps Dodge–funded building with a thin red line of stained glass running the width of the altar, the communion line split in two—one filing toward a strike-supporting deacon, the other toward a strike opponent. Mike heard strikers whisper "scab" to strikebreakers even as the deacon offered communion with the holy utterance, "Body of Christ."

"You're receiving what the Catholic Church believes is the Lord himself through the Holy Communion. You're receiving Jesus for strength and spiritual nourishment. [The whispers] were maybe even a sinful thing. And people were doing that." Mike's mother broke down one day and told Father McGrenra that she couldn't attend church anymore. She could not understand how strikebreakers could come to church praying the same prayers and to the same God while taking away her husband and her friends' jobs. Nor could she bear teaching Sunday school anymore. For Mike, the problem was also soul-wrenching: despite his preparation to enter the priesthood, he couldn't forgive those who tore apart the community and took his father's job. "I decided then that I could never minister here—in my own hometown."

Church v. Church

James Carter's voice and appearance suggested Gomer Pyle. He didn't say "Ga-a-w-lee" the way the televison character did, but he had that same inflection, boyish face, and small-town friendliness. His father was Clifton's Chevrolet dealer. In addition to helping out with the car sales, James Carter was spiritual leader and bishop to Clifton-Morenci's 605-member Church of Jesus Christ of Latter-day Saints. At thirty-three, he was one of the youngest leaders of any Mormon ward in the country and way too friendly to be accused of organized church-led strikebreaking.

There was one unavoidable ethnic fact in the Phelps Dodge strike. Mexican-Americans (who were mostly Catholic) largely honored the picket line and many Anglos (who in this region were mostly Mormon) did not. Several months into the strike, by the union's count, there were some 640 strikebreakers at Morenci. Of these, about 500 had Anglo surnames and 140 Hispanic. Before the strike, the same count would have shown half of all employees with Hispanic surnames. (An attorney for a Mexican-American rights group attempted to convince the Department of Labor that these replacement results showed discrimination against Mexican-Americans, but for reasons explored in chapter 7, the unions never formally pursued this complaint.)

Some observers, like Bishop Carter, said that the higher numbers of Anglos or Mormons crossing the line did not indicate any effort by the church to sway workers. Mexican-American miners built their communities around the union, they said, and whites, in general, not just Mormons, did not. Others, including many members of the Mormon church, however, felt the correlation was quite direct: the church leadership was antiunion. These tensions all boiled over into public view on the day James Carter found the large brick Mormon church at the base of Shannon Hill in Clifton defaced with large white graffiti saying, "Church of the Latter-Day Scabs."

Inquiring later into the tensions behind this and other incidents, the *Tucson Citizen* newspaper quoted an unnamed Mormon church member who belonged to a union: "We are very strong, family-oriented people as a religion. This is one of the reasons why I wanted to go back to work. I, for instance, believe I owe my family more than the unions." Such a decisive statement of loyalty had been encouraged directly by church leaders, according to other members quoted in the article, which was headlined, "Church Strikebreaking Charged; LDS members contend they were urged to defy pickets."

Arizona's Catholic leadership made public statements that tended to support the union cause. For example, the Archdiocese in Phoenix seemed to speak directly to Phelps Dodge when it issued its 1983 Labor Day Message: "Nothing can be gained by an unwillingness to compromise. There is no economic justice for either side when the people suffer, and there is no dignity in breaking the human spirit." Nor was this the first such "message."

Over the years, the Catholic Church had been at odds with Phelps Dodge on other matters of the human spirit. The notorious "26 and 2" work schedule—twenty-six consecutive days on the job followed by two days off—played havoc with family life, according to church leaders. But workers were reluctant to ask for a change because they were accustomed to these hours and the overtime pay padded their wallets. The company wanted to keep the schedule because productivity was high, and hiring and training new workers was expensive.

When Father John Bardon became the priest at Clifton's Sacred Heart Church in the early 1970s, he challenged both the company and union over this policy. A huge, round man with a relentlessly sermonizing voice, Bardon summoned fire and brimstone at a Sunday service. "I used certain words you don't usually hear in church. I told them that there was only one difference between a whore in Nogales and a Phelps Dodge worker on the 26 and 2. At Phelps Dodge, you're better paid." With the Church's encouragement—and Phelps Dodge's resentment—the union bargained the "26 and 2" schedule out of the contract.

In the ensuing years in Clifton, Father Bardon kept himself informed about union negotiations with Phelps Dodge, and he thought the summer of 1983 was a bad time for a strike. "Everybody knew this was strike-busting time—look at what President Reagan had just done to the air traffic controllers." But he also understood the foundations of the community. "Yes, I did support [the strikers]. I didn't want to get up and tell the people to go back to work. Most of my parish was Hispanic and they were trying to be loyal to their unions and their families.

"I got really peeved when the Mormons told their people to go back to work. They were pragmatic as opposed to idealistic. They were also raging capitalists."

For his part, Mormon leader Carter denied ever directly encouraging members to cross the picket line. Nancy Foster, a Women's Auxiliary member and devout Mormon churchgoer, recalled that one Sunday Carter began a sermon: " 'You really need to go to work because you have a family to support and that's what you're supposed to do.' He didn't come right out and say that you need to go to work so you can pay your tithing. But he was using his position to stand up there. The guy sitting next to me may have felt just as strongly for the union, but most people are going to take counsel from the head of the church."

Foster said that Carter's sermon took on even greater meaning the next day. "On Sunday he spoke and on Monday he went to work for PD. So he had already committed to go to work. When he went to work the next day, we said now we understand why he's saying it.

"It seemed like after [Carter's sermon] it was, 'Oh, it's okay to cross the line. We're doing what's right, so let's do it.' I just quit going to church. I told [Bishop Carter] that I don't think I can go and say 'Good morning brother, Good morning sister' and shake their hands when they're stabbing us in the back by taking our jobs."

Carter took a job as a security guard, which was nonunion, so he argued that he wasn't really crossing the picket line. "It did weigh on my mind that I didn't want to do anything that would cause real bad feelings with people," he said. As for whether his leadership influenced others, Carter said, "The bishop is not the church. The bishop is an individual who makes his living and supports his family and tries not to offend or hurt or do damage to any other people.

"My own personal feeling was that the union wasn't very smart. I'm not talking about the local union people. Local people were caught in this thing. They'd say 'I want to go in, but I can't do it. My family thinks this, or my dad thinks that.' They should have seen the writing on the wall. Times were bad, and PD was serious. PD needed some concessions. The union wasn't willing to make them. My own personal belief was they should have settled. They should have taken it."

For Carter, taking the job as a security guard didn't help much anyway. It paid less than positions elsewhere, and his town was in an uproar over the strike. So Carter eventually quit as bishop and quit town. He found work at a power company sixty miles away. "I loved Clifton, but it was not the same place. The feelings weren't the same. Passing people on the streets wasn't the same. And the church had a lot of problems. There were feelings that people just didn't get over easy."

The Flood

Union leaders found themselves praying for some cathartic event that might make the strikers' miseries disappear. Steelworker negotiator Alex Lopez had a dream that the price of copper suddenly climbed, Phelps Dodge agreed to continue COLA, and everyone was called back to work. Steelworkers publicist Cass Alvin, the union's senior spokesperson, drafted a mock press release (he called it a "laff release") headlined, "PHELPS DODGE GIVES UP COLA FIGHT." The story was datelined Phoenix and announced that Phelps Dodge was planning

> The immediate dismissal of all replacements the company hired and a return to the original workforce. . . . "It came right from the top in New York where all big issues are resolved," said Pat Scanlon of Phelps Dodge. The news had an immediate impact on the unions. Angel Rodriguez, president of USWA Local 616 in Morenci was elated. "Hurray, now I can go back to work and maybe visit some of my old friends who were scabbing all this time."

Other Steelworkers wished for the price of copper to fall—something that could send the company into bankruptcy. If union justice could not triumph, at least evil would be punished.

Instead, the unions were hit with one more blow of misery. In the last week of September, a matter of days after the company had sent out letters announcing that all strikers had been permanently replaced, a deluge began. For seven days, storms crashed through one town after another, and on October 1 the flood sirens in Clifton started to wail. Like the threats of Phelps Dodge, these alarms, too, had been heard before. "We'd had lots of close calls," said Marty Montoya, whose husband was a striker in the Operating Engineers union. "I just didn't believe it would happen. We've never seen anything like this."

The Montoya home stood a few hundred feet above a retaining wall along the San Francisco River, a river that usually looks more like a creek. But in a series of tidal-like waves at midday on Saturday,

October 1, 1983, the river rose up and swallowed 300 homes, hit 86 of Clifton's 126 businesses, caused $12 million in damage, and added the category "homeless" to many of those who had recently learned they were officially jobless.

Montoya had watched the river climb. "I had chosen a marker—first a rock, then a wall, then a tree," she said. "The electric poles began to spark. Then I saw a wave come up about ten yards from the house and I started running up across the street and up the hill."

Mud flowed through town, and tarantula spiders crawled onto dry land. The Sears Roebuck catalog store disintegrated into the river—just after two men trapped on the roof were rescued. Strikebreakers passed by, shouting out, "We've got your jobs and now the river's got your houses!" Believing that law enforcement was helping replacement workers get to work through the flood, strikers "rocked" the Clifton police chief's brand-new Ford Crown Victoria cruiser, denting it and knocking all its windows out. More rocks followed the strikebreakers through Clifton's flood-ravaged streets. The one-hundred-year-old town newspaper, the *Copper Era*, was flooded out but still produced a one-page issue with typewriters and mimeograph machines. A Phoenix paper wrote, "There is nothing left of Clifton," to which the *Copper Era* editorial responded, "I say bull. We are here. . . . Although I wonder about our sanity sometimes."

The National Guard, which had departed from its August assignment at the Phelps Dodge gate after just one quiet week, was called in for the second time—this time to bring in sandbags and sandwiches, not gamma goats. But when the guard flew helicopters onto Phelps Dodge property with provisions for some five hundred refugees, the unions immediately accused them of favoring Phelps Dodge and its employees over the strikers. Then Babbitt himself came to visit Clifton. He was greeted by the vice mayor, Edward Marquez, who was still enraged over the National Guard's previous visit. As television reporters followed Babbitt, Marquez moved in and called the governor "Scabbit"—an outburst that became the lead story on the evening news.

Miraculously, no one was killed in the flood, but the family losses were devastating. "I just started crying. Everything was ruined," said Montoya. "We lost all the furniture, lost the kids' confirmation dresses, the newspaper clippings, the photographs. And we didn't have any insurance. We couldn't afford it."

At the time of the flood, Boo Phillips had been counseling her husband Glenn to stay strong on the strike. He had twenty-eight years with the company, and two more would get him a full company pension. Boo had helped build up his resistance to crossing. "And you know what?" she said. "That flood hit only the strikers. The scabs were all living in Morenci or Safford." The flood was not only a disaster—it was an unjust disaster.

The *Arizona Daily Star* reported that "the psychic damage was bad. Some residents loaded their undamaged possessions into pickup trucks and headed out of town, their jobs gone and now their homes. 'I'm gone for good,' said Reuben Sanchez as he joined the sad parade." The waiting list for U-Hauls grew longer.

Reporter Paul Brinkley-Rogers witnessed a rock-throwing confrontation between strikers and strikebreakers. He wrote, "Windshields shattered. Dents appeared in doors. People scuffled in the mud but couldn't get in a good punch because a swing would put them off balance in all that slime on the ground." Brinkley-Rogers later spoke with Phelps Dodge officials about a proposal to sell land to Clifton in order to move homes to safer ground. "Personally," an unnamed Phelps Dodge official said, "I would not mind at all if the whole town of Clifton went away. Some of the people there are animals. Our people have taken a hell of a lot of abuse from them."

With the strike and now the flood, Clifton's population of 4,250 began to shrink. It dropped by 500 within a few months of the strike. Another 500 people moved out soon after. A local poet tried to make sense of the one-two punch that Clifton had experienced in a poem he sent to the *Copper Era*:

> Many won't believe me when I say God brought this flood
> For many hearts were mended as they shoveled and they dug
> The copper strike already had our town torn all apart
> And Jesus knew what he must do to cleanse our bitter hearts.

Others found in the flood only the sum of all their frustrations. David Velasquez, the seventy-year-old cofounder and president of the old Mine-Mill union, the union that had come in to rescue Mexican-Americans from racism in the 1940s, was among those sent running for higher ground by the flood waters. Velasquez escaped, but a manuscript he had been working on for years—a history of the Morenci Miners Local, 1942–1983—did not.

The momentum of the strike had turned harshly against the strikers. In late September, a small copper company near Tucson called Duval (which had not drawn much press or union attention, because it was on a different contract schedule than the rest of the industry) declared that, like Phelps Dodge, it was terminating cost-of-living allowances. Unlike Phelps Dodge, it offered a wage increase of $1 an hour over three years in return. The International Brotherhood of Teamsters, who had been known to go their own way in other years, precipitously abandoned the union coalition. On October 4, two days after Clifton's flood, Duval announced that two unions had accepted their terms. Copper conference spokesman Cass Alvin tried to downplay the events, pointing to the historical differences between Duval and other copper companies in the industry and to the fact that 75 percent of Duval's work force was already on furlough. But the picture was becoming clearer: Arizona's copper unions were on the run.

Dr. O'Leary and the People's Clinic

The unions needed to find a new way of inflicting damage to Phelps Dodge from the outside even as families tried to hold together on the inside. They got some unexpected support in mid-October, 1983, from a company doctor fed up with Phelps Dodge's tactic of pressuring workers back to work by threatening to withdraw medical coverage. When Dr. Jorge O'Leary criticized Phelps Dodge and offered free medical care to strikers, mine manager John Bolles sent a termination letter to O'Leary, writing:

> It is important to both the company and the Clifton-Morenci communities that the unfortunate tensions caused by the strike be defused. . . . You nevertheless have continued through public appearances and statements—which often have been inaccurate and misleading—a course of conduct which serves only to increase the hostilities we should all be trying to mitigate. . . . It is not appropriate for us to appear to condone your inflammatory behavior by continuing you in our employ.

Shortly after Phelps Dodge fired him, O'Leary, who was said to have delivered more than twenty-five hundred babies in his twelve years in Clifton and Morenci, put up his own money to open a clinic for strikers. In a converted seed store on Route 666, the "People's Clinic" was born. At about the same time, O'Leary's wife, Anna, began taking a leadership role in the Women's Auxiliary. The clinic and the Women's Auxiliary together attracted a radical wing of strikers and strike-supporters that would drive the company, the state police, and sometimes even the mainstream union leaders into fits. The group's impact on negotiations was negligible, but these supporters launched a war of attrition that picked up its own life independent of the Steelworkers negotiations.

Solidarity

If there had not been a Jorge O'Leary in Clifton, it would have taken a substantial imagination to invent one. Doctor, protester, revolutionary, son of a Mexican Yaqui Indian mother and Irish brewmaster father, Jorge O'Leary believed with all this heart that the strikers had justice on their side. He believed these unions were America's version of Lech Wałęsa's *Solidarność*. He believed that if Americans could comprehend the history of discrimination against Mexican-Americans and the present Phelps Dodge union busting, they would put a stop to the tragedy in Clifton and Morenci.

Dr. Jorge O'Leary had a vision: one day, he imagined, a million Steelworkers across the nation would walk off their jobs in protest against Phelps Dodge's replacement of the union strikers. The autoworkers would stop work, too. Then the coal miners. Union members throughout the nation would see on that judgment day that the strike against historic labor outlaw Phelps Dodge affected them all. Surely, O'Leary argued, the American labor rank and file could see the harm being done to unionism by the events in Clifton and Morenci.

But even if unions in the Reagan '80s understood that they needed to support the Phelps Dodge strikers, there was not much they could do. Labor was taking a severe bruising during the decade. There were far fewer than a million active unionized Steelworkers left. The country was just climbing out of a recession and neither steel nor copper seemed to be climbing with it. Worse, public opinion had turned against labor unions. Replacement workers like President Reagan's new recruits in America's air traffic control system were the most visible workers across the nation, not union members.

Finally, the law itself was against the unions. Most sympathy strikes such as the ones Dr. O'Leary imagined were unlawful. As for stopping the permanent replacements, the labor movement was plainly straitjacketed in legal procedures.

But if Dr. O'Leary's national vision failed for lack of supporters, his effort was strengthened by his own seemingly boundless energy. Like the union workers, he had himself been replaced. O'Leary was providing his services for free and speaking his mind. Phelps Dodge called this taking sides.

In the end, O'Leary invented a new side. He told *People* magazine in a two-page article (that included close-ups of the clinic and O'Leary at work), "These people are still my patients. How can I leave them?" In addition to his commitment to the Hippocratic oath, O'Leary also had a broad labor consciousness, shaped by the leftist union tradition in northern Mexico, especially among the copper miners of Cananea and Nacozari in his home state of Sonora. This was where early twentieth-century American radicals had seen the brightest potential for a workers' revolution on the North American continent. American mining union radicals even signed up to fight alongside Pancho Villa, hoping to bring the workers' revolution to reality. Steeped in this tradition, O'Leary had gone to medical school in the late 1960s at the University of Mexico in Mexico City, the school where Mexican federal police opened fire on leftist student protesters before the 1968 Olympics, killing dozens. That shooting had left O'Leary with strong feelings against military intervention in protests—feelings he felt return during the periodic police actions against strikers in Clifton and Morenci.

O'Leary took his medical degree in Mexico, completed his residency in surgery in Tucson, and joined Phelps Dodge in 1971. In 1980, three years before the strike, he became an American citizen. In an interview, he told reporter Paul Brinkley-Rogers: "When I studied to become an American citizen I quickly realized how important is the First Amendment. That's why I can't understand how PD could fire me just because I chose to express myself about the strike. When I studied the Constitution, I came to believe that democracy ends when you are not able to express yourself. In Arizona, that's true, too, isn't it?"

These formative events in O'Leary's life made him instinctively resentful of the role that Phelps Dodge and the Arizona state government had played in suppressing the strikers. O'Leary felt that a Zapata or a Pancho Villa was needed to show rank-and-file union members the way in Clifton and Morenci. The Steelworkers, he said, hadn't come up with that man.

"The local leadership was incompetent, not a match for the company," O'Leary said. "And the international union leadership was afraid to make a stand. They tried to win the strike through negotiations. But so many people wanted to be more active in the strike and really feel it. They weren't just fighting for one more penny. They were fighting for their rights.

"These are people whose families weren't buried in the same cemeteries as white workers. There had been so much discrimination against the Mexican-American and Indian. They were fighting for their dignity."

Strikers appreciated O'Leary's support as well as his fiery personality. Dr. O'Leary's Route 666 clinic fast became a community meeting place. As many as fifty strikers and their families came in for treatment each day—a measles shot, pregnancy care, or a wound suffered in the line of picket duty. Banners went up on the clinic wall calling Clifton "Solidarity U.S.A." after the struggle of Lech Wałęsa and the independent Polish union movement, which had just been quashed by Polish troops. Dr. O'Leary's clinic also became a kind of clearinghouse for information and informal counseling about strike-related incidents and events.

Several months into the strike, the Steelworkers leadership began to see a shift away from interest in the union's "no progress" briefings and newsletters and toward O'Leary's more radical leadership from the People's Clinic. As more time passed, it was no exaggeration to say (as O'Leary often did) that, from a local angle, he "was in complete control of the strike." But many, especially the union leaders, wondered what that control was being used to promote—the strike or Jorge O'Leary's own dream of leading a revolution.

"Blow his damn head off"

In tandem with Dr. O'Leary's rise to prominence, new forms of strike leadership emerged from Morenci Miners Women's Auxiliary. At the beginning of the strike, the women's group was mostly a cooking circle. Within a few months, new leaders had turned the auxiliary into one of the few largely minority, working-class women's groups in American labor history—a center of strike activism. "Initially our women's auxiliary was patterned after the auxiliaries of prior strikes—a support group for the unions," said Fina Roman, a former Clifton town councilwoman who helped change the auxiliary when she became president three months into the strike. "It was mostly domestic and geared for family support. They were to make burritos, hold bake sales, arrange parties for children, and plan fundraisers."

Then came the court injunctions, the permanent replacements, and the National Guard. By expressly limiting the number and activities of union members, the court orders all but invited other supporters to become involved. The women were angry—they saw perhaps more clearly than the men that families and the entire community were also under attack in the strike. (After all, they had been watching much of the strike activity unfold from home.) But their husbands were not always comfortable with the notion of women taking to the picket line. The unions encouraged such support, but union leaders also attempted to control the women's group, initially helping to select a local insurance representative as its president. When the auxiliary supporters saw a leader with painted fingernails and false eyelashes in charge, some of them rebelled and called their own meetings. "We saw them eyelashes afluttering and we said no way," said Toni Potter, one of the earliest auxiliary members. "This isn't going to be a 'Ladies' auxiliary. Kiss that shit good-bye. This is going to be the Women's Auxiliary."

As the women became more involved in the strike, they became more and more resistant to accepting pat answers either from the company or the unions. Auxiliary members came to harbor deep resentments about being left out of the all-male club of early decision making on strike tactics. They never had any choice about stopping that first strikebreaker. At that time they were still accepting traditional definitions of their roles as wives and mothers—and no female worker held a union leadership position. The union had allowed a ten-day cooling-off period rather than force a complete shut down; union leadership had allowed Governor Bruce Babbitt to bring in the National Guard without a good fight; and under union leadership, the company had permanently replaced everyone. "We thought that not enough was being done," said Roman. "Not enough information filtered to the rank and file for negotiations. It was amazing how many members didn't really know the reason for the strike. They denied that PD was out to bust the union. They had all the faith in the world that a contract would be signed. . . . The men seemed to give the union leadership the power to make all the decisions without question." Through the auxiliary, women began to demand more of a voice.

"I don't know what [the strike] brought out in women—independence, maybe, the right to think for themselves. After a while the strike itself kind of became secondary," said Roman. The auxiliary moved to punish the company for destroying the union community and, at the same time, to deliver a message that union members had better start respecting the full participation of women.

Two women in particular piloted this activity—Roman, a secretary and sometime town councilwoman, and Anna O'Leary, wife of Jorge O'Leary and the daughter of a Clifton shoemaker. Roman was born to Spanish parents who had immigrated to Clifton in the 1920s to mine and cut lumber. She knew from her parents the tumultuous relationship of Phelps Dodge and labor. But Roman also had the kind of personal experience that could drive a political movement. In the mid-1970s, Roman said, she was fired by a construction company after Phelps Dodge protested that she was helping to organize migrant workers. That activity had consisted of hosting United Farmworkers union leader Cesar Chavez during a tour of southern Arizona. Chavez came from Yuma, Arizona, and had long hoped to bring more Arizona farmworkers into the union.

Roman remembered the Chavez visit vividly: "I was on the Clifton town council at that time, and I knew the Farmworkers. We had planned a place for a rally when Cesar got there." Chavez, two bodyguards, and two German shepherd guard dogs stayed at Roman's house for four days. "He was a most interesting man, very soft-spoken, very powerful. I also remember—one of the shepherds' names was 'Huelga' [strike] and one was 'Boycott.' "

A few days after the Chavez visit, Roman's boss at the Phelps Dodge subcontractor where she worked as secretary asked her to resign. "Mr. Poster called me into his office and said [a Phelps Dodge official] wanted me fired. I wanted to know why and he said 'because Cesar Chavez was a guest in your home and spoke to all these union members and he doesn't approve of it.' " She refused to quit. "I told him 'You'll have to fire me.' For about six months he continually tried to get me to resign. Finally one day Mr. Poster called me into the office and handed me a termination slip. 'Instructions from headquarters,' he said. He apologized." Roman was certain that the real force behind the firing was Phelps Dodge. She moved in with her sister and brother across the border in New Mexico.

A few years later, when Roman had moved back to the Clifton and Morenci area, she saw Phelps Dodge fighting off unions again. She decided to start attending the auxiliary meetings to see if she could help. Not long after the National Guard had moved into town, Roman vented her views in a long, angry letter to the Clifton newspaper, the

Copper Era. "The morale of the strikers has been lifted higher by the show of force sent by [Governor] Scabbitt," wrote Roman. "Unfortunately the news media doesn't find peaceful rallies and talk of working within legal boundaries as interesting as so-called acts of violence." One of the stories that had been ignored was about a group of women who, in order to boost the men and take a more active role in the strike, had organized an all-women picket line. It was a transformative event for women who had been relegated in past strikes to duties behind the lines. "Unlike some women in a neighboring county who believe they belong at home," Roman wrote, referring to the mostly Mormon community of nearby Safford, the women on the Morenci picket line "believe their place is at their men's side in defense of their principles and the rights that affect future generations." Soon after, although she had no family members on strike, Fina Roman was asked by the women on the line to become the new auxiliary president. She accepted the nomination and was elected at a subsequent meeting.

Very quickly, the organization developed into a self-help group and activist cell. "Everybody had their specialty," said Roman. "Angela Alvillar was director of the college extension office in Clifton and she gave us this idea: don't go to union members who know less than you do. Ask for papers from the NLRB, official documents." On a local level, the women often had trouble getting accurate information from the men about the negotiations. So they began consulting directly with the many activists who flocked to Clifton for the strike—like writers from the New York–based left-wing newspaper the *Militant*.

Of the hands-on strike activism, Roman said, "Everybody did what they did best. . . . It didn't bother me to be a public speaker since I had done that before." Some took these roles to poignant (and sometimes humorous) extremes. For example, when the company asked the courts to amend the picket injunction to include all pickets, not just union members, a group of women arrived at the picket line dressed up in disguises, like Donald Duck and Dolly Parton, in an effort to avoid that injunction as well.

But for most, the new activism was dead serious and deeply moving. Jessie Tellez, wife of engineer Fillmore Tellez, became the Women's Auxiliary scribe, often reading her soulful poems at meetings. "Angustia" mixed Spanish with English, and read, in part:

Tristes y desconsolados,
  Barrios silencios y abandonados

. . . .

We work to line your pockets with silver,
  You the people from New York,
 All we ask is a share of the profits
  Just as we share in the work.

. . . .

When it's time to meet your Maker,
  And you don't know what to say,
Tell him of the tears of mothers
  Separated from their sons.
Tell him of the sleepless nights they spent,
  Praying for their loved ones.

Tell him of the broken families,
  Tell him of the ruined towns,
Tell him of the misery,
  That your ignorance spread around.

Women with counseling experience helped others whose children were having trouble in school or who were experiencing family upheaval. The turnover rate of teachers at Clifton and Morenci schools tripled and no one could begin to measure the family strife. Many auxiliary members went town-to-town giving speeches and raising funds for strikers' families.

Of the women who joined in this strike activism, Roman said, "Some of them did horrendous things and they went to jail. But that's what they did best." For example, one group of women learned that a neighbor who had crossed the line had purchased a new car with what they called his "scab money." In the middle of the night, they strung cans of acid across his driveway. When he backed up in the morning without seeing the cans, his car's finish was spattered and scarred.

"These women made the scabs' lives miserable," said Roman. "It didn't help so much with the end result. But we reminded them that they didn't come and take over without a fight."

There was also a certain amount of apocrypha that entered the strike saga—stories of daring and sometimes fiendish assaults carried out by activists with no fear of the consequences. According to Roman, one dynamic pair in particular carried out the most imaginative assault on strikebreakers. She said the two auxiliary members decided that their best attack route against strikebreakers driving into town would be by horseback. The only thing they lacked were the horses. Said Roman, "Both were expert riders. So they went to the sheriff's corral at his house in Loma Linda and took two horses." From there, according to the story, they galloped bareback across the hills and timed their assault on strikebreakers on the highway. They heaved rocks from horseback, then swiftly fled into the hills to return the horses. Unfortunately, when asked, the two women Roman named as the perpetrators of this act said it didn't happen, and one of them doesn't know how to ride a horse.

Nevertheless, the true tales were enough to drive strikebreakers, company officials, and law enforcement officers into a fury. Writer Barbara Kingsolver noted in her narrative of the auxiliary, *Holding the Line*, that a frustrated state trooper declared in the middle of the strike, "If we could just get rid of these broads, we'd have it made." Some auxiliary members became so militant, they said to each other that if they, rather than the men, could start the strike over again, their strategy would be, "First scab that tries to cross the line, blow his damn head off."

For others, a more personal sort of radicalism developed. Rosemarie Martinez, wife of crane operator Ralph Martinez, found herself doing and saying things that she never knew she had in her. For example, she said before the walkout she never would have lifted a middle finger in a gesture of anger. It struck her as unseemly for a housewife. But as the strike wore on, "I called people scabs, and I threw the finger. One day I was at the grocery store and I saw our neighbors. I called them 'scabs' just when they were walking by. I never thought I would have a reaction like that to a friend, but it came out. I said it."

Auxiliary members' aggressiveness and independence caused its own problems at home as well as at the union hall. "The auxiliary caused a lot of conflict among couples," recalled Roman. Husbands weren't keen on their wives leaving town on their own for fund-raising trips or speaking engagements. Said Anna O'Leary, who succeeded Roman as president, "Here's a bunch of women who'd never left home, never been any place before, and now they're out making political speeches. That was part of the evolution. For twenty-five or thirty years, they'd never even slept away from their husbands." Kingsolver told the story of one member, Alicia, whose husband had gotten fed up with his wife's hours away from home. He demanded that she return early from a speaking trip to Chicago, or he would move out with the children and divorce her. She decided to stay for the remainder of the trip. Wrote Kingsolver, "Dead tired at 2:30 A.M., Alicia came home to an empty house. True to his word, her husband had packed up the kids and gone to Tucson."

Then there were the clashes with the union itself. As the auxiliary gained its own footing and confidence—and budget—it committed gaffes such as inviting an alternative candidate for United Steelworkers president to speak to them. Ron Weisen, a union leader from Homestead, Pennsylvania (location of a famous and violent strike in the nineteenth century against Andrew Carnegie), accused the modern-day Steelworkers of "betrayal" for failing to provide enough support to the Phelps Dodge strikers. Like Dr. O'Leary, Wiesen felt that Steelworkers around the country should have traveled to Morenci to join the picket line. At the first Steelworkers local meeting following Wiesen's visit, union president Rodriguez and others castigated the women. When an auxiliary representative tried to speak, they cut her off. A union officer said that women should leave the issues to the men and "stay in the kitchen." Others were even more vocal and insulting, criticizing the women with obscenities.

The women were infuriated and Roman wrote back to Rodriguez:

PD violates the rights and freedoms of strikers. Are we now going to do this to each other? . . . Patience is required. You advocate this yourself at the negotiations table. Why were the words of a woman at your meeting so formidable that a vicious attack was thought necessary—an attack upheld by two men who are also looked on as leaders?

Apology requested, Fina Roman.

Rodriguez wrote a formal apology, but the tension was never fully resolved. Instead, the organizations operated as mutually suspicious allies in a common cause.

The union cause had vital high points for the women, in addition to low points such as the flood, arrests, and battles with the men. For Roman, the most memorable moment occurred in New York in 1984, during her first trip east of New Mexico. She was asked to address a strike rally organized in front of Phelps Dodge headquarters in midtown Manhattan. In front of thousands of protesters who had helped shut down Park Avenue in the middle of the day, Roman unleashed her fury:

We have become union "soldiers" and of necessity have become involved
in some pretty unladylike behavior. We object to being called a "Ladies"
auxiliary. We are the Morenci Miners WOMEN'S Auxiliary. We fight for
our homes, our livelihood, our children's futures and dignity as productive
human beings.

It is obscene, some say, that small children witness gestures and listen
to adults shouting profanities at scabs. There are many kinds of obscenities
and profanities. It is obscene for an industrial giant like Phelps Dodge to
exploit its employees. It is obscene that a man or woman is subjected to a
sub-human level because of ethnic origin. It is obscene that men and
women who risked their lives to preserve civil and human freedoms face
guns in the hands of their own countrymen for exercising those very
freedoms. . . .

We have adopted Emiliano Zapata's Mexican Revolutionary War Cry
"Better to die on your feet than live on your knees." Brothers and sisters,
join the ranks of the Arizona Copper strike that continues firmly on its
feet, never on its knees!!

Roman traveled throughout the country giving speeches and recruiting supporters. Under her leadership, the auxiliary helped wage
a national corporate campaign that, however belatedly, put a scare
into Phelps Dodge creditors. The auxiliary also brought important
national publicity to the remote copper towns. And perhaps most
important, the auxiliary changed the lives of individual members.

For example, Anna O'Leary began the strike as a housewife struggling to complete a college degree part-time while caring for six
children and a husband. Two of her brothers had been Phelps Dodge
employees, and one of them crossed the line while the other stayed
out. She knew the anguish of a family at odds over the strike, so she
went to an auxiliary meeting for support. One day, she spoke uneas-
ily about the need for women to support each other. Gradually, she
began to take a leadership role. Later, she was selected by the Ford
Foundation to speak about women's labor struggles at a conference
in Kenya, and then she began studies for a Ph.D. in anthropology.

At first, she said, "I'd go and sit in the back. I was not inclined to
actively do anything. Later on, little by little, I started participating.
The difference between our concerns and the union's was that we
had to take care of the household—the children, the family. We
would share bits of information. Like how to cook ten thousand ways
with government cheese. We got big old blocks of it. And it wasn't
even Velveeta."

But gradually O'Leary came to believe that the women could do more; after all, the men were failing at their own "job," which was to lead. Her language and actions became more aggressive. "The union and union members abided by union rules and bylaws. . . . The men were legally castrated as union members and subject to what the union governed. Maybe that accounts for the lack of violence. The union was concerned about its image to the public.

"The women, on the other hand, had been historically excluded. They weren't counted and had no means of control. But of course, that also meant that the men had nothing they could control us by." O'Leary and Roman became frequent road partners, speaking about the community—not just the union—suffering.

Said Roman: "I never thought, and I'm sure neither did the other women, that the union was losing the strike. How could we? We hadn't ever lost before. . . . There was a loss of union representation, yes," but gains in many other ways. In her account of the auxiliary, Kingsolver wrote that "a new bunch of confident women came rolling hell-for-leather out of the strike, for the norms of Arizona's old, stagnant mining camps had been turned upside-down and dumped like a laundry basket."

From the soul of the strikers, the Martinezes, to the strikebreaker, Mary Beager, to the feuding Tellezes and Torrezes, families were tested during the Phelps Dodge strike response—and many came unraveled. Why they came unraveled had much to do with their own particular circumstances—but much also to do with a common conundrum. As many of the local residents began to realize, there were really two separate, simultaneous strikes going on in the Arizona copper towns. One, led by the international unions, was a strike about economic matters: the union was concerned about preserving a bargaining legacy dating back to 1967. The other strike was about values, tradition, place, power, and, most of all, justice. The differences help explain why the Phelps Dodge strike became such a bitter, protracted, and violent affair.

Some families interpreted the strike issues as essentially economic questions and found the decision to cross the picket line uncomplicated. Feeding their children meant more than an abstraction such as pattern bargaining or COLA—the fractional cost-of-living adjustment. To them, neither pattern bargaining nor COLA were central to survival. But to others, these same questions contained the kernel of union and community life.

The outside press questioned whether families should have responded the way they did to the strike. Was it worth it? If the threatened demise of the union and the battle for rights as a Mexican-American community demanded their unyielding attention and support, did the cost-of-living allowance demand such regard as well? There was no objective answer to the question. Both the company and union leadership had created circumstances in which it was difficult for the strikers to determine what they were really striking for. The company appeared to be challenging the workers rather than seeking compromise. And the union appeared to be inciting loyalty through the old rhetoric rather than educating the rank and file about the more complicated details.

Many families supported the union because it had been right before when the company was wrong. There was reason within individual and collective memory to continue to believe in the union. The Martinezes had grown up in Morenci where "PD" stood for both Phelps Dodge and "Police Department." Fred Torrez, like the Andazolas, had participated in the transformation of his family from virtual serfs in Morenci to "lords" of their own property in Clifton. Many families in the area had some experience of having to migrate from site to site as the mine expanded. At the onset of this strike, they knew that high unemployment and high debt had weakened the unions' bargaining power with Phelps Dodge. But for these families, union power was not a stock market indicator, rising and falling according to daily circumstances. Union power was an investment built up over time, a confidence in their union's ability to provide a counterweight to the company. Power in the minds of these families was also moral power—the force of being right, of having justice on their side.

Strikers drove home these connections between the power of union and the commitment of family in stunning acts of faith—or perhaps acts of retribution would be more accurate. For the Tellezes and Torrezes, for example, betraying the union meant a betrayal of family. Fred Torrez confronted his brother, and the battle between the two symbolized the dissolution of Clifton families. Only by staying on the union side of the line could strike power be maintained.

For the Tellez family, who lived just a parking lot from Clifton's Catholic church, the decision to disown their daughter contained an important element of moral justice. The union had helped improve the quality of life from which their daughter had benefited—not just through better wages but through advances in civil rights. The union was, in a moral sense, presumptively "right." Violation of it—even for a perceived medical need in the family—was wrong. In the ideals of these families, such justice should prevail over all.

Issues of morality created a tangible picket line and community spirit. This spirit shook and transformed families—and changed the tenor of the strike. For Brother Mike Martinez, the moral force of families in this strike could be transformed into a tangible commodity. He delivered sermons on the line and stared down acquaintances who crossed the line. Mike's mother suddenly found that she, a warm, peaceful woman, could also throw a finger and scream, "Scab!" Women's Auxiliary leaders took bolder action yet, using a grassroots feminism to empower women and to demand answers from the men that ran both the unions and the company.

Was it reasonable to turn a dispute over wages into a moral question? Outsiders posed this question as they watched the strike lengthen and intensify. But such a question would have sounded strange to most of the strikers of Clifton and Morenci, Arizona. The older generation had grown up amid injustice, and no one had ever declared the battle over. On the contrary, an old enemy of justice was suspected to be lurking behind the terms and conditions that had now been imposed. To the strikers, this struggle was not about an acronym called "COLA"; it was about whether, after all they had struggled for and won, they would again be forced to wear Phelps Dodge's copper collar.

 *Chapter 6*

Hard Change

Another difficult year lies ahead.
　　　　　—Engineering and Mining Journal, 1983

A s the human response to the strike became increasingly desperate, the economic issues grew more and more urgent. In the
copper towns, union members counseled each other on how life on
$40-a-week union payments and government cheese could hasten
Phelps Dodge's defeat, while strikebreakers let their earnings speak
for them. Entering and leaving the mine gate, the strikebreakers
began a ritual of waving paychecks and flicking pennies at the
strikers. There was an ironic symbolism in the crude acts: a broader
economic justification of the strike—for both sides—could be found
on the head of a penny.

Every penny up or down in world copper prices caused a $10
million shift in annual income at companies the size of Phelps Dodge.
In 1981–82, as recession slowed the auto and housing sectors of the
economy (among the most important copper consumers), world
exchange prices for copper steadily declined from a little over $1 per
pound to under $.80 a pound, Phelps Dodge's nominal break-even
point before the strike. Cheaper imported copper began to erode the
market for American-made metal. Finally—speaking of pennies—the
U.S. mint delivered another blow to the industry. In 1980, when
copper prices were temporarily at a high, the government decided to
switch the bulk material in pennies away from copper (the only other
time was during World War II). New pennies would get a zinc
core with an electroplated copper coating, reducing domestic copper
consumption by thousands of tons. Despite the subsequent price

decline, the mint never switched back to copper. The industry saw insult added to injury.

What was the merit of these grievances when the unions and Phelps Dodge collided? That was the strike's $74 million question— Phelps Dodge Corporation lost that amount in 1982, its worst loss since the Great Depression. To anyone unfamiliar with copper, $74 million in red ink might seem to justify just about any cuts or concessions that management might demand. But copper economics were not all that met the eye. Phelps Dodge was a conglomerate, and in 1982 its mining operations accounted for about $40 million, not all $74 million, of the company's losses. More important, copper was a complex, volatile commodity that underwent radical shifts in price and demand depending on global business cycles. One or two years of losses were just a blip (albeit a real blip) on long-running balance sheets of both union and company economists. Short-term losses did not make or break heavily capitalized copper companies. For example, even though Phelps Dodge lost $74 million in 1982, it earned profits of $110 million in 1979 and $94 million in 1980. As for predicting how long a cycle might last, analysts relied partly on hard information (world inventories, interest rates, economic growth rates) and partly on astrology. Although Phelps Dodge president Richard Moolick had a pessimistic outlook that he called the "Moolick treatise," other companies, labor unions, and investors held fast to the regular movement of the stars: copper prices always came back up, it was just a question of time.

The Experts

There were three basic resources available at the time of the 1983 negotiations for guessing the direction of the copper industry: published reports of the experts, labor contract decisions by the other companies, and short-term results in the industry. An account of each of these helps bring into relief the merit and motives of Phelps Dodge's strike decisions.

Just before the strike, different industry experts predicted widely different futures for the health of copper. One reason for this was uncertainty over what would happen to the most important industry variable, world copper market inventories. If the excess stockpiles of copper eased as economies recovered, prices would rise. But if inventories remained high, the market would remain stagnant. Standard and Poor's summed up copper's future this way: prices would dip to the lowest level since the depression but recover by the mid-1980s to perhaps the highest mark in history. "Seeds are being sown today that should yield substantially higher prices and perhaps record profits for the industry by the mid-1980s," stated Standard and Poor's annual industry report for 1982–83.

Other analysts were more cautious. The U.S. Chamber of Commerce predicted a best-case scenario of prices rising to more than $1 per pound (assuming increases in demand for copper from the durable goods, automotive and construction sectors) and a worst case of continued stagnation. Meanwhile, in its 114th Annual Review and Outlook, the *Engineering and Mining Journal* was the least sanguine. "A rundown of developments during 1982 makes for very gloomy reading—not unlike the obituary pages," the publication reported. "Even so, U.S. copper consumption should show some growth this year." The journal limited its projections to 1983, commenting only that "While the desperate shape of the industry should result in more modest union demands, the companies might insist on 'give-backs' and that could lead to a fight." The article concluded, "It seems another difficult year lies ahead."

The Companies

The company negotiators had begun the spring 1983 contract talks with these reports well in mind. Yet, within a matter of weeks, Kennecott, Magma, ASARCO, and Inspiration had all agreed to a wage freeze and continued cost-of-living allowances. Union members, of course, felt that the settlements provided a kind of local truth about the market. If four of the biggest producers in the world felt they could afford this contract (in the most peaceful negotiations in fifteen years), why not Phelps Dodge?

The first to the table and first to settle was Kennecott Corporation. Although Phelps Dodge (the number two producer) had lost $74 million in 1982, Kennecott (the largest producer), had lost $187 million. Yet, despite the bad times, according to company labor relations director Judd Cool, "We took a congenial approach to the unions." One reason for this approach may have been that the company had an anchor during bad times. Kennecott had been bought by SOHIO, a cash-rich oil company, two years earlier. In its analysis of the copper company's afflictions, SOHIO was more concerned about the triennial strike-related losses than market losses, which would certainly be reversed at the end of the recession cycle.

After the SOHIO takeover, Cool had worked on a campaign the executives called "Strike Free in '83." In 1981, the unions and Kennecott began a dialogue on particular concerns of both groups. They even published a newsletter of complimentary quotes and photographs of union and company officials at the table together. By 1983, Kennecott had convinced the unions to unload one particularly burdensome vestige of the more free-spending 1970s, a jobs security program that locked in high employment levels. In exchange for the unions giving up this program and accepting a wage freeze, Kennecott agreed to the unions' request to continue cost-of-living allowances. "I thought '81 and '82 had been bad and '83 would be up," said Cool. "I expected a better economy, plus we were making some major changes in cost reduction. . . . When we concluded our negotiations, all of us in Kennecott's management felt very good. We had satisfied our objectives."

As for the dialogue, "When the early talks failed at Phelps Dodge, Phelps Dodge stopped talking," said Cool. "Because of [the company-union dialogue], Kennecott had a natural way to continue."

Within a few weeks of the Kennecott settlement, Magma and Inspiration had also agreed to the basic economic package set by Kennecott. The most resistant company was ASARCO, a close third in production behind Kennecott and Phelps Dodge. Like Phelps Dodge, ASARCO had no oil company parent as a cash cow. Still, shortly before the midnight, June 30, 1983, contract deadline, ASARCO bought the pattern as well. "ASARCO, like the other companies, felt that we could get a fair enough deal" without a strike, said company labor relations chief Douglas Soutar, one of the most respected wage strategists in the industry. "We used the COLA issue more as a wedge or a bargaining ploy," meaning ASARCO's position against COLA was really a strategic way of winning other concessions before accepting the pattern. Soutar said that this was precisely what happened, with the company cutting back on medical and other costs. As to the costs of keeping COLA, "There was a good chance of the cost of living tapering off," Soutar said.

In sum, apart from Phelps Dodge, the four largest copper producers—Kennecott, Magma, ASARCO, and Inspiration—decided that based on their predictions and economic standing, they could afford a wage freeze and continue to pay cost-of-living adjustments. How the market actually played out, at least in the short run, provides some insight into the Phelps Dodge dissent.

Phelps Dodge on the Record: Some Numbers

Analyzed on a purely economic basis, how reasonable were Phelps Dodge's demands when the company made them? One way to answer the question is to measure what the company demanded as against what it reaped from its tough stand. Any publicly traded company that asserts its wage-cutting prerogative must eventually face a public reckoning: did the numbers play out the way they claimed they would? The answers in this case suggest that Phelps Dodge's historical obsession with controlling the labor pool— perhaps even more than its interest in controlling the amount of wages—drove management decisions.

Newspapers and trade publications periodically updated the critical numbers in the strike. When the negotiations reached an impasse in June and July 1983, Phelps Dodge was insisting on $14 million in savings over three years, including termination of quarterly cost-of-living adjustments, a lower wage scale for new hires, termination of some vacation benefits, and copayments on medical care. The unions quickly countered that the company was hiding reductions and that the proposed changes would cut out more than $20 million from workers' take-home pay and benefits. Less than two months into the strike, the company acknowledged the accuracy of the unions' claim—and raised them one: the proposed savings would be $25 million. A few days later, the company adjusted the figure even higher—to $50 million.

This bartering game had complex roots. Both the company and union strove to win over their immediate constituents (workers), as well as the press and the public. Initially, Phelps Dodge had an incentive to make its dollar claims appear realistic—especially since the other companies had agreed to the pattern contract—whereas the unions had an incentive to make the cuts seem drastic and unreasonable. But once the company's strike plan was in place and workers began to cross the line, the company could afford to reset the boundaries. When Phelps Dodge was at its most confident—the week in late August 1983 when the National Guard protected the company gate—its demands for relief peaked at the $50 million mark.

But, as the strike wore on, Phelps Dodge's reported savings varied drastically from what the company had claimed in the early articles, leaving the impression that their numbers had all along mixed propaganda with economic analysis. Illustrating these discrepancies calls for a few simple calculations.

Phelps Dodge based its final demand of $50 million in savings (over three years) on an expected 5 percent rate of inflation, along with projected savings from lower-cost new workers and lower benefits. Because the wage package that was finally imposed on workers contained all the clauses Phelps Dodge had demanded, the company's actual savings should, if their estimates were correct, have roughly corresponded to the $50 million claim. Yet, as the first year of the strike dragged on and the company operated with much cheaper permanent replacement workers (many without union seniority), Phelps Dodge announced much more modest cost reductions, a total of $6.8 million for the year.

The company had insisted in 1983 that ending cost-of-living adjustments would save $35 million over three years and that wage and benefit reductions would save an additional $15 million. But by the end of the first year of the strike, with an inflation rate of 4.5 percent—very near the 5 percent rate predicted during the negotiations—the company reported savings of just $2.8 million in COLA for the year. In addition, the company claimed an additional savings of $4 million in wages under the dual-wage system that paid new hires less.

These numbers were utterly at odds with the company's early strike claims. The $2.8 million in COLA savings, even spread over the three-year term of a union contract (totaling about $20 million saved), did not come anywhere near the amount demanded in earlier negotiations by the company. That's because Phelps Dodge had included nonunion management and office staff in its numbers for negotiations. But the union had neither control nor responsibility over those employees' wages. (Phelps Dodge was never under any obligation to pay cost-of-living increases to its three thousand nonunion employees.) When Phelps Dodge made its final economic arguments to the press, the company was multiplying its demands on the union (and its claimed savings) and no one called it to task for the inflated numbers.

The company's largest reported savings for the first year of the strike—$4 million—came mostly as a result of hiring cheaper nonunion workers. There, too, the numbers did not fit the earlier claims.

The original contract demand by the company anticipated savings of $5 million per year, but because of the unions' strike discipline, the company had to hire more than one thousand new workers. Less-skilled workers received the lower entry-level wage rate of $7 an hour (compared to an average of $9 an hour for new hires before the strike). According to figures supplied to newspapers, Phelps Dodge reduced its average wage in 1983 from $12.60 an hour (an average of $26,000 per year, plus benefits) to an average of $11.80 an hour (about $24,500 per year). The company's savings should have been much greater than the $5 million it had predicted because of the cheaper replacement workers, but, on the contrary, the balance sheet showed a total of only $4 million in wage savings for the year.

In retrospect, with both the COLA and wage numbers, it is clear that Phelps Dodge's original predicted savings contained major exaggerations. The possible reasons for these inaccuracies ranged from the benign to the malicious: undue optimism, bad math, bad faith, and all of the above.

Another insight into management's "one year after" representation of the company's fiscal health came in an obscure federal labor board hearing. In August 1984 the company sent its lawyers to argue before the National Labor Relations Board that, even though it had laid off some of its replacement workers, they would soon be back on the job and should therefore still be eligible to participate in the decertification vote. Phelps Dodge lawyer Timothy Greaves III used the opportunity to tell the hearing officer about the company's view of the copper market.

Given the company's arguments leading up to the strike, one might have expected Phelps Dodge to repeat the pessimistic views voiced by Moolick or labor relations director Jack Ladd. After all, the strike was still on, the price of copper was low, and the company was demanding even bigger reductions from the unions. But Phelps Dodge's short-term interests—decertification of the union—were different now, and so were its numbers.

Greaves presented an article from a respected industry publication, the *Metal Investor*, which predicted an increase in copper consumption that would send prices (still languishing below $.70 a pound) up to $1 a pound by mid–1985 and as high as $2 not long after that. These were precisely the numbers that the other companies had relied on in their earlier negotiations and that Phelps Dodge insisted it did not find credible. Yet now the company not only adopted them, it introduced them into evidence in a federal hearing. In August 1983, the company beat the unions by pessimistically inflating union costs; in August 1984, the company beat the unions by optimistically going along with mainstream market predictions. (By convincing the labor board that the market was headed upward, the company could ensure that laid-off replacement workers—but not the permanently replaced union workers—could vote in a decertification election). If those on the union side might have called the company's behavior hypocrisy, those on the management side surely considered it effective strategy.

A footnote to the company's 1983 fortunes: Phelps Dodge lost $63 million, almost all of it in the second half of the year after the strike began. Union researchers attributed the losses to the costs of replacing the union members, while the company asserted that the new workers were even more productive than the union workers and that the losses were caused by a continued slow market.

The Professors

Two more technical schools of thought later emerged about the merits of Phelps Dodge's crisis claims. In the early 1980s, former Labor Department official, copper industry arbitrator, and Cornell University professor George Hildebrand began writing a landmark study of the copper industry, *Capital and Labor in American Copper, 1845–1990: Linkages between Product and Labor Markets*. With University of Utah professor Garth Mangum, Hildebrand came to believe that overcentralized (and overly powerful) labor unions had forced Phelps Dodge into a wage structure that was driving the company into bankruptcy. A young graduate student, Ruth Bandzak from the University of Notre Dame, began doing research at about the same time on the Phelps Dodge strike, and she reached almost exactly opposite conclusions. Their intellectual battle, carried on in separate universes, offers another vantage point from which to judge the positions of the company and unions in 1983.

Hildebrand essentially agrees with Phelps Dodge's argument that cost-of-living adjustments were the bête noire of the industry. Part of union contracts since the 1970s, COLAs were the quarterly wage increases pegged to the U.S. inflation rate. The unions won COLAs in 1971, meaning that, no matter what happened to copper prices, union wages and benefits would stay roughly even with increases in the cost of living. (More exactly, when the basket of consumer goods that constitute the U.S. Consumer Price Index went up by three-tenths of a point, wages increased by $.01 per hour. A 7 percent inflation rate brought on a $.69 per hour wage increase, which also augmented other benefits, like pensions.)

The Hildebrand argument against COLA in copper is this: high interest rates, low growth, and third world dumping were devastating the copper industry. Meanwhile, COLAs went up as copper prices declined. Economists describe this divergence as a wage "scissors" because, plotted on a graph, the wage line heads up without a break while the copper price line heads down. To complete the metaphor, Hildebrand believes that the companies were being economically cut apart by this COLA–copper price anomaly.

If the American copper industry had been able to control prices—or at least inventory, Hildebrand argues—the wage escalation might have been less important. But structural changes in world copper production and the U.S. economy upset what might (loosely) have been called market equilibrium. High interest rates made U.S. copper more expensive abroad. Correspondingly, foreign goods became cheaper at home. Needing hard currency to finance high debt, foreign copper producers increased production, forced prices down, and ate away at the domestic copper producers' share of the market. (Overall, foreign producers enlarged their share of the American copper market from 7 percent in the 1970s to more than 20 percent by the mid-1980s.) Hildebrand argues that, by 1982, the market was out of sync because nationalized mines, especially in Chile and Peru, were producing copper more out of an incentive to bring in hard currency than to earn profits. But President Ronald Reagan refused tariff protections of domestic copper and, meanwhile, although the market was down, inflation continued to push wages up by an average of 5 percent annually in the early 1980s. The "scissors" school holds that the way to reestablish a rational relationship with the market is to terminate COLA and connect wages back up to copper prices.

At Phelps Dodge headquarters, with his ideological aversion to unions, President Richard Moolick took on this scissors issue as a personal obsession, fellow executives said. (At the negotiations, Phelps Dodge representatives adapted an old soft drink advertisement and pasted a sign to the pressroom windows that said: "Phelps Dodge: The UnCOLA Company.") On the other hand, as ASARCO's labor relations chief Soutar had noted, the worst inflationary period was over and companies could hold costs down elsewhere. In any case, Phelps Dodge had enough authoritative support for the COLA position (whether it was based on an antiunion crusade or on economic thinking) to convince the NLRB that the negotiations had reached an impasse on this issue. If the company could decertify the union, it could ensure that, as the sign said, Phelps Dodge would forever be known as the "UnCOLA" company.

Enter the "solidarity school." Less mainstream than the Hildebrand "scissors" thinkers, those taking the solidarity view were led by Ruth Bandzak, who now teaches at the University of Redlands in California. Bandzak does not deny that there was a crisis in copper in the 1980s, but she asserts that neither COLA nor the price depression in copper justified Phelps Dodge's actions. Instead, Bandzak believes that the company was attempting to conceal antiunion motives behind spurious claims that labor costs were at the root of its economic hardship.

Cost of living and copper prices are central to the scissors school analysis, but productivity questions drive the solidarity analysis. Bandzak finds that one of the unique features about copper as a commodity (unlike, say, blue jeans) is that reducing the cost of production by lowering labor costs does very little to bring in more buyers. Competitive advantage comes mostly through technological or geological superiority (for example, an exceptionally high grade ore). Even though its ore was only average in grade, Phelps Dodge was already well known by virtue of technology and productive workers as the most efficient producer in the industry. Thus to Bandzak, the answer to the question of whether or not labor was earning its keep depends not merely (as Hildebrand asserts) on whether wages and copper price keep pace with each other, but whether worker productivity keeps pace with wage increases. Hildebrand never provides these numbers, arguing in his book, "The only offset available to producers was increased labor productivity. But it was impossible to match the growing gap by these means." Bandzak, however, finds that, between 1980 and 1985, the period in which Phelps Dodge and the scissors school made the most of its COLA claim, overall worker productivity in the industry rose at a whopping 12.4 percent annually—more than double the rate of COLA increases during that period and just below what had been the average wage increase.

One note of caution about the Bandzak analysis, however: Bandzak neglects to calculate the before-strike/after-strike productivity of union workers versus nonunion replacement workers. Despite the accuracy of her numbers, if Phelps Dodge could show that lower-paid replacement workers operating without union work rules were significantly more productive than union workers, this might help vindicate Phelps Dodge's decision on pure economic grounds—and, in addition, present something of an indictment of the industrial relations system. Indeed, Phelps Dodge attempted to make this very claim in its 1984 "strike-in-review" for the Arizona newspapers. But that claim was not supported by the numbers derived from government sources. Federal and state surveys showed that during the critical three-year period of the 1980–83 contract, productivity followed roughly the same upward trajectory. Moreover, Price Waterhouse conducted an audit of Phelps Dodge just prior to the strike and observed that during the first two quarters of 1983, as the company operated with a union work force, Phelps Dodge was already showing "significantly lower production costs."

Although Phelps Dodge boasted throughout the strike (and afterward) that nonunion workers were more productive, its claims must be tempered by the technical strategies that Phelps Dodge intentionally employed to make the nonunion workers "look" more productive. For example, company president Moolick said in an interview that the company did a great deal of blasting in anticipation of the strike in order to speed up production during the walkout. Moreover, company productivity figures after 1984 (with a nonunion work force in Arizona) were skewed by the introduction of new chemical production methods that began to radically reduce the labor needed for capturing certain types of ore found in company waste dumps. (This ore had actually been mined years earlier by union workers, although the company's productivity statistics credited nonunion workers with the improved efficiency, because these later workers physically extracted the copper.) The figures also fail to show a cost that Phelps Dodge was especially reluctant to publicize: work-related injuries to strikebreakers. Excluding minor incidents that are easy to conceal without union surveillance, work-related deaths at both the Ajo and Morenci properties during the strike were arguably attributable to the company's intensive replacement strategy. At Ajo, a sixty-seven-year-old engineer who had come out of retirement to work at the mine was run over by a train and killed. At Morenci, a young replacement worker from Utah (the nephew of union striker Fred Torrez) was crushed under a spilled load of ore. There is no certainty that union workers could have avoided these incidents but, according to union reports, age and inexperience, respectively, may have contributed to these deaths—a high cost to pay for continuing operations.

On the whole, Professor Bandzak overreaches her point only slightly when she argues that "increases in labor costs for the U.S. copper industry were more than offset by the large increases in productivity." Union miners had by no means priced themselves out of the market. Depressed markets made U.S. labor look expensive by one measure: the wage-price graph. Such graphs, with their aura of rigorous market logic, could be used in the press and before the labor board to disguise Phelps Dodge's ill will toward unions. (Phelps Dodge ran newspaper ads throughout Arizona showing the scissors graph.) By broader and more realistic measures, however, as Bandzak has pointed out, labor represented just one-fourth of Phelps Dodge's total production costs in copper, with capital costs constituting the primary expenditure. Any reduction in labor costs represented only a fraction of the total cost in producing a pound of copper—and an even smaller fraction of a company like Phelps Dodge's overall operations.

The focus on productivity numbers does not alter the fact that there was still a crisis in copper—but it suggests that the real crisis was not the one that Phelps Dodge or the scissors school claimed. The scissors school theorized that Phelps Dodge had every reason to panic in 1983—it was being cut up by labor costs. But the company's economic position was certainly no worse—and probably better—than that of other companies with respect to labor. Indeed, the solidarity school account probably explains why other, less efficient copper producers accepted the pattern contract in 1983. Worker efficiency was increasing, inflation was decreasing; the scissors wasn't the root of all evil. Phelps Dodge had the industry's highest productivity, and overall industry productivity continued to rise even more in subsequent years. The essential question was not whether abolishing COLA could save $3.5 or even $12 million per year, but whether Phelps Dodge could, as it had done until the era of union power, run the show the way it wanted—that is, on its own.

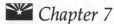 *Chapter 7*

Wars of Attrition

We have decided to take our case to Wall Street.
                                    —Lynn Williams

O
n the afternoon of August 19, 1983, when he got word of
the National Guard deployment to Phelps Dodge's gate, Ray
Rogers, a stocky, mercurial union consultant from New York,
declared to his associates that it was time for a trip out to copper
country. Rogers had all the qualities of a labor savior: a quick grasp
of companies' weaknesses, personal charisma to charge up the union
troops, savvy in playing the media. Even his name made him sound
like a man in a white hat—and Ray Rogers did have a rare reputation
for heroism in an era of union defeats. Business and labor experts
alike credited him with designing the so-called "corporate campaign," a sophisticated program to fight back against antiunion
companies with an economic war of attrition. His primary weapons
were public shame and private economic pressure. Rogers wanted to
bring his strategy to bear against Phelps Dodge—if the Steelworkers
would invite him in.

The Academy Award-winning movie *Norma Rae*, starring Sally
Field, dramatized the early 1970s organizing campaigns that brought
on Rogers's renown. In the film, Norma Rae mobilizes workers in an
effort to improve conditions at one of the South's most notorious
union busters, textile company J. P. Stevens. The company moves to
crush the incipient union local at a North Carolina plant by firing
workers and threatening the organizers. Norma refuses to give in
and, as she is carted out of the mill by force, her fellow workers cheer
her on and decide to join the union, the Amalgamated Clothing and
Textile Workers (ACTWU).

Ray Rogers cleared the way for such local victories with a gritty high-level fight against J. P. Stevens, lobbying the company's financial sponsors and exposing the company's antiunion tactics to a wider public. When, following Rogers's strategy, ACTWU used its pension plans and other accounts as leverage against financial institutions like Manufacturers Hanover Bank, J. P. Stevens suddenly started to look vulnerable. The union planned to transfer as much as $1 billion from pension funds, which business analysts credited as the cause of the resignation of a J. P. Stevens board member from the boards of both Metropolitan Life Insurance and Manufacturers Hanover. That little detail of a billion dollars, in particular, seemed to bring a response. J. P. Stevens relented and the workers won an even bigger victory than the one portrayed in *Norma Rae*, breaking—at least temporarily—a southern stranglehold on labor. Rogers and ACTWU had proven that outside pressure could be used to influence the internal decisions of a known union-buster.

Following his work with ACTWU, Rogers launched a nationwide consulting firm that sought to bring back labor's power through corporate campaigns. Sometimes the unions came to him, but often he saw a strike that he felt certain he could win—or that just plain needed to be won—and he went to the unions. In Arizona, Rogers sensed the same knee-jerk antiunion attitude as he had found in the Southeast, and he believed he could hit Phelps Dodge where it would hurt the company most: in the bankbook. But the unions' initial response to the company's replacement of workers troubled him. "When I saw on TV that the workers went to the gate with baseball bats," said Rogers, "I thought, they're going to be crushed. The union was out there by the copper pits and the price of copper was way down. There was no way they were going to bring the pressure [in Arizona]. They needed to bring it to New York. There the union could have rung the company's bell." Rogers believed that Phelps Dodge had an exploitable weakness in its bank debts and could be pressured back to the bargaining table. With the support of Carl Morris, one of Frank McKee's assistants, and Morenci local president Angel Rodriguez, Rogers got an invitation to make his pitch in Phoenix.

Ray Rogers's Phoenix Whirlwind

Rogers arrived at Sky Harbor Airport at the end of August in the middle of what residents call the "monsoon" season—it was hot,

humid, and overcast, with wind and dust storms every afternoon.
Without so much as stopping for a glass of water, he handed out his
twenty-two-page proposal to union representatives and began an
excited narration. Rogers argued on two tracks: first, the unions
needed to hit the banks that supported Phelps Dodge. He pointed to
a diagram in the proposal that illustrated his argument. It resembled
a waterbug: Phelps Dodge was the body and the company's bank
debts were the legs enabling it to stay afloat. Rogers explained that
his first priority was to attack company creditors, the legs, where
one Phelps Dodge board member—like William Seidman, Arthur
Kinneberg, George Munroe, or the scion of the company founders,
Cleveland Dodge himself—sat.

Second, the unions needed to take advantage of whatever national
public support they might be able to garner. The unions were only
playing into the company's hands by picking up baseball bats—"like
residents in a ghetto burning and blowing up their own community,"
he said. Rogers felt that the American public would be more sympathetic to the copper strikers if they knew how dangerous mining and
smelting operations could be, how much they polluted, and how
badly workers had been treated in the past—including how Phelps
Dodge had discriminated against Mexican-Americans. Another
strong pitch could be made to the public with an issue that was then
stirring protests on campuses and in Washington, D.C.—companies
doing business with apartheid-driven South Africa. Phelps Dodge
had a 49 percent stake in a silver mine in the western Cape Province
and fully owned a fluorspar mine in the Transvaal. These mines
employed hundreds of blacks who lived in flimsy worker hostels and
worked at low wages.

The key feature of the campaign, which Rogers stressed over and
over, was the need to bring all the union members into the campaign
as a team. His introduction stressed the need for a new philosophy
of fighting companies:

> In the most intense conflict situations, a Corporate Campaign is relentless,
> constantly attacking an adversary and escalating pressure from every
> conceivable angle. It takes on the power behind a company. . . . It
> recognizes powerful institutions as both economic and political entities,
> which must be attacked in both the economic and political spheres. It
> shifts the workers' struggle from their own doorsteps to the doorsteps of
> the corporate and financial power brokers, thereby transforming the

workers' customary defensive and reactive stand into one that places [the companies] on the defensive.

Rogers had supporters in his original sponsors, McKee aide Morris and Morenci local president Rodriguez. They had admired Rogers's work in the Southeast, but, given the Steelworkers hierarchy at the time, the corporate campaign would go nowhere without McKee's support. Technically the decision about whether to hire Rogers was up to international president Lloyd McBride, and McBride was said to be leaning in favor of a campaign. But, in the end, McBride deferred to McKee's judgment.

McKee felt little but disdain for Rogers and his methods, later calling the whole notion of a corporate campaign "monkey business." Rogers "outlined what they would do—contact the banks and all this stuff. I was absolutely against that corporate campaign. In my own mind, I knew it wouldn't create a bubble," said McKee.

McKee felt that a mining company was too remote from the public to be hurt by publicity, and that the unions had too little leverage to exert financial pressure. McKee still believed in the old textbook principles of power bargaining. To McKee, whose strike vocabulary was full of words like "honesty" and "toughness," this struggle was still a picket-and-notebook battle between unions and companies. If a union won, it won at the bargaining table or on the picket line; if it lost, it looked for the next place to defend its principles. Other Steelworkers leaders agreed with McKee's rejection of Rogers, but not because they thought a corporate campaign wouldn't work. The problem for these other leaders was Rogers's swirling and sometimes overwhelming personality—he had earned a reputation of going his own way at the expense (both in dollars and authority) of the union leadership. Even then Rogers was enmeshed in a trademark suit with other prounion consultants in which he was claiming the sole right to use the name "Union Corporate Campaign" in his business. One union leader told the *Village Voice* that Rogers was "delirious with his own ego." Rogers's price tag to the Steelworkers coalition was reported to be $300,000 for an Arizona campaign.

McKee issued his "no" to Rogers's plan in September, meaning that the strike would move ahead for the time being with a conventional approach. Rogers was despondent, feeling that the Steelworkers had failed to use their strongest means of resistance when these might have counted most. One of those methods was, of course, to

strike at the banks. Another—perhaps the unions' best opportunity
to strike back while it still had a measure of picket-line bargaining
power—could have been to quickly publicize the civil rights issues
inherent in the company's replacement of union members.

Years earlier, the copper companies and unions had been the subjects of a federal inquiry over the channeling of Mexican-Americans and Native Americans into the lowest-paying jobs under a
virtual caste system. Now, with Phelps Dodge's permanent replacement plan, minorities who had benefited from changes in personnel
practices after the suit were being replaced by Anglos at a rate of
nearly five to one. To many of these workers, this replacement
recalled the discrimination and sometimes outright exile they, their
parents, and grandparents had experienced for more purely racial
reasons. How, they asked, could laws that protected them in their
right to equal opportunity also allow Phelps Dodge to replace them
and force them out of town? In a feeble attempt to bring these
principles to light, a Tucson-based union organization wrote a letter
of protest in September to the U.S. Department of Labor. But the
protest never went beyond letter writing, and the unions didn't work
the racial angle of replacement.

One institutional reason for that decision (in addition to the decision not to go with Rogers) was that, when the strike began, some
senior union officials apparently felt that the race issue was a red
herring. The company might have been trying to bust them, but it
was not discriminating, said then chief negotiator Alex Lopez. Lopez
administered the Steelworkers territory that included the famous "Salt
of the Earth" union, a mostly Mexican-American local that had won an
important strike against wage discrimination in mining in the 1950s.
As a Mexican-American who had himself been denied job opportuni-
ties, Lopez was the last person likely to give the company a break on
such a matter. But he was also wary of playing the race card. "I had
to work with Juan Chacón, who portrayed the president of the union
in *Salt of the Earth*," said Lopez. "His attitude [toward management]
was 'I'm Chicano and you're a gringo and you're fucking the Mexican.' That was his thing. I'm not denying that there was once a hell
of a lot of discrimination. But it was being resolved." The unions
steered clear of such claims—even if the replacement action seemed,
to an outsider at least, to have merited that kind of attention.

Even without an ethnic or racial element, the company's permanent replacement policy could have been fought as a civil rights issue.

International bodies like the United Nations' International Labor Organization, which helped bring attention to Lech Wałęsa's struggle for the Solidarity union in Poland, had criticized dismissals during strikes as violating international principles of freedom of association—and replacement basically had the same effect. With South Africa and the United Kingdom, the United States was among the only industrialized countries in the world whose laws permitted giving union jobs away permanently to nonunion workers during strikes. In the United States of 1983, no strong union opposition to permanent replacements had ever arisen—perhaps because there was no evidence that companies had regularly used the law in a strategic manner to break unions. Arguments about the law had usually taken place among theorists. To participants enmeshed in the day-to-day strike fight, the Phelps Dodge action may not have looked like the beginning of a trend, a more sophisticated way of fighting unions. Certainly the unions were unaware of the Wharton School participation in the strike. A Ray Rogers-style corporate campaign might well have discovered the saliency of combining the replacement issue with Phelps Dodge's record of discrimination against Mexican-Americans. But in the early phase of the strike, no such effort was made.

Guerrilla Warfare

The battle on the ground, meanwhile, gave McKee fresh reasons for why traditional union power, not a corporate campaign, was the appropriate language for disputes between companies and unions. First, during the week of Thanksgiving (less than two months after the flooding San Francisco River wiped out a portion of Clifton), Phelps Dodge announced aggressive plans to evict strikers from company housing. The *Arizona Republic* headlines rang with echoes of Phelps Dodge's 1917 Bisbee deportation: "Phelps Dodge Strikers Should 'Pack Up,' Firm Says." Company negotiator Jack Ladd told reporters after a frustrating bargaining session, "The sooner those people in Morenci and Ajo realize that they are finished, the better off they will be. There are no jobs for them. It would be better for them to pack up and leave and find a job elsewhere." Permanent replacements had taken all the jobs, and now the company wanted the housing back, claiming that more than two hundred strikers were delinquent in rent payments. The company had aimed an additional blow at the strikers by unilaterally cutting off all medical benefits, a move suggested by the Wharton School strike "bible," which Phelps Dodge was following. McKee kept a high profile during this period, promising strikers that the union would pay their back rent—in all, more than $100,000—and accusing the company of being heartless and exhibiting an "Old West" mentality by evicting strikers and cutting off benefits during a holiday season. The strikers got a boost when an arbitrator ruled that the company had no right to cut off medical benefits because the benefits had been promised even in the case of a strike under the previous contract. (Phelps Dodge was so determined to carry out its strike plan that it refused to provide benefits while the ruling was pending, and then challenged the ruling in federal court where a judge again ordered the company to provide coverage.)

At about the same time, union efforts on a political front began to bear fruit. In October, Congressman William Clay, a Democrat from Missouri and chairman of the U.S. House of Representatives Subcommittee on Labor-Management Relations, launched an investigation of union charges that Phelps Dodge had set out to break the union. He sent staff investigators to the mining towns, retracing the early-century route of presidential investigator Felix Frankfurter. The subcommittee report stated that "for the first time settlements were possible in the copper industry without resort to strikes, [but] Phelps Dodge deliberately has chosen to provoke one." The report continued, "It is probable that . . . busting the unions is now the only objective that can justify the amount of money, energy and reputation, both personal and corporate, that has been expended in pursuit of the strike policy." The inquiry concluded that the strike was a disaster to Phelps Dodge shareholders and to "families [that] have lived in those communities for two and three generations." Publications like *People* magazine soon devoted space to the suffering of the copper strikers, featuring articles that portrayed them as refugees.

McKee for President?

On November 6, 1983, steelworkers president Lloyd McBride died of a heart attack. An intense and sometimes bitter election campaign began between McKee and Secretary Lynn Williams. Their constituency included a million Steelworker members in the United States and Canada. In announcing his candidacy, McKee said, "I am openly declaring war on concessions, vacillation, timidity, discrimination and apathy in our union." He obliquely attacked the legacy of his friend McBride, asserting that management had begun to "walk all over our hard-won rights." The sixty-three-year-old McKee faced an uphill battle against Lynn Williams, sixty years old, who had the support of most of the Steelworkers district directors. Labor writer John Hoerr wrote later that Williams, a college graduate with broad union policy experience, "had demonstrated his willingness to shuck old concepts and rigid union behavior if the times called for it." Hoerr quoted Williams as calling for "a place in the new world." If Williams offered a new era of participation, McKee offered confrontation—not only in his leadership style against companies, but in his campaign against Williams as well. McKee criticized Williams for failing to show enough concern for local unionists' concerns and even urged Steelworkers that "It would just not be right to have our union dominated by a Canadian," meaning Williams.

As the election campaign brewed, events in Clifton and Morenci continued to smolder. One more futile negotiations session passed on January 23, 1984, in Phoenix. (There was less bargaining than arguing: union spokesman Alex Lopez accused the company of being out to break the union. Jack Ladd responded for Phelps Dodge by accusing the Steelworkers of being out of touch with their membership, and he said of the company's actions, "The point is, we didn't mislead anybody.") The next morning at 3:00 A.M., a vehicle drove past Angel Rodriguez's rented Morenci house, and one of the occupants opened fire with a .22 caliber rifle. In all, seven shots were fired at the house—one into the front door. Rodriguez and family members were thrown awake but escaped injury. Two weeks later, the Greenlee County sheriff's department arrested two Phelps Dodge strikebreakers, Lorenzo Gonzales and Edward Dropulijic, and charged them with the shooting. Phelps Dodge responded to the incident by giving each of the accused $2,500, money that they would repay only if found guilty. While on bond, both men continued to work at Phelps Dodge, and one, Gonzales, even continued to work after pleading guilty to a misdemeanor. On the other hand, the company's policy for those strikers who had protested company replacement policy by raising bats at the mine gate, was to bar them from ever again working at the company.

In March, the election day between International Steelworkers Williams and McKee finally arrived, with Williams soundly defeating McKee by a vote of 193,000 to 136,000. McKee won a plurality among the U.S. membership, but Williams won 90 percent of the Canadian vote. The defeat meant more than the end of McKee's dream of leading the union—it also meant that his philosophy of a traditional approach to union-management relations had suffered a defeat. The Phelps Dodge strike was still technically McKee's to guide, but Williams and his new guard would play a much greater supervisory role.

Lynn Williams's First Round

Williams would have his hands full. Williams's first test at the bargaining table would come in May 1984, when Phelps Dodge withdrew the "offer" of a concessions package from the previous June—wage reductions for junior hires, an end to cost-of-living adjustments, and assorted other reductions. Union negotiators Lopez and Rodriguez asked for a green light from Williams and McKee to make one last effort at saving the union by offering a package of concessions. They were ready to give ground on COLA. Williams gave the go-ahead, authorizing an offer of a $2 per hour pay cut, copayments for medical care, and, the key feature, a two-year freeze on cost-of-living adjustments. In short, the unions were offering more savings than Phelps Dodge had ever asked for—and the negotiators might still save face for McKee on COLA by avoiding the word "termination." Preserving COLA in some form had been McKee's one last demand to preserve some uniformity with the other company contracts. Rodriguez was conciliatory in announcing the new offer: "We've been listening to [Phelps Dodge] for a long time and basically what we offered is what they asked for." But the company had no reason to settle and immediately pulled away from the offer. "Our offer was to delete COLA," complained negotiator Ladd. Another sticking point was the company's firm insistence that no replacement worker would be let go for a returning striker. As if to underline the futility of the entire exercise, the Tempe Inn Suites, where the talks were convened, had to be evacuated temporarily due to a bomb threat. Phelps Dodge formally rejected the offer a few days later.

The Phelps Dodge rejection left the Steelworkers at a dead end, with nothing to show the despairing residents of the copper towns as the strike's first anniversary approached.

Flying Rocks and Wooden Bullets

Williams, for the first time in his career, was now looking a Phelps Dodge challenge in the eye. Would he recommend that the unions finally renounce the strike and get onto the company's list for rehire? Or would Williams continue the war? If there was any doubt about how aggressive Williams's Steelworkers should be, events in May and June 1984 helped seal the decision. First, on the festive Mexican holiday known as *Cinco de Mayo*—a traditional celebration of the Mexican Army's nineteenth-century victory over Napoleon III—Clifton residents, most of them strikers, held a party that ended at the same time as the shift change. A strikebreaker leaving Phelps Dodge after the shift aimed a weapon at picketers, drawing the wrath of a crowd that had been attending the holiday events. The anger turned to rage when the Department of Public Safety was called in to protect the departing Phelps Dodge workers. A crowd of angry union supporters began to pelt the DPS with rocks, causing extensive damage to their vehicles and putting a scare into the officers. Governor Babbitt responded to the incident by calling out a small contingent of the National Guard again for several days until tempers subsided and an investigation was launched of the strikebreaker who had caused the riot by raising the weapon. But no measure short of a contract settlement was likely to quell the frustrations of a community that had been on strike and out of work for nearly a year.

On the boiling Arizona afternoon of June 30, 1984, Williams (and anyone else watching) could see that the Phelps Dodge strike had begun to take on historic proportions. Dr. Jorge O'Leary and the Women's Auxiliary organized the strike anniversary rally that led to Bobby Andazola's lonely stand. This day marked the clearest split between the union's traditional leadership, which held its own anniversary rally at a park away from the highway, and the new, radical wing that had emerged from the People's Clinic. After a march on the highway by hundreds of members of O'Leary's faction, a heckling line of perhaps twenty strikers took up position to hoot, leer, and take an occasional swing with their picket signs at strikebreakers driving home after the shift change. At about 4:30 P.M., an unmarked DPS car slowly rolled by the protesters. Union member and striker Janner Nessler slapped the trunk of the car twice with his hand.

Unknown to Nessler or the crowd or Bobby Andazola, DPS captain Bill Reutter radioed to riot-ready officers, "Okay, that's it. Bring 'em down."

The state troopers had been stationed near the company gate. Now they climbed into buses and, still concealed from the strikers' view, disembarked at a mountain curve less than half a mile from Clifton's business district. From there, several deep and perhaps twenty across, they marched down Route 666 toward the Sonic Drive-In, a few hundred feet from the alleged lawbreakers. A trooper ignited a smoke bomb to gauge wind direction, filling the highway with a swirling brown and white smoke. Another officer declared through a megaphone that the highway gathering constituted an "illegal assembly" but the crackling amplifier and distance made it difficult for anyone to hear.

At this point, Bobby Andazola made his way from his parents' house, through the crowd of picnickers in front of Clifton Liquors, to try to stop the troopers. The columns of troops and Bobby marched toward each other on the highway, with Bobby holding his arms out and shouting at the troops to turn away from Clifton. A beer bottle was thrown at the troopers (some troopers later said during federal court testimony that they believed it might be a Molotov cocktail) and the troopers launched tear gas. Bobby Andazola launched his clothes at the troopers and was arrested. Meanwhile, one gas canister was tossed into the small, enclosed space of Clifton Liquors to smoke out anyone who had run there for refuge. The troopers said later in a civil rights suit that they didn't know that pregnant Alice Miller, an elderly man, and a child were in the store at that time. In one of the trial exhibits, it was clear that DPS had planned in advance for "Mission: Restore Peace in Morenci." In a visit with company officials exactly sixteen days before the strike anniversary, an officer said, "DPS is here to keep the peace, but we will take care of any situation that is started by the strikers. No more turning the other cheek." The results of that day: ten injured and twenty arrested strikers and supporters, six injured troopers, more than a dozen civil rights complaints. (With civil rights complaints from this and other strike incidents, state and county governments eventually paid out nearly a million dollars in settlements or liability.) Clifton looked like a town under siege, complete with burning tires, barricades, and a declared state of emergency. In a day of strong symbols and dreadful reality, Phelps Dodge got in the last word: while DPS troopers battled and arrested the strikers, the company bulldozed with impunity the union picket shack.

Next Stop: Wall Street

On receiving a full report of the events, Lynn Williams set a team of lawyers to work on civil rights charges against the state troopers and reconvened Steelworkers officials to consider a corporate campaign to punish the source of these explosions, Phelps Dodge. If the unions couldn't force Phelps Dodge to agree to a contract and rehire workers, Williams believed, a corporate campaign would at least send a message: busting unions was bad for business.

The Ray Rogers thesis was revived—even though Rogers himself was not the one who carried it out. By late 1984, the copper industry, and especially Phelps Dodge, was in its worst financial shape yet. The company was relying on loans while awaiting an upturn in copper prices. A loss of bank confidence would mean intense pressure to pay off debts, and possibly even bankruptcy. Following on its 1982 and 1983 losses, the company was now heading toward its largest losses yet, some $250 million. The price of copper was stagnant at $.68, well below the break-even point. Though analysts called a turnaround in prices imminent, there was no longer any doubt that, in the short term, all domestic producers were in trouble. So the unions used the bad times as an arrow in their meager quiver. If the company could be forced to lay off the new work force, it might have difficulty bringing the replacements back on the job and some degree of union bargaining strength would return. At the very least, the unions might punish Phelps Dodge for its replacement of members and for the expected decertification of the unions. If the unions could mount a strong campaign, other producers would think twice before repeating Phelps Dodge's tactics.

At a meeting of Steelworkers executives in Denver on August 21, 1984, Williams made the long-awaited announcement: "We have learned that the Wall Street creditors are the company's only hope for survival. Consequently we have decided to take our case to Wall Street." In a national letter to union members, Williams elaborated:

> If Phelps Dodge were to succeed in breaking our unions, other copper companies might try the same. We recognized that it was necessary to expand the dispute beyond the picket line and into the corporate boardrooms, the legislature, the community and government regulatory agencies—places where we thought the company might be vulnerable.

Opening Days

Williams began the corporate campaign by hiring the Kamber Group, a Washington consulting firm with a reputation for having a more open, team-oriented approach than that of Rogers. To kick off the corporate campaign, the Kamber Group began a coordinated series of visits to Wall Street, university campuses, city council chambers, the copper-domed capitol in Phoenix and, finally, the U.S. Congress. During the eighteen-month-long campaign, the Steelworkers spent millions of dollars (no one ever gave an exact figure) in an effort to dissuade banks from lending to Phelps Dodge and to persuade state and federal environmental authorities to clamp down on the company's pollution violations. The campaign also tapped a vein of popular support, as recommended originally by Rogers, by attacking Phelps Dodge's role in a South Africa mining venture and attempting to unseat the company's directors from boards of other firms and foundations. The campaign especially personalized its attack on CEO Munroe, pressuring the Metropolitan Museum of Art, the YMCA, and Dartmouth College to drop him from their boards. In short, the campaign included almost everything Rogers had promised and Frank McKee had rejected one year earlier.

Union supporters shut down Park Avenue in New York with a solidarity rally. A group called "Dartmouth Students and Faculty Concerned about Phelps Dodge Strikers" packed a college auditorium to witness Steelworkers president Williams debate an empty chair (representing alumnus and trustee Munroe). The campaign got an unsolicited boost from rock and roll's "Boss"—singer Bruce Springsteen—who dedicated his song "My Hometown" and $10,000 to the strikers during a November 1984 concert in Phoenix. (Although fourteen thousand Springsteen fans in the Arizona State University crowd applauded for the song about workers displaced from an industrial town, the singer's appeal for additional contributions netted only $600, less than a nickel per person.)

In the New York rally just before Christmas, 1984, more than one thousand protesters converged across from the Colgate-Palmolive Building, Phelps Dodge's Park Avenue headquarters. Organizers set up a thirty-by-twenty-foot stage and disrupted midtown traffic with a picket line nearly a city block long. Six union members were arrested at the nearby South African consulate while protesting Phelps Dodge's holdings in South Africa. The crowd chanted "Say No! to Phelps Dodge from South Africa to Arizona" and "Hey-hey, ho-ho, Union Busting's Gotta Go." (Or, alternately, "Hey-hey, ho-ho, George Munroe's Gotta Go.") The Dartmouth activists built South African shanties at the rally and at the Metropolitan Museum of Art. A representative from the African National Congress told the protesters that, at Phelps Dodge's South Africa mine, black workers in 1980 earned forty cents an hour working sixty-hour weeks and sleeping twelve to a room in a migrant hostel. Other speakers included a U.S. congressman, state assembly members, a coal miner direct from a huge miners' strike in England, Fina Roman of the Morenci Women's Auxiliary, and Morenci local president Rodriguez. Rodriguez's announcement at the rally that Phelps Dodge president Richard Moolick and senior vice president Arthur Kinneberg were retiring added an immediate air of accomplishment to the rally. Rodriguez claimed that the strike and corporate campaign were responsible. (In fact, as detailed in the concluding chapter, Moolick departed under some pressure and Kinneberg had planned to retire). Still, the rally confirmed that a low-profile copper company's operations could be turned into national news in the streets of New York.

For Fina Roman, the New York appearance represented the apogee of the women's movement in the strike. The Women's Auxiliary was no longer merely incidental but had become a nationally recognized force for change. She gave a speech that had the Manhattan crowd on its toes, cheering and raising fists. The next day, the strike force of Roman, Rodriguez, Williams, and others moved on to Boston, where Mayor Raymond Flynn declared December 15, 1984, "Boston's Day of Solidarity with the Arizona Copper Strikers." The schedule included television interviews, a meeting with the mayor, radio and newspaper interviews, a march through the downtown shopping district, and a rally of several hundred people at an Episcopal church. Rodriguez lambasted Boston's banks for supporting Phelps Dodge and called on the public to condemn the company's South Africa holdings. These events raised more than $25,000 for the local Arizona unionists.

Because the concept of a corporate campaign was still somewhat new, business experts could not decide what to make of the Steelworkers sudden onslaught. *Business Week* reported that "a short-term victory is not likely at Phelps Dodge." But the magazine also quoted Chase Manhattan vice president Edward D. Henderson, Jr.: "I certainly think the union is serious. But I have never seen this kind of campaign before, and I just don't know whether it will have any effect."

As public rallies and media spots drew the copper maker into the limelight, the environmental and pension fund drives began to score a few direct hits. The unions knew that Phelps Dodge was filling the air and water at the mine sites with toxic pollutants. For example, runoff from Phelps Dodge mining dumps polluted Clifton and Morenci rivers with acid, arsenic, and other chemicals. Back when the paychecks were still coming, the union did little about these matters except when a worker's health was directly threatened. Now the corporate campaign brought various interest groups together in a coalition to push a legal and media effort against the company's environmental policies. The unions drew support from a fledgling environmentalist movement in Arizona (where the radical Earth First! organization was born), as well as from Governor Babbitt, whose advisers now wanted to make amends for sending the National Guard to Morenci. Responding to pressure from these groups, the U.S. Environmental Protection Agency eventually filed suit against Phelps Dodge and fined the company $1 million for the water pollution.

A memorandum after one corporate campaign visit with Babbitt indicates just how extensive the campaign had become. The forty-minute meeting at the state capitol in early March 1985 was attended by the governor and his two top aides, George Britton and Ronnie Lopez. According to the memorandum from corporate campaign director Harold Leibovitz,

> The length of the meeting and the location indicate that Babbitt went out of his way to be cordial and deferential. . . . Babbitt sincerely desires to close the Douglas smelter. . . . To this end, Babbitt has spoken with the EPA Administrator Lee Thomas. Babbitt asked Thomas to adopt this position when the [Mexico-U.S.] border commission meets at the end of March. . . . Eddie [Steelworkers treasurer Edgar Ball] and Bob [Steelworkers district director Bob Guadiana] agreed to help the Governor.
> "Specific actions include: 1) direct contact with [EPA administrator] Lee Thomas; 2) lobbying the "copper caucus" in Congress to speak with Thomas. . . .
> On other issues, Babbitt agreed: 1) to routinely hold permits for new leaching facilities at the Morenci-Metcalf mines; 2) to pressure EPA to investigate potential superfund sites associated with the Douglas and Morenci smelters; and 3) to pursue groundwater quality analyses at Douglas, Morenci and Bisbee.

Of course, the campaign leaders' views of their own influence were more hopeful than realistic—there was no evidence that Babbitt ever ordered any specific action against the company in response to their pressure. But the breadth of public debate and pressure were extraordinary for Arizona. In the same busy week as the Babbitt meeting, Leibovitz also organized protesters to present testimony in a public hearing on smelter pollution in Douglas, attempted to limit Phelps Dodge's access to industrial development bonds in Morenci, and met with other statewide interest groups to enlist their support. What might otherwise have been a routine meeting of local environmental activists with U.S. Congressman Jim Kolbe in Douglas turned into a mass protest of more than three hundred people as a result of the Kamber Group's organizing. The corporate campaign also claimed victory when the company decided to shut down its Douglas smelter ahead of regulatory mandates. As the corporate campaign made abundantly clear, that smelter had been for years the country's largest single industrial polluter of sulfur dioxide—and now someone had done something about it.

Bank Raids

The most sophisticated and potent weapon in the Steelworkers' corporate campaign arsenal was the union bankbook. The reason was that whatever media campaign the unions mounted, they faced one unavoidable fact—copper was not subject to brand loyalty and could not easily be boycotted. No one was going to respond to a bumper sticker that said, "Boycott Phelps Dodge: Don't Buy Motors." Moreover, the environmental campaign faced the limitation that politics could bend the law only so far in the union's direction, and judges would eventually decide these issues. But if the unions could heighten the already unfavorable business climate for Phelps Dodge—perhaps even forcing the company to dismiss its antiunion strikebreakers—retribution or even victory could be achieved.

In the early and mid-1980s, many American banks were reeling from large loans they had made to third world countries whose governments could no longer afford to pay them back. One of the leaders in dangerous loans—and coincidentally Phelps Dodge's largest creditor—was Manufacturers Hanover Trust Company. The bank was saddled with more than $1 billion in loans to Argentina, whose economy was in a slide. The bank was registering huge losses from bad oil and gas loans and was facing a federal investigation for failing to report certain transactions. Finally (and most relevant to the unions), Manufacturers Hanover Investment Company, a subsidiary that held many union pension funds, had over the past several years turned in one of the worst performances of any investment company in the country. In 1984, Manufacturers Hanover alone held some $50 million in outstanding Phelps Dodge debt. If the unions could turn off or reduce this spigot of loans, the Steelworkers argued, Phelps Dodge might begin to see that replacing the union members in Arizona was not the end of union strength. Indeed, a mere perception of unexpected power by unions might have the desired impact. At the very least, a viable financial or voting threat could give the company a few more bad headaches.

The corporate campaign's first strategic move was to withdraw union pension funds from banks supporting Phelps Dodge. As fiduciaries with a responsibility to their pensioners, the unions were forbidden from using the funds for political ends, but they could shift funds elsewhere if the host banks were not otherwise performing well. The first action came from the Steelworkers themselves. In October 1984, shortly after announcing the campaign, the union withdrew $11.5 million of its own Strike and Defense Fund investments from Manufacturers Hanover and Chase Manhattan. Steelworkers president Williams declared, "As a matter of sound financial practice, we should not keep our funds in any institution which has a dubious loan policy." The Steelworkers also announced a plan to convince fifteen other unions holding hundreds of millions of dollars in funds to withdraw them from Phelps Dodge lenders, especially Manufacturers Hanover. In particular, the Kamber Group set its sights on several huge pension accounts held by public teachers' unions. For example, the New York State Teachers Retirement System held more than $1 billion in funds with Manufacturers Hanover. The American Federation of Teachers (AFT), which administered the system, had already moved to withdraw substantial amounts from the fund, but the Kamber Group saw an opportunity to link the funds withdrawal to the Phelps Dodge strike. They drafted a speech for AFT president Albert Shanker and picked an annual AFL-CIO conference, always attended by top labor reporters, to get the biggest news bang for the announcement.

It was on a bright, warm February 1985 morning in Bal Harbour, Florida, when Albert Shanker interrupted the union congress to announce a sudden new turn in the Phelps Dodge strike. To a bevy of national reporters attending the meetings, Shanker declared that New York's teachers planned to withdraw nearly half a billion dollars in pension funds from Phelps Dodge's biggest creditor, Manufacturers Hanover. Pennsylvania's teachers were pulling out another $300 million. In all, the teachers were withdrawing more than $750 million. At the press conference, Shanker said that Manufacturers Hanover's poor investment performance could not justify keeping the funds there. Then he added that "the bank had made substantial loans to Phelps Dodge throughout the year-and-a-half-old strike . . . which is still continuing."

Furthermore, Shanker added, George Munroe, the Phelps Dodge chairman, sat on the bank's board of directors. Shanker called the Phelps Dodge participation at Manufacturers Hanover an "additional and obvious concern"—a barely concealed plug for the Kamber Group's corporate campaign. Articles in the *New York Times* and *Washington Post* the next day keyed in on the corporate campaign tie—the Phelps Dodge story, not the bank's poor performance, got most of the national attention. Thus, after countless efforts by the Steelworkers to punish the company for replacing the union members, after marches down Park Avenue in New York, and fund-raisers all over the country, it looked as if the union effort might finally show some results through the account leverage.

Until the next day. On February 20, something caused Shanker to change his mind. No one directly involved has spoken about it, and, years later, Shanker refused repeated requests for an interview. *New York Times* reporter Kenneth Noble reported on the turnabout:

> Labor leaders who have been migrating for years to the east coast of Florida for their winter conferences say they have never seen anything quite like it.
>
> At just about every turn the other day Albert Shanker, the president of the American Federation of Teachers, was seen apologizing for having announced a pension fund deal that never existed, and hinting darkly that someone had taken advantage of him.

Shanker denounced the previous day's event as a "publicity stunt." The union leader intimated that the Kamber Group had lured him into an "outrageous" misstatement. The New York teachers union had withdrawn just $200 million, all of it more than a month before the current meetings, and none of it was related to the Phelps Dodge strike, he said. Shanker also corrected the record on the Pennsylvania withdrawal, saying it occurred "within the last year," not within the past month—and it, too, was unrelated to Phelps Dodge. The retreat was especially poignant because it backed the unions away from bank disinvestment on the order of the successful J. P. Stevens corporate campaign—$1 billion. That number had been wielded by Ray Rogers's textile workers' union—ACTWU—against precisely the same bank as in the Phelps Dodge campaign—Manufacturers Hanover. The ACTWU campaign had shown that, when subjected to strong economic pressure in tandem with voting power on the boards of directors, other company directors listened. This time, a corporate campaign had gotten the numbers into the mouth of a national union spokesperson but had to stage an embarrassed retreat.

Responding to the debacle, Victor Kamber, head of the Kamber Group, tersely told the *New York Times*, "We're paid to take the blame, so we're at fault." Still smarting from the earlier Steelworkers slight, Ray Rogers himself lashed out at the Kamber Group's tactics as "all puff and no substance." The Bal Harbour incident "really hurt the whole concept" of corporate campaigns, Rogers told the *Village Voice*. To Morenci union president Angel Rodriguez, the funds withdrawal "would have had PD on the ropes at that time. Once [the pension fund] was withdrawn, PD would have really hurt. We thought it gave us a lot of leverage and would have put pressure on them to settle. Of course when [Shanker] said they couldn't do it, we were not too happy." Although Kamber never explained what happened, Rodriguez, who spoke with corporate campaign leaders, said, "It was a fiduciary problem—they could not withdraw funds for a labor dispute. Maybe they didn't think it through. Or maybe the teachers thought that the Kamber Group had cleared all the legal hurdles." In any case, Shanker and the Kamber Group had briefly lit up the union members' brightest hopes, only to have to tell them that it was all an illusion. The only remaining hope for the unions was that they might be able to avoid what was known as decertification, the federally administered procedure in which replacement workers could reverse the 1942 decision to unionize. But the unions had faint hope. Union lawyers believed that the Reaganite NLRB director in Phoenix had his own reasons for wanting to see the end of the Phelps Dodge unions. Strikers had not been allowed to vote in an election to determine the future of their own union, and only appeals of that vote stood in the way of a formal declaration of defeat. So, as the strike took a legalistic turn, even the rules of warfare seemed to be tilted against the unions.

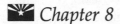 *Chapter 8*

Slant of the Law

*The investigation established that the Employer has at all
times bargained in good faith.*

—Milo Price

Washington, D.C., and Arizona labor union consultants tell
the following story about an unpublicized dispute with new
president Ronald Reagan during the first weeks of his administration.
The dispute, two years before the explosion between the unions and
Phelps Dodge, would, in a curious way, help shape the final outcome
of the Phelps Dodge strike.

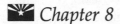

Frank Fitzsimmons, Jimmy Hoffa's successor as president of the
International Brotherhood of Teamsters, was furious with President
Reagan. After everything Fitzsimmons had done to help elect the
new U.S. president (for example, assuring the Teamsters' endorse-
ment) and even after Chief of Staff Edwin Meese's promises that
Fitzsimmons would be consulted on major labor decisions, the administration was about to make its most important federal labor
board appointment without his input. So Fitzsimmons asked for a
word with the president, and, of course, the stubby, wheezing,
gruffer-than-life chief of the nation's largest union got the meeting.

He wore a characteristic, dark, American-made suit and a pair of
gold cufflinks bearing the presidential seal, a gift from Richard Nixon.
His heavy breathing stemmed from the advanced stages of lung
cancer, an illness that caused his death a few months later. He carried
nothing in his hands: no briefcase, no briefing notes. That's the way

he met with presidents—trucking-line presidents or U.S. presidents. Fitzsimmons wasn't there to negotiate. He barely got out a "hello" before delivering this demand to the president: "Mister Reagan don't bring in Milo Price. He's a sonofabitch."

Teamsters' Veto

At the time of the Fitzsimmons visit in 1981, Milo Price was the Arizona and New Mexico regional director of the National Labor Relations Board, and number one on the president's list to become national chairman of the NLRB—the most powerful labor-management administrator in American government. Price had gotten where he was by being intelligent and by having the right conservative pedigree. He had been an up-and-coming attorney with the NLRB Southern California office when Ronald Reagan was governor. Price was a protégé of Ralph Kennedy, a California NLRB director who was later named NLRB chairman under President Richard Nixon. Kennedy brought Price along as his chief of staff. As a labor board lawyer, Price was a specialist in "secondary boycotts"—the illegal effort by unions to cut off a struck company from other producers and suppliers. Hostile union lawyers came to call him "Mr. 10-L," after the federal labor code section which Price applied against the unions. Price developed influential political contacts as a result of his Washington assignment and anti-boycott work, and, in 1972, he was named director of the NLRB southwest office.

Nine years later, Price a registered Republican, was ready for a promotion. He had high-level support in Senators Barry Goldwater and Orrin Hatch as well as many of California's top management-side lawyers; they advanced Price's name with the new president. Candidate Reagan had often said that one of his first priorities would be to deregulate American industry, which meant dismantling or radically reordering the federal regulatory agencies, including the NLRB. When President Reagan set his sights on weakening labor's power, his advisors recommended Price as the man to carry out the conservative revolution.

When word that the president was tapping Price as chairman of the NLRB made its way West, Arizona labor leaders began a furious campaign of opposition. Even management attorneys acknowledged Price's reputation, telling business publications that Price "shares the viewpoint of management." Phoenix labor lawyer Michael Keenan, whose cases were ruled on by Price, helped put word out that Price's rulings usually went against labor. Keenan's grandfather had been a labor aide to President Truman, and the Keenan name commanded respect among Washington labor leaders, including the Teamsters. Arizona conservatives, meanwhile, pushed hard the other way. The *Arizona Republic* newspaper, a bastion of Goldwater Republicans, published an editorial with the headline "Price Is Right," and declared, "Price's appointment to the NLRB may well help correct the pro-union course to which it has hewn during the past three years." The paper even aimed a message at the Teamsters, urging them to look past Price's secondary boycott work (which the paper noted had resulted in prosecutions of some Teamsters) and support him. It was Keenan who convinced Fitzsimmons's aides that Price should be knocked off Reagan's list.

As Fitzsimmons quietly laid his plans, there was some public suspense about the president's choice of a new director. For example, the *Wall Street Journal* reported in its Labor Letter column on January 19, 1981, that the Teamsters were opposing Price. The column quoted an unnamed presidential transition team official as saying that the Teamsters were "a major constituency" but that politics would not determine the choice. On March 31, 1981, the same column, bearing the headline "Teamsters Get Their Way with White House," reported that "the administration often consults the big union . . . and occasionally heeds it. Thus the Teamsters seem to have blocked . . . Milo Price." According to one Washington labor consultant with extensive first-hand knowledge of Teamsters politics, the rejection of Price occurred as a direct result of the Fitzsimmons White House meeting, although the meeting was never reported and never appeared in any public White House documents. That individual, who requested anonymity, explained the political spin: "Fitz was not a guy with a big ego. He just did the job. It would have been embarrassing to Reagan to publicly say 'I, Frank Fitzsimmons, stopped Milo Price.' Then Reagan's phone would have been ringing off the hook from the right wing. . . . Had he done that, he might never have another favor done.

"The president's people were desperate during the campaign to get some labor support. Fitz had been one of Hoffa's assistants who still harbored some bad feelings, whether just or not, against Teddy, Bobby, and Jack [Kennedy]. Meese and a delegation came to visit Fitz and told him he would be labor's man for this administration, and they would seek his advice concerning appointments. This was pretty heady stuff: he would be *the man* that would have input with the administration. So the Teamsters endorsed Reagan and then threw their political support to him during the campaign. And when President Reagan came to the Teamsters building after the election, before the inauguration, that was quite a coup. Since FDR's day there hadn't been a president who had come over there."

Thus, in 1981, Price's career was stopped short. After the rebuff, according to associates at the NLRB, Price held the unions responsible for his failure to get the top NLRB appointment. When the United Steelworkers alleged unfair labor practices against Phelps Dodge during the 1983 strike and sought labor board protection, the Steelworkers' lawyer was Michael Keenan, one of the union lawyers who had lobbied against the appointment. And the front-line referee of this dispute would be Price himself.

Milo Price's Phoenix NLRB

Milo Price had always been seen as a somewhat prickly NLRB regional director. He was generally regarded as intelligent, but behind his back, labor and management attorneys and even his own staff complained about his character and his legal analysis, calling him variously "petty," "vindictive," and "biased." Milo Price stories—some innocuous and some positively damning—were legion. There was the story about how Price ordered one of his attorneys to stop wearing turquoise bola ties because Price felt that they didn't meet his official dress code. The attorney infuriated Price by not only appealing the order in an administrative hearing but winning the hearing by showing that bolas were the official "state tie" of Arizona. (The attorney left the Arizona NLRB office soon after.)

Price's "office rules" sometimes had a more sinister edge. One board employee recalled, "If you came up with a recommendation contrary to [Price's] anti-union views, he would criticize your work and force you to rewrite your recommendation as many as six or seven times until he broke you down. Eventually you would give him what he wanted. That meant that you had better recommend dismissal of union unfair labor practice charges against the employers he favored."

A variation on this theme was Price's periodic intervention in cases by reassigning investigators without explanation. Career officers saw it happen often enough to speak of a pattern at the Phoenix office. Price tended to step in and appoint the investigators in cases involving certain companies or law firms, they said, and the reassignment, more than once, limited the latitude of Spanish-speaking NLRB investigators in cases that involved Spanish-speaking employees (often these were low-wage workers attempting to unionize in Arizona's antiunion climate).

Two particularly memorable incidents involved investigator Hector Nava, originally from South America, who was considered one of the brightest young officers at the Phoenix office. Nava (now a high official in the Miami NLRB office) declined to be interviewed, but other NLRB employees and Phoenix lawyers described the incidents. A Flagstaff textile manufacturer was alleged to be illegally blocking Mexican and Mexican-American workers from organizing a union. The company was represented by attorney Dan Gruender, a partner in the Phoenix law firm that had lobbied Washington to hire Price as regional director during the Nixon Administration. The assignments officer, who routinely made these staffing decisions, put Nava on the case—a natural choice because he was the Spanish-speaking officer with the most experience. But Nava needed help because the case involved a large number of workers who did not speak English. Price refused to send help, and instead sent the only other Spanish-speaking investigator to Tucson, the opposite direction, to investigate a much less substantial case that had been filed against a union and did not call for a Spanish speaker. Nava was left with an almost impossible task. "The implications of what [Price] did were disgusting," said one of the union attorneys in the case. "He was spending all kinds of resources on a case [against the unions] when he could have spent them on [the case] requesting back pay orders" for the Flagstaff textile workers. In another case filed by unions against a mining company—again involving Spanish-speaking workers and the same law firm as in the textile union dispute—Nava initially handled the case until Price abruptly took him off it and assigned an inexperienced law clerk, ordering her to avoid any overnight expenses. In both of the Nava cases, according to the sources, full investigations were impeded by Price's involvement. (In a 1994 interview, Price said that assignments were shifted on the basis of need only, and he denied that political considerations ever dictated assignments.)

The NLRB Role in the Phelps Dodge Strike

The National Labor Relations Board could not in and of itself decide the outcome of the Phelps Dodge strike, but the board played an important role in determining the bargaining power of the company and the unions. Created by Congress in the 1930s, the NLRB was conceived as a vehicle to end open warfare, such as violent strikes, between unions and companies. The labor board would restore industrial peace in two ways: by conducting elections to give workers a chance to determine whether they wished to be represented by unions, and by investigating and remedying alleged unfair labor practices by employers (and eventually also by unions). Of all the federal officials invested with authority to carry out these purposes, the one with the most power in the field was the one in Price's position—regional director. If the regional director issued a complaint against a company, the allegations would receive a hearing, first before an administrative law judge, then, if necessary, before the board as a whole and federal appeals courts. If, on the other hand, the regional director declined to issue a complaint, that was usually the end of the case. The union could appeal to the NLRB general counsel's office in Washington, but regional directors' decisions were almost never reversed, especially if the directors had political clout in Washington. Said one high-level NLRB employee, "There was a widespread feeling in Washington that nobody better cross Price because he still had a chance to become a board member or even general counsel. Although he was disliked, everyone avoided confrontations with him, including his superiors."

When the first charges were filed by the unions in the summer of 1983, Price immediately inserted himself into the Phelps Dodge-Steelworkers dispute, directing and monitoring virtually every aspect of the unfair labor practice charges against the company. "There had never been a case that the regional director monitored in such detail," said an NLRB official familiar with the union's proceedings. "Ordinarily a regional director is not involved in the assignment or direct supervision of investigation of charges. However, the opposite held true in regard to Phelps Dodge."

The official added, "Phelps Dodge's only real [legal] concern was a possible conclusion by the NLRB office that the company's bargaining with the union was in bad faith. If that were alleged in the complaint and ultimately established [in court] that would mean that the strike was an unfair labor practice strike and that the strikers could not be permanently replaced." Had the company been found to be bargaining in bad faith, the unions would have kept their status as representatives of all the employees, and Phelps Dodge would have had to lay off replacement workers when the strike was settled. The NLRB official concluded, "So PD's greatest interest was in making sure that no complaint should ever issue. Its strategy was therefore to convince Price never to issue a complaint, and Price was glad to oblige."

In practical terms, the NLRB could limit or augment Phelps Dodge's power through its answers to each of four critical questions. Was Phelps Dodge acting with an antiunion bias during the strike? Was Phelps Dodge bargaining in good faith? Was the company authorized to hire permanent replacement workers—new workers who need not be displaced from their jobs even if the union offered to settle? Were replacement workers authorized to decertify the active unions at Phelps Dodge? According to several sources, Milo Price's answers to these questions clearly favored Phelps Dodge. More broadly, Price's actions during the strike revealed the free hand with which Reagan-era labor administrators could alter the rules of engagement between American management and labor unions.

Unfair Labor Practice

The unions filed their first two charges against Phelps Dodge early in the strike, on July 21 and August 1, 1983. They alleged that the company had unfairly discharged union leaders and other union members at the Morenci and Ajo properties. On September 2, 1983, the unions filed a third charge, asserting that Phelps Dodge refused to negotiate in good faith at the bargaining table.

The first two cases alleged relatively routine instances of company interference and discrimination stemming from the company's firing of more than a dozen union leaders. NLRB assignments coordinator Robert Jackson put investigator Martin Dominguez on the case. Dominguez had worked for several years at the NLRB, and, if not as impressive on the job as his colleague Hector Nava, he was considered a perfectly competent investigator. But John Boland, Phelps Dodge's private counsel, disliked the choice of Dominguez. First, Dominguez, like many of the workers who had filed the charge, was Hispanic. Second, he had once upset Boland during an unrelated hearing, and Boland preferred to avoid him. During the second week of August, when the uprisings over the company's hiring of permanent replacements were beginning, Boland, through his assistants, asked that Dominguez be taken off the case. Why couldn't Gordon Jorgensen, the senior NLRB investigator, be assigned instead, they asked. On August 15, 1983, Price took Dominguez off the case and assigned Jorgensen instead. NLRB internal records show Dominguez's name on two file cards dated July 21 and August 1, 1983. A line has been drawn through "Dominguez," with "Jorgensen" replacing it. The date "August 15" (1983) is circled next to Jorgensen's name.

Asked about the changes, Dominguez, who now works in labor relations for private industry, first explained, "I believed at the time that all of us had bits and pieces [of the case] and it was getting pretty damn large. I thought they had consolidated it." When he was informed that Price had taken him off the case only after pressure from company representatives, Dominguez responded in a slightly changed tone, "That's very likely. Keep in mind, Milo Price was pro-management." Price responded that such a change in personnel at the request of one of the parties would have been improper and that no such changes occurred.

Curiously, when its decision was issued in early September, the NLRB stated that it planned to issue a complaint regarding the discharge of thirteen union members. Company representatives might have been bewildered at this turn of events—until they saw the signature at the bottom of the case. Price had been out of town, so acting regional director Peter Maydanis wrote the decision. This substitute arrangement would not occur again. The decision on the firings was the only union victory before the NLRB during the entire strike—and the only time that Milo Price's signature failed to appear at the bottom of a major decision. Phelps Dodge agreed to review the discharges, and the issue was resolved without a finding of unfair labor practices.

❧

On September 2, 1983, the same day as the decision on the strike-related firings, the union filed its most serious NLRB charge—one whose success could save the union members from being replaced:

> Since May 4, 1983, and continuously thereafter, the Respondent (Phelps Dodge) has engaged in surface bargaining with each of the various charging parties. . . .

Continuously throughout the last six-month period, the Respondent
has made various threats and promises designed to coerce individual
employees from exercising their various rights. . . .
Since July 1, 1983, and continuously thereafter, the Respondent has
failed to present at the bargaining table any representative who has
authority to enter into the terms of a new collective bargaining agreement.

The unions' three assertions had one primary goal: to win reinstatement for all striking workers at the end of the strike by showing that
the company had committed an unfair labor practice. If Phelps
Dodge was required to bring striking workers back, then its plan to
restructure operations without the union would be foiled. The outcome of this battle depended on another investigation and on the
legal interpreter of the investigation.

A company commits what is known as an unfair labor practice
when it refuses to bargain on certain required subjects, such as
wages or medical care, or when it conducts what is called "surface
bargaining"—bargaining without authority to reach agreement or
failing to bargain in good faith. The union affidavits claimed that
Phelps Dodge was violating several of these provisions. For example,
the union said that the company's bad faith was illustrated by a
company program of distributing antiunion literature and by allegedly hiring a psychologist to retrain foremen in how to undermine
union procedures. The unions also claimed that Phelps Dodge had
refused to bargain over wages when it refused to consider granting
cost-of-living adjustments.

Lawyers for both Phelps Dodge and the unions agreed that, regard-
less of the investigator, the ultimate decision about whether the
NLRB would file a complaint against Phelps Dodge lay with Price.
There is, however, no evidence that Gordon Jorgensen, the NLRB
investigative officer who replaced Martin Dominguez, went beyond
the routine in his investigation. He never interviewed the top company officials. He said later that he believed that the impasse was
strictly economic—cost-of-living adjustments and wages. He recommended that the board reject the charge of unfair labor practices
against Phelps Dodge—a finding that was put into words by Price a
little more than a month later in a one-and-a-half page decision:

The investigation . . . has disclosed no evidence . . . that the Employer
attempted to bargain directly with employees or made threats or promises
of benefits to employees. Additionally, the investigation disclosed

insufficient evidence to establish that the Employer engaged in surface bargaining, that the representatives of the Employer did not have sufficient authority to negotiate a contract, or that the Employer failed to bargain to impasse before implementing its last contract offer. . . .

The investigation disclosed no evidence that the Employer entered into negotiation with any unlawful objectives. To the contrary, the investigation established that the Employer has at all times bargained in good faith.

Of course, there is no guarantee that the board investigators would have learned anything different had they interviewed top company officials. But the statements made by company officials in interviews for this book arguably included some elements of an antiunion bias. (Any potential for legal liability expired long ago.) These statements included:

- Moolick's comment that "I had decided to break the unions" after the unions refused to give up cost-of-living adjustments.

- Company board member William Seidman's statement that the permanent replacement plan "was not designed to kill the union. It was designed to kill the cost of living [increase] and a lot of productivity problems. In the end it became clear that the only way you could win was to kill the union."

- Senior attorney Jack Boland's comments (shortly before his death from cancer), "You must keep in mind that dear to the heart of Moolick was to get rid of the unions. . . . Dick had an effort going forward from time to time . . . of getting together enough genuine sympathy and confidence to get rid of the unions. . . . I'm sure that the decisions by Moolick as the strike progressed were influenced by his long range decision to obtain a union-free shop. In other words, if a decision is doubtful about 'do this or don't do this'—and the possibility of ultimately getting rid of the union was a factor anywhere in there—why that's the one he'd choose."

A federal labor official familiar with the unions' charge, who spoke on condition of anonymity, said, "Assume the decision had been made to issue the complaint. If we allege that it's an unfair labor practice strike, Phelps Dodge has a tremendous burden. If at any time the striking worker offers to return, Phelps Dodge owes all the back pay from that date until reinstatement. What Price did was effectively exclude that possibility. . . . Procedurally, if the [NLRB] charge had been handled in an objective manner, with fair procedures, the outcome might have been different. In the ordinary case where the facts and legal issues are not clearly resolvable, it has been the agency's policy to let the issue be decided by judicial tribunals, not by administrative fiat."

Union lawyer Gerald Barrett said that his team of attorneys tried to bring out an argument of lack of good faith at the bargaining table, "but we never got to the point where we could put these people on the witness stand to find out what their intent was. The regional director cut us off at the pass."

Decertification

The formal, legal end of the strike also depended on the NLRB. Decertification is, technically, a federally supervised "yes" or "no" referendum on union representation. But when union members have been permanently replaced, decertification elections mean certain death for the union. After one year of a strike, the replacement workers' rights are strengthened—for example, replaced union members are no longer permitted to cast ballots in that union–no union decertification vote. Without the union members' participation, a decertification vote would be a certain victory for Phelps Dodge.

When requests for decertification petitions began to come into the Phoenix NLRB office after one year of the strike, according to an NLRB source, Price took a direct role in distributing and filling out the petitions—a practice that had never before been observed. On a Friday afternoon in July 1984, Price ordered one investigator to drive the four hours to Morenci to help process petitions. In all, strikebreakers at thirty bargaining units—one per union at each company property—filed decertification petitions. In a break from normal procedure, the board accepted decertification petitions simultaneously from employees and from the company. Prior to the Phelps Dodge strike, the board dropped company filings when it received one from union members. When the board allowed both in this strike, it effectively provided Phelps Dodge a kind of decertification insurance.

After summer hearings to determine whether any strikers were eligible to vote (Price held that none were), Price set the decertification vote for October 9, 1984. The election was to last three days in order to cover all the Arizona PD properties—Bisbee, Ajo, Morenci, and Douglas. Union officials weren't exactly sanguine about their chances: "It's a stacked deck, and we're not planning to win the election," said Rodriguez. He added: "That doesn't mean we're giving up the fight. We're going to be on strike for as many years as it takes to win." Tom McWilliams, Phelps Dodge assistant labor relations director, told reporters, "It would be presumptuous for us to predict how the employees will vote, but after what they've been through it's inconceivable that they wouldn't vote to get those people out. Certainly the unions have not represented the best interests of the employees."

During the week of the vote, Morenci manager Carl Forstrom distributed a letter that said, in part,

> You have absolutely no need for a union. . . . Remember, one of the union's main goals is to try to get you out so the strikers can come back to work. WE WILL NOT LET THIS HAPPEN TO YOU. But, with "friends" like these unions, you certainly don't need any enemies.

In the middle of the Arizona voting, Price visited El Paso, Texas, and released the results of a decertification vote at the Phelps Dodge refinery there—a release that outraged union leaders and led to further protests of NLRB bias. Radio and television stations available in the Arizona mining towns reported the overwhelming Texas results even as voting continued in Arizona: 372 votes against the union, 4 votes in favor. Although the Arizona vote was completed within a matter of days, legal appeals of various issues (including publication of the Texas vote) delayed the count for three months. On January 24, 1985, Price tabulated the results. Replacement workers had voted to abolish all thirty union locals at all the Phelps Dodge properties by a combined vote of 1,908 to 87. Shortly after this vote, Phelps Dodge gave another presentation at the Wharton School that included a forty-five-minute videotape on how it broke the unions.

Objections

The unions had legal rights of appeal, called "objections" in this phase of the labor board proceedings, but members were unaware at the time of earlier incidents, such as the alleged personal involvement of Price, and the allegedly improper delivery and typing of petitions that would have supported an appeal. One well-placed observer noted, "After the election, the unions made allegations about Price. [But the unions] didn't really know what the real objection was. For the board, even the appearance of impropriety is enough to set aside an election. Board agents must avoid even the slightest appearance of prejudice or bias. This principle was completely discarded in the PD case. In fact the opposite was true. Jerry Barrett and Mike Keenan knew they had a tough opponent. What they didn't know was the extent that Price had taken it upon himself to sabotage their efforts."

The union lawyers' primary claim against Price was that he abused his administrative discretion by announcing votes of the Texas decertification election just when the voting was beginning in Arizona. The objections against Phelps Dodge included complaints about election day signs that said, "Fuck the Unions" and "Don't Get Mad, Get Even," and a protest about an impromptu party held while the voting was still taking place in which company officials toasted each other with champagne along Route 666. But U.S. Administrative Law Judge Earldean Robbins recommended dismissal of the objections against Price and the company in a fifty-three page opinion that was upheld later by the NLRB as a whole.

"That [administrative] hearing was a sham from beginning to end because it didn't address the real issues," said an informed NLRB source. "When a board agent is involved and there's any question of impropriety, it is in the public interest to set aside the election. Here the board agent Price virtually sponsored the decertification petitions. This case violated all the known rules.

"If objections to an election are investigated we're required to investigate not only those objections but also any unalleged matter that the investigator is aware of. We investigate A, B, and C, and if we come across issue D we're supposed to investigate D. 'D' in the PD proceeding was Price's involvement and handling of the petitions.

"Had any hearing officer heard the facts about Price's conduct on behalf of PD and had that evidence been brought before the board, the election would have to have been set aside."

The union loss underlined how, despite the failure of Milo Price to become the nation's chief labor lawyer, he nonetheless carried out the Reagan administration goal of cutting down labor's strength. Price pursued a promanagement agenda with unique zeal and commitment. If career labor board officials are for the most part bureaucrats who speak a specialized procedural language, some take an altogether different tone when the subject is Price's administration. By the last months of the Phelps Dodge strike, said one official, Milo Price, in effect, "was acting as counsel to Phelps Dodge."

Anyone who doubted Price's drive to promote management's views had another opportunity to judge shortly after Price retired from the board. On June 15, 1986, the *Arizona Republic* published a dispatch from the Associated Press stating that Price was facing a federal criminal investigation for unethical practices stemming from his first private legal work after retirement. In early 1986, Price went into private practice for a management-side labor law firm called Beus, Gilbert, Wake and Morrill. At this time, the firm represented a produce company, Great Western Produce, Inc., which was accused of firing workers for union activities and of giving cash and gifts to antiunion informants. Price dealt with the case in the same way he had been accused of treating cases while NLRB regional director: he played both sides. Price had already been involved in this case at the NLRB, attending a conference on the union's charge and ordering an extension of a hearing after a company request. Now, as a private attorney representing Great Western, he allegedly communicated with the board on a union representation election and attended the election. (The union initially lost its representation election by a vote of 17 to 15). In the Phoenix newspapers, Price called his NLRB involvement "really procedural, not with the merits of the case" and asserted that the investigation was "a vendetta, a personal vendetta against me."

But what Price called a "vendetta" others might have called a proper federal inquiry. Investigators pointed to Chapter 18, section 207 of the United States Code, in which federal employees must wait at least six months before representing in the private sector any party over whom they had federal jurisdiction. In addition, an NLRB rule forbade past employees from ever having any private involvement in a case that they had worked on at the NLRB. In early 1987, Price signed an agreement with the NLRB forbidding him from practicing law before the board for one year. The Justice Department, meanwhile, dropped any criminal investigation and Price retired.

❦

Strike Out

The legal end of the Phelps Dodge strike arrived on February 19, 1986, with the final rejection of the unions' decertification appeals by the National Labor Relations Board in Washington, D.C. In all, more than one thousand unionists from the Steelworkers coalition had remained on strike and in contact with their unions for the full thirty-two months—some taking jobs elsewhere, some unemployed, and a few working for the struggling locals. But now that the strike was over, the cleanup and the explanations were far from complete.

Angels and Demons

*Our struggle must always be remembered as a courageous
struggle.*

—Angel Rodriguez

With the NLRB's final declaration of defeat, Angel Rodriguez
went back to the union hall to look for what was left of his
membership lists and to write one last letter. As Morenci local
president, he would now have to be union eulogist as well. Rodriguez
got out of his beat-up Pontiac station wagon and looked down
narrow, crumbling Chase Creek Street toward the castle-like ruins of
the early-century smelter. During the strike, visitors had commented
that Chase Creek looked like a ghost town—once grand but now
tumbling structures like the 1902 Spezia Building, the high flood-
worn curbs, the boarded-up store fronts. Rodriguez had always
insisted that the street and the town were very much alive: there was
still the Clifton Social Club, the El Rey lounge, and the Wagon Wheel
bar. Women's Auxiliary leader Toni Potter liked to say, "You can still
hear the women of the night calling out from the windows"—
confirming that there were ghosts but also plenty of people around
to hear them. Then, of course, there was still the busy union hub,
Morenci Miners Local 616 of the United Steelworkers. But now, as
Rodriguez's feet hit a cracked section of the street, Chase Creek truly
did feel as if it were going under. If the union had been the hub, then
the center no longer held. The hub was shutting down. For the first
time in his working life, Angel Rodriguez had to think about life
outside of Clifton and Morenci.

Rodriguez unlocked the union office and entered a front room
lined with strike posters, photographs, and mementos. It was as

quiet as a crypt. The silence filled his mind with questions: if the union was dead, what did that make him as union president? A phantom? An outcast? Or, since he could still write and speak, perhaps a seed of return and redemption. Rodriguez believed in both an angry God and a powerful union. A just struggle must have its reward. So surely Chase Creek would come back, and from this crypt, union members would some day walk again down these streets.

Rodriguez saw a hopeful sign: the strike mural. Two folk artists, David Tineo and Tomas Bandariés, had come to Clifton some months earlier (Tineo from Tucson and Bandariés from Paris, France) with the conviction that the Phelps Dodge strike carried a lesson for the world. They asked if they could paint the union story. Rodriguez liked the artists' proposal, so he gave them the long, inside north wall of the union hall. He felt a mural would provide a counterpoint to the open pit "landscape" paintings on the opposite wall, works donated by a Navajo painter during more peaceful times. For twelve days and nights, the artists worked to record the dying union's life. Rodriguez and other union members and residents had roamed in and out of the hall, watching the mural take shape and suggesting ideas.

Now, Rodriguez again stepped into the hall, the site of so many lively meetings and speeches since the first days of the union in 1942. He flipped on the light and stood before the forty-by-ten-foot explosion of color, history, and—at least Rodriguez still believed—hope.

The mural's narrative began at the entrance of the hall with a trio of young, multiethnic union members signifying solidarity. Arms out front like superheroes, they flew out of a corner of the past filled with steam trains and old cars over the hills of Morenci. Ahead, the smelter steamed and snarled, part furnace, part dragon, as a line of scabs with "on" switches embedded in their backs was conveyed inexorably toward the fires. Beyond the smelter, an unattached arm—perhaps the amputated arm of one of the mine's accident victims—seemed to grow from the ground near a crucible that spilled molten copper, forging the United Steelworkers insignia. Further on, a team of muscle-bound workers pulled a gear that shattered the copper collar, symbol of mining company power over workers. In all, from left to right, the mural recorded a journey from harsh past, to hopeful future, to dismal end. The most vivid testaments to union glory were undermined by images of defeat: a National Guard helicopter circling in the sky, state troopers igniting tear gas canisters,

union members on the highway sinking and disappearing into the
smoke. The sequence ended with the image of a grieving angel
hovering over everything, head buried in her hands.

With those last scenes—the National Guard, the smoke, and the
tearful angel over Route 666—the muralists suggest an apocalypse, a
cataclysmic end to union history. But Rodriguez had convinced
himself that, if the angel signaled the end, then surely the angel's
tears would be followed by some sort of judgment day against the
company, a chance for justice and resurrection.

He signed the last letter to unionists on March 15, 1986:

> *Dear Brothers and Sisters:*
> *The Unions that represented workers at Phelps Dodge's Arizona properties are
> now decertified. Over forty years of union representation is over. It is not a defeat
> of the Unions, but it surely is a defeat for the scabs who crossed our picket lines.
> [Decertification] has made it possible for Phelps Dodge to deal with them as it sees
> fit. They have no right of representation and no voice in how they are treated or
> what their working conditions, wage or benefits will be. They have little to
> rejoice for.*
> *We have witnessed the politicization of the National Labor Relations Board to
> the point now that a just labor law as it was intended has fallen by the wayside.
> The Reagan administration can be held directly responsible for the union-busting
> rage going on throughout this nation. . . .*
> *What about Phelps Dodge? Will it be content with decertifying the Unions? I
> think not. The "Copper Collar" will tighten on those scabs and elected public
> officials who will remember, perhaps too late, that they were the beneficiaries, either
> direct or indirect, of a strong union influence.*
> *Our members have nothing to be ashamed of. Yes, there may be memories that
> hurt, but they have had a learning experience that has made them stronger and
> proud that they kept their character and dignity. They won't have the betrayal of
> their fellow workers on their conscience like the scabs who crossed our picket lines.*
> *Our families are better for the experience. Our children know what it means to
> stand up for your beliefs. . . .*
> *Our struggle must always be remembered as a courageous struggle by people
> who believed in their right to a better life for themselves and their families and
> [were willing to] sacrifice for that right.*
> *We thank you from the bottom of our hearts. . . .*
>
>   *Sincerely and Fraternally,*
>   *Angel Rodriguez, President*

With the letter, Rodriguez included instructions to union members
on how they could get back on the company's hiring lists should they
want to return to work at Phelps Dodge. (Only if a replacement
worker quit and the ex-striker's job still existed would the company

have a legal obligation to contact the striker.) He swore to himself that he never would go back. Rodriguez prepared the letters for mailing and then got to work on his next task: tuning the car for a move to Phoenix. He would try to catch on with another union.

Rodriguez's words acknowledged the end of forty years of union history, but the strike continued to have its own life in the towns, in the minds of the participants, and in the federal courts. Calling the strike a "courageous struggle" didn't answer the remaining questions—it only raised more. No single account could really explain what had happened to the union. Clifton residents talked about the struggle over at the flower shop along Route 666. Replaced and retired union members gathered at the home of *el papa de todos*, David Velasquez, in Tucson, to curse the company bosses and sometimes, too, the international union leaders. Lawyers argued out conspiracy charges against the company (for the Ajo arrests) and civil rights charges against the state police (for the attack on union strikers in Clifton at the one-year anniversary).

For years after that first midnight gathering at the gate, for years after Angel Rodriguez's last letter, the questions persisted. What had killed the unions? The possible answers wound around the towns and the dead union halls like the labyrinthine turns of a murder mystery. Understanding this strike took something more than praising solidarity and cursing Phelps Dodge. It took an inquest. Jessie and Fillmore Tellez invited friends over to their Chase Creek home, where they took out the newspapers, reviewed the court papers, and wondered how it could have happened to them. Engineer Ray Isner and Rodriguez kept up the conversation as they took on jobs with the American Federation of State, County and Municipal Employees (Isner usually took up the conspiracy angle and Rodriguez pieced together the negotiations account). After Pete Castañeda was permanently replaced, he carried the questions in him like burning cinders as he journeyed from shipyards to auto test tracks to boiler rooms looking for a job. He asked how a country that claimed to lead the world against repression could permit this peculiar form of exile.

To the participants, then, the strike could be all these things at once: it was a trap by the forces of corporate greed to destroy the forces of union good; it was two giant institutions (a multinational company and an international union) battling each other for position, victimizing local residents. The strike was police power and capital conspiring to beat down the workers. The strike was a mistake. The strike was an act of bold martyrdom that may someday save the labor movement. To each character, a scenario; for each scenario, a set of causes. But it all began at the gate. And it all led to two indisputable ends: Phelps Dodge survived to become one of the most profitable mining companies in the world ("an emerging superstar," in the words of the business press) and the union locals were dead.

Industry Spikes and Streaks

With these continuing conversations, the former Phelps Dodge miners watched closely the fate of the industry and the trends in negotiated contracts. They did this by habit, but they felt they might also find some further clue or perhaps the moral of the story they had lived. Indeed, their struggle had carried them almost into another triannual round of negotiations. But there were no Arizona negotiations at Phelps Dodge—collective bargaining occurs only at companies that still have unions. They watched the previous negotiations' pattern-setters, Kennecott, ASARCO, Inspiration, and Magma. What bargaining they saw looked more like collective retreat.

For the first time since 1967, one company, Phelps Dodge, now had a clear competitive advantage on labor costs. Even though the unions no longer had anything to do with the lower wage at Phelps Dodge, the other companies continued to count on the union coalition for providing an equivalent savings. The unions had always promised that no major copper producer would be undercut by a cheaper union contract elsewhere in the industry—they called it the "most-favored nation clause" of the pattern contract. When Phelps Dodge broke free of the pattern by eliminating cost-of-living adjustments and instituting a dual wage, this industry wage discipline was thrown into chaos.

What's more, the price of copper still had not risen to expected levels, adding urgency to the companies' demands. The unions had earlier offered across-the-board cuts of as much as $2.50 per hour to match or even drop below wages at Phelps Dodge, but Kennecott, the former pattern setter, had recognized that it was now a new world in copper. Kennecott capitalized on the unions' weaknesses and refused any modified "pattern" of reductions. The company preferred to wait for the 1986 round of bargaining when it, too, might break from the pattern altogether. Industry experts George Hildebrand and Garth Mangum write, "No longer could the pattern-following technique be relied on to 'keep wages out of competition' because one of the largest employers was now immune to the pressure. The approach had to be company by company, and it would be crippled from the start by the competitive power of the big nonunion producer [Phelps Dodge]."

An important change in Steelworkers' contract approval procedures also hastened the demise of the pattern contract. In the Phelps Dodge strike, no separate vote had been taken on whether to consider the company's final offer. That prerogative lay with the representatives of the copper conference. Even those conference votes came to be seen more as a show of unity than considered judgment—one blunt union leader called the conference action "pissing in a blue serge suit. It feels good but it doesn't mean anything." In other words, the power resided elsewhere—with the conference chairman and the top international representatives of the other unions. At the request of various locals at the Steelworkers International 1984 convention, the first under President Lynn Williams, the international had voted to end total coalition control over contracts. Now, although a coalition still established bargaining goals and certified the pattern contract, the unions directly affected were offered the option of going their own way. In the name of local union democracy, the coalition was breaking down.

In the 1986 copper bargaining, the tremors from Phelps Dodge's victory created a series of visible stress fractures. Each company had a list of specific demands—and a determination to stop at nothing to win them. Kennecott, which was being spun off from its oil company owner, SOHIO, wanted a promise from the unions of a four-year contract with major wage concessions. (Because the coalition depended on common contract expiration dates, the expiration date change alone had the potential to destroy the pattern.) Magma wanted a complete rewriting of job definitions and substantial wage cuts, asserting that its underground operations deserved different treatment from other companies' open pit mines. The Steelworkers had hoped that the corporate campaign against Phelps Dodge would limit the temptation of the other companies to use permanent replacements. Instead, all the companies threatened to follow Phelps Dodge's example. Facing the threat of another copper war—one that would be impossible to fight on so many fronts—new union coalition chief Edgar Ball asked Governor Babbitt to help mediate. If the governor could not get a settlement despite the union's cooperation,

Ball wagered, he might be less willing to call in the National Guard to protect the company gates.

Babbitt attended much of the May–June 1986 Magma negotiations, often until the early hours of the morning. When a settlement was reached five days before the contract expiration date of June 30, the unions had agreed to a 20 percent cut in wages and the end of cost-of-living adjustments. The cuts would be compensated by bonuses if the price of copper rose well over the profit margin. Similar cuts were negotiated at ASARCO. But now Kennecott, the one-time pattern setter, was determined to go its own way. The company wanted to slash production costs at its Bingham Canyon, Utah, mine (which produced a higher grade ore and was even bigger than Phelps Dodge's Morenci open pit) and insisted on wage cuts and a four-year contract in exchange for new investments. Reticent union leaders declined to issue recommendations on these contract proposals—no one wanted to sign the death warrant of pattern bargaining—but, applying the new union procedures of an independent vote, the union locals ratified the four-year contract.

Ironically, with these concessions and the abandonment of pattern bargaining, the world price of copper started its upward march. Recovery had come later than expected (and losses at all the companies had been significant), but the magnitude of recovery easily made up for the lean years. In 1987, prices rose to an average of $.83 a pound. In 1988, prices jumped to $1.18 and in 1989, to $1.29. During these same years, mining productivity took another leap forward, primarily as a result of new technology. Companies brought on-line a chemical copper reduction process called "electrowinning" that dropped costs for producing each pound of copper by more than 50 percent. Electrowinning had been available since the 1960s but, perhaps a sign of just how sanguine the companies had been about their financial health, no company had used it extensively. Between 1984 and 1986, Phelps Dodge built electrowinning plants (called "SX-EW" for "solvent extraction-electrowinning"), at its Tyrone, New Mexico, and Morenci properties and by the late 1980s, Phelps Dodge was producing 30 percent of its copper with the electrowinning process.

Because electrowinning percolates acid through waste rock that has already been mined, most of the labor cost for this processing had been covered years earlier—with the work of union miners. The miners could not have known just how large a windfall this "waste" would one day bring for Phelps Dodge. As the price of copper rose to nearly $1.20 in 1988, Phelps Dodge was producing electrowon copper at $.30 a pound—an unheard-of $.90–margin of profit on every pound of copper. In 1988, the company paid out bonuses of about $8,000 per worker with these profits—much of this to the nonunion miners at Morenci. Phelps Dodge's annual profits were $29.5 million in 1985, $61.4 million in 1986, $205.7 million in 1987, $420 million in 1988, $504 million in 1989 (which was reduced by a one-time write-down to $267 million), and $455 million in 1990.

As former union members watched the upswing of the industry and, in particular, Phelps Dodge, it became even more difficult to understand what had happened back in 1983. The inquest continued. Could a company that earned a $100 million-plus profit in one quarter, much of it dependent on union-mined rock, be justified in permanently replacing the unions as a result of one year's $74 million loss?

The Industry View

With the passage of time, Phelps Dodge officials and industry analysts have developed their own own narrative of what the company did, and why, in 1983. Essentially, the account reduces to this: Phelps Dodge was facing bankruptcy in 1983, which justified big cuts in labor costs. The United Steelworkers, meanwhile, were facing an international election that stifled any realistic attention to the company's demands. Drastic cost reductions and the use of permanent replacements were justified by the dangers of bankruptcy at home and gridlock in the union. If the unions were dead, it was because Phelps Dodge had acted in self-defense.

A review of the record, however, reveals the inaccuracies of this narrative. Press criticism (such as in *Business Week* in 1982) and market uncertainty, rather than bank threats, had nettled company officers and led to published rebuttals. As the 1983 negotiations approached, the company chiefly showed concern about restructuring its unprofitable investments and labor cost reductions. Public statements about the company's future in copper tended to be upbeat. Munroe himself told the business press less than two months before the negotiations that he thought conditions would soon improve. The company reported a profit for its second quarter of 1983. No one at Phelps Dodge sounded a bankruptcy alarm at that time.

Then, in 1987, well after the unions had been replaced, Phelps Dodge drew reporters to the dramatic story of how a company management team had devised a way to make a profit even during cyclical drops in the market. In 1989, that post-strike story had grown into a kind of American corporate parable about how to restructure and avoid bankruptcy, as the *Wall Street Journal* published a page-one article whose headline declared, "How Phelps Dodge Struggled to Survive and Prospered Again." In this retelling of the 1980s, the company executives represent the risks of failure as bankruptcy; the demands for concessions in 1983 are cast as an element of the survival strategy. But only in hindsight—and by juggling the order of events—can the company argue that replacing union members was a necessary element of that survival.

As for the company's account of union electoral politics as a cause of gridlock, Phelps Dodge again distorts events in order to construct its story. Company officials have asserted in interviews that Frank McKee's run for the Steelworkers presidency caused him to take the position he did against Phelps Dodge. Such an argument offers cover for any company policy that might have led to the unions' demise—the unions' own presidential politics did them in. This revisionism ignores the fact that union politics on the national level did not directly affect the strike until the death of Steelworkers president Lloyd McBride—two months after Phelps Dodge had already replaced its union work force. McBride's death and the subsequent election fight between Frank McKee and Lynn Williams may have sharpened the issues and prolonged the strike, but these events cannot account for the positions taken.

PD: The Strike as Sport

More revealing than Phelps Dodge's public rationalizations about the strike are its private discussions and "cinematic productions." I was invited by retired vice president Arthur Kinneberg to view one of these productions at his home in North Phoenix. A large Hungarian pointer greeted me first at the door followed by Kinneberg, his wife, and daughter. "You wanted to see some videos on the strike?" asked the tall, heavy set former Navy officer. "The guys made this for me on my retirement." Everyone sat down to watch.

The video began with the pirated graphics and theme song from a cable sports network. Playing the role of "sports" announcer was a

Clifton school teacher and old friend of Kinneberg. The announcer was drinking Budweisers and acting drunk, declaring that "Coach" Kinneberg and the "Union '83–ers" were "in great shape and ready to play. Here's the pitching staff" (cut to video clip of strikers throwing rocks). "They're loose and ready to smoke 'em" (cut to video clip of state troopers with tear gas).

The video went on for more than ten minutes, identifying union spokesman Cass Alvin as a "professional scout," strikers as "players," and strikebreakers as the "visiting team." Fired company doctor Jorge O'Leary appeared on the screen, and the narrator made a slur against O'Leary's Mexican heritage and accent by pronouncing his name "Hor-hey Ho H-Leary." A dubbed voice came on and declared "Beesboll been very, very good to poor workers. Must horganize." Governor Babbitt appeared on the screen with a dubbed voice saying, "My team is really fired up," followed by an unaltered clip of Kinneberg saying, "We have to improve the efficiencies of the operation" and "We're going to win."

Finally, the "game" moved into the main event, with the video showing state troopers firing wooden bullets and tear gas at the strikers. A close-up showed a trooper with his nightstick at the throat of a striker, and the narrator declared, "You'll go far with the team that wears the star."

The video concluded with a flourish. The state troopers headed toward their fateful clash with the residents and strikers in Clifton on the one-year anniversary on June 30, 1984. When the naked man marched into the picture, waving his arms at the troopers, the narrator's voice returned: the strike was almost over, he declared, and it came to "a very bitter end." The camera panned down to Bobby Andazola's naked behind: "The End."

This was retirement party material, of course, a satire. Nonetheless, it was produced by Kinneberg's colleagues and friends—people who knew that away from cameras and away from NLRB investigators, rather different topics were discussed than Phelps Dodge's survival.

⚜

Not long after undertaking the research for this book, I asked two Phelps Dodge officials, then vice president Steven Whisler and employee relations director Stuart Marcus, to allow me to see company video productions from the strike. Retired officers had indicated that they had seen such videos, although Marcus responded that Phelps Dodge had only news footage and surveillance films. I was welcome to watch the news footage. Perhaps they didn't consider the Kinneberg video a serious record of the strike. But they withheld another video that could not have been considered trivial—I located a copy only years later on the shelves of the Wharton School library. It was a forty-five-minute company-produced documentary about how Phelps Dodge decertified the union, including voice-overs with chants of "Union! Union! Union!" during scenes of violence. What was presented as a joke at Kinneberg's home appeared in dead serious form here. The film was part of a series that Professor Herbert Northrup had called "the Phelps Dodge case study."

The Leaders, the Critics, and the Fates

Phelps Dodge's Kinneberg wasn't the only executive to retire from the company or the union before the strike was formally over—but his may have been one of the few retirement parties. At the time of the strike, Frank McKee and company president Richard Moolick occupied the top decision-making positions for the Steelworkers copper coalition and Phelps Dodge—only to be pushed out their respective doors. Why? The answer to that question provides one key to understanding what killed Morenci Miners Local 616 and the other unions.

Frank McKee

Not long after losing the March 1984 international presidential election to Lynn Williams, Frank McKee retreated to his summer home in Ontario, California. The battle with Williams had been a bitter one, and nobody overlooked the fact that McKee skipped a series of post-election meetings with Williams. Steelworkers tradition demanded McKee's presence, and his absence was understood by other unionists as a measure of the lingering discord between McKee and Williams over both personality and program. Technically, McKee was still the International Steelworkers treasurer and head of the copper conference, but he carried out his duties from an increasingly long distance. Williams eventually turned the job of copper conference chairman over to someone more in his own likeness—Edgar Ball, a Texas district director who had earned a reputation as a skilled negotiator while working for the Texas and Arkansas operations.

But McKee couldn't step entirely out of the history that he had helped make.

Shortly after McKee's retirement, the first historical analyses about what had happened to the unions were published. These first evaluations seared like a wave of heat from a Pittsburgh blast furnace. In a book about the decline of the United Steelworkers, former *Business Week* reporter John Hoerr assessed McKee's no-concessions view of bargaining:

> [McKee's] personal opposition to wage cuts . . . led to a spectacular defeat for the union in the copper industry. . . . As the strike wore into the fall months, even McKee's friends at USW headquarters in Pittsburgh believed that he had made "a big mistake." . . .
>
> The unions' intransigence brought about their own downfall. Pro-strike sympathizers deplored tactics employed by the company, such as evicting strikers from company housing, and the sometimes violent methods of the state troopers. But deploring could not alter either the economic circumstances that forced the company to take its tough stand or the labor laws that enabled it to hire permanent replacements for the strikers. . . . Finally, in 1985, some directors openly attacked McKee for his administration of the strike. Williams, then president, removed McKee as chief copper negotiator. . . .

Hoerr's account demonstrates how the Phelps Dodge strike discredited McKee among some of his peers, but the critics may have made a bit much of McKee's "personal" view against wage cuts. McKee clearly thought he was giving voice to something deeply embedded in Steelworkers history and membership. McKee was the kind of union traditionalist who derided number crunchers and lawyers, and who relied instead on an almost mystical belief in the powers of instinct. He had lived through the ups and downs of labor, from the early corporate abuses of workers, to the depression, to the first comprehensive U.S. labor laws, to the heyday of union power embodied in the Steelworkers giant headquarters in Pittsburgh. McKee believed that this experience had endowed him with all the essential tools for leading the Steelworkers into the future.

In many ways, his record backed him up. No one had more experience in copper than McKee, and no one had as many marks in the "win" column. His experience told him that Phelps Dodge was not endangered by the crisis in copper and that, if the other companies could agree to a deal, so could Phelps Dodge. His instinct told him that the company was out to break everything that tens of thousands of union members had won in the 1960s and 1970s, and McKee's instinct about Phelps Dodge was in many ways dead accurate.

But institutions need a way to discern when a leader's commitment to unbending principles produces unwilling or unknowing martyrs. McKee saw himself as a protector, even a savior, of a no-concessions wing of labor. In this role, however, he was willing to sacrifice democratic decision-making at an altar of institutional authority. If he had earned his authority, he had also assumed a trust. On the summer day in 1983 when he silenced the union representatives at a solemn executive meeting in Phoenix, he violated that trust. By McKee's refusal to entertain debate, the rank and file in Clifton, Morenci, Ajo, Douglas, and Bisbee, Arizona, as well as in El Paso, Texas, were never fully consulted about what the McKee stand might entail. The alternative at the time of the Phoenix meeting was to honor grassroots union democracy and allow the resisters to be heard. A number of different proposals might have been added to the union debate, including a reconfigured pattern bargain for the first time in fifteen years; rather than destroying the unions' pattern program, the move might have saved the structure of bargaining. If the Steelworkers could rely on a resurgent industry (as they had argued to the companies), then any concessions could have been returned another day, if necessary, with a unified front against the companies. Certainly the unions at Phelps Dodge would have been preserved for the next fight.

In declaring that the strike must go on, McKee needed to show that a full-fledged assault was worthwhile and winnable. (In the 1950s "Salt of the Earth" strike in New Mexico, to which local Phelps Dodge strikers sometimes compared themselves, an often-quoted line from a striker's wife was, "I don't want to go down fighting. I want to win.") Absent a commitment to an immediate corporate campaign and a national appeal to organized labor, the unions were vastly outgunned. McKee relied on his reputation and instinct, but what he needed to apply was a combination of innovation and guile. Phelps Dodge would be his first major defeat, and also his last. Frank McKee's imposed retirement represented more than a dispute over new directions by the Pittsburgh Steelworkers leadership—it was also the local voice of disapproval finally coming through.

Richard Moolick

In a visit to Richard Moolick's retirement house near Aspen, Colorado, I learned that he and McKee were shown the door at almost the same time. Copper was Moolick's religion, and he had won a holy war against labor. Moolick once thought, "You know, I'm going to be a hero, because what I did for this company is unbelievable." But for the company, as for the unions, these were new times. No one else could have held the company's line on the strike—probably not even George Munroe. And yet standing firm was also part of Moolick's undoing at Phelps Dodge. Other executives felt that Moolick became obsessed about labor issues and the core copper operations to the exclusion of the company's diversification needs.

Moolick may also have underestimated the public relations and other costs of the Phelps Dodge stand. Some current and retired executives acknowledge that there was this effect—they even bristle at a generally favorable 1989 *Wall Street Journal* article that noted the company's "sheer ruthlessness" during the strike. Before the strike was over, Phelps Dodge decided to hire one of New York's top public relations firms, Ruder and Finn, to help retrieve the company reputation. On a more conventional level, the company reported a loss of $100 million in its copper operations and an anomaly of another $100 million write-off in 1984, the year of the union corporate campaign, making the hourly wage reductions a relatively minor savings for the company. Moolick also had to bear the union corporate campaign tactics, which proved a thorn in Phelps Dodge's side—at least in terms of public protests and the frequent environmental pressure leveled at the company. The union also exerted a negative influence over new Phelps Dodge mine acquisitions. (New Phelps Dodge president Robert "Bull" Durham eventually arranged a meeting with Steelworkers president Williams at which an agreement was reached to call off the union corporate campaign in exchange for union certification at a new mine in New Mexico.)

Finally, an analysis by researchers at the City University of New York asserted that Phelps Dodge stockholders had lost $220 million in share value during the strike, or $92,000 per striker. None of the comments of company officials suggests that Phelps Dodge regretted replacing the unions. But in October, 1984, George Munroe informed Moolick that the board wanted him to step down in favor of a younger leader. Moolick's sudden retirement even before the strike had ended gave the appearance that, far from being appreciated as a savior, he was yet another liability.

Earlier, during the execution of the company strike plan, Moolick had wanted to be invisible. His preference, he said, was not to be recognized as "*the guy* [leading the company strike response]. . . . There's a lot of advantage to not being recognized. Don't ever let anybody know that you have the hand on the trigger."

Yet, Richard Moolick fell precisely because of his single-minded quest. Phelps Dodge knew that Moolick was not leading the way into a new economic era for Phelps Dodge. If Moolick had succeeded in his strike role of the radical Rasputin to a conservative Munroe, Moolick's mysticism had finally run its course.

Phelps Dodge might now ignore Richard Moolick, but labor historians should not. He was, for the 1980s, the corporate counterpart to Ronald Reagan. President Reagan demonstrated to the American public that skilled public service workers could be replaced and airplanes would still fly. Richard Moolick achieved the same role in private industry, demonstrating that industrial workers belonging to the country's strongest unions could be replaced—even in a legal strike—and furnaces would still roar. But there was more. Moolick's Arizona crusade assembled corporate power with rare efficiency: academic intelligence, police power, and administrative authority all operated at optimal capacity in the Phelps Dodge strike. With such an arsenal field-tested at Phelps Dodge, antiunion campaigns would be stepped up throughout this country. Although he was gone, Richard Moolick had shown the way.

Sam Franklin

In addition to McKee and Moolick, one other figure who failed to survive the strike deserves mention. It was federal mediator Sam Franklin, the man who told friends, family, and colleagues that the differences in the Phelps Dodge strike could be resolved. In the most difficult moments of the Phelps Dodge negotiations, Franklin had said that there was no strike short of the flight of the Israelites from Egypt that couldn't be settled. But Sam Franklin couldn't settle the Phelps Dodge strike, and on February 24, 1985, one month after the union decertification vote was counted, he died of a massive heart attack. Franklin's colleague at the Phoenix office of the Federal Mediation and Conciliation Service, Ron Collotta explained, "Sam was concerned that after Phelps Dodge . . . the whole industry might go on strike [in 1986]. There would be a lot of victims." Collotta concluded, "The stress and pressure of the copper industry killed my partner."

Bruce Babbitt

The strike also put one would-be peacemaker's career in extreme danger—that of Arizona Governor Babbitt. The *New Times*, an iconoclastic but usually liberal Phoenix weekly, declared Babbitt's future political hopes "mortally wounded" in an article early in the strike headlined, "Has the Copper Strike Ruined Bruce Babbitt?" Union spokesman Cass Alvin told the paper that "The best thing [Babbitt] can do is join the Republican Party. He'd have to live a thousand years to overcome this in the eyes of organized labor." Frank McKee had declared himself Babbitt's most fervent enemy, insisting that any national Democratic leader who supported Babbitt would earn labor's wrath. As Babbitt moved from running Arizona to running for president in the 1988 Democratic primaries, the controversy followed him. In several states, such as Oregon and Wyoming, Babbitt received invitations to speak, only to be disinvited or boycotted when labor leaders protested to local Democratic Party officials. At other speaking engagements, labor sometimes trailed Babbitt to question him on the Phelps Dodge dispute so that his actions in Morenci would not be forgotten.

When AFL-CIO president Lane Kirkland invited presidential candidates to make a pitch for labor's support in the spring of 1987, Babbitt confronted the issue head-on: "Let me be blunt," he began his video presentation. "For some of you, the only thing you know about a guy named Babbitt is that he called out the National Guard during a copper strike in 1983." Babbitt presented the Chandra Tallant shooting in Ajo as the primary reason for calling in troops—he couldn't allow a repeat of such an incident—and he cited his efforts as copper industry mediator in 1986, as well as vetoes of anti-union legislation, as proof of his good faith with labor. Perhaps the most important turn of events for Babbitt was the union criticism of Babbitt's own worst critic, Frank McKee. When McKee's stock dropped, Babbitt's seemed to rebound. New Steelworkers leaders like Edgar Ball even spoke favorably of Babbitt's assistance to the unions during later negotiations. Babbitt had a brief run of popularity as a dark horse candidate, but he failed to place in the top three in the 1988 Iowa or New Hampshire primaries and he dropped out. Still, Babbitt's relations with the leadership of organized labor underwent a minor catharsis during the primaries. By 1993, when President Bill Clinton chose Babbitt as U.S. Secretary of the Interior, and later held him up as a finalist for a U.S. Supreme Court seat, the Phelps Dodge debacle was never raised as a disqualifying factor.

How should Babbitt's role in the strike be judged? Neither with the plaudits that Babbitt has earned on other issues that required careful negotiations (such as state water rights reform while he was governor or federal range and mining land reforms after he became interior secretary) nor with the animus that labor attached to his name early in the strike. Babbitt was a reactant rather than an innovator in the strike. He made the same miscalculation that so many others made of Phelps Dodge, as he acknowledged early on: "I had thought we were beyond the days of these troubles in Arizona. I thought all that was in the history books," he told *New Times* in 1983.

Babbitt's early warning system failed him in the Phelps Dodge strike. He had employed a labor relations adviser from 1978 until 1981—the state AFL-CIO had insisted on it when an official with strong ties to management was appointed to another political position. But there never seemed to be enough work for the labor aide and the position was eliminated. Whether that individual might have offered a helpful assessment will never be known. But clearly none of Babbitt's other staff members predicted the fury of the strike and those who later proposed solutions were largely pragmatists who knew little about the history of Arizona mining negotiations.

Once the negotiation openings had passed him by, Babbitt—and his reputation—depended largely on the role and rule of law enforcement. Here, Babbitt looked more like an old-fashioned law-and-order conservative than an innovator. Over the course of the strike, state police repeatedly sided with strikebreakers and the company, violating the strikers' civil rights in the process. In photographs, news clips, and congressional reports, the Arizona strike helped advance the 1980s image of state-sponsored suppression of labor; Babbitt could not avoid being associated with these images.

At times, looks may have been deceiving. For example, early in the strike, Babbitt allowed only a minimal law enforcement presence at the mine gate, giving strikers an opportunity to exert pressure in numbers. Some of the union minutes also show periodic off-the-record efforts by Babbitt to bring about a compromise on the contract dispute. But in the end, Babbitt's worst problem was that he had no alternatives in reserve. The entente fashioned years earlier between labor and management had collapsed, and neither he nor anyone else in government could offer a response.

A Place in Labor History

As time passed, the Phelps Dodge strike took on its own life as a symbol of defeat for American unions. Industrial relations studies, like the 1986 landmark work *The Transformation of American Industrial Relations*, as well as management school texts like *The Economics of Labor Markets*, singled out this strike as the beginning of overt company strikebreaking in the 1980s through the tactic of permanent replacement. Journalists referred to the copper miners' strike as a precedent for labor's failure in the 1980s. A Duke University professor even used a Barbara Kingsolver short story based on the strike in an ethics seminar at the Central Intelligence Agency—to instruct agents on how not to treat subjects.

From these accumulated post-strike accounts, it became evident that an era of American labor history ended in the 1980s along the desolate highway between Clifton and Morenci, Arizona.

Solidarity Lost

The Phelps Dodge strike is emblematic of the decline of two vital achievements of the American labor movement: solidarity and the right to strike.

Solidarity is the bedrock idea that workers should join together to fight exploitation by management. In its most basic form, solidarity means winning members and forming a union community. In the current industrial climate, solidarity has been defeated in part by companies well-armed with strategies to impede organization. (By 1993, union representation in private industry had plunged to 11 percent, one of the lowest recorded levels ever.) In addition, as the Phelps Dodge strike demonstrated, union leaders themselves sometimes failed to justify solidarity as the form of protection and community that workers need to flourish at the modern workplace.

In the traditional conception of solidarity, of which Clifton and Morenci were once prime examples, workers and their families educated each other about their rights and goals and supported each other as they provided labor to run the American industrial machine.

Solidarity meant putting the community above individual interests, although unions held out the hope that these interests would converge. Between 1967 and 1983, union solidarity in the copper towns had brought a string of wage and benefit victories, as well as a new sense of social dignity for many of the Phelps Dodge workers.

But over those years, solidarity also lost its innocence. The union "community" grew from locals fighting their battles in relative isolation to a sophisticated and complex bargaining network. The International Steelworkers and the local union members never fully communicated to each other about how union life was changing. If the union families of Clifton, Morenci, Ajo, and Douglas had transformed themselves from being economically undervalued, racially abused, and politically ignored, they had not fully taken notice of the costs of that transformation. Complex new social and economic arrangements—and even words—entered the union members' lives. The "new" solidarity meant taking action and holding together in groups much broader than the old local membership—and for reasons far more complicated than the traditional local reasons. The highest achievement of this institutional solidarity was pattern bargaining—bringing the local unions into one tent and constructing one leading industry contract. This structure had won the unions increases in wages and benefits averaging 14 percent annually since 1967. But when local solidarity and institutional solidarity (in the form of pattern bargaining) were challenged simultaneously—in the Phelps Dodge strike and in many strikes elsewhere throughout the decade—something fundamental to unionism failed. Getting at that failure of solidarity in the Phelps Dodge strike is essential to understanding the fall of American labor in the 1980s.

At least part of the failure was in union leaders believing too much of their own language. They believed in their copper conference mantras of COLA (cost-of-living adjustments) and pattern bargaining. But neither COLA nor pattern bargaining meant much to the wider public. Strike language became almost incomprehensible. Unions—and Frank McKee in particular—failed at one of their most basic tasks: educating the workers and the public about labor's needs. The union members understood the impact of pattern bargaining and they knew the importance of showing unity at the picket line at midnight. But they also thought that the rest of America would appreciate the connection between this strike and fundamental civil rights like basic health, dignity as a minority community, economic justice, political power in their communities. They were wrong.

The unions instead might have acknowledged both the power and pitfalls inherent in the new solidarity. Pattern bargaining was a kind of bargaining technology: it was modern, sometimes obtuse, and dangerous when used without precision. The international unions had at their disposal a growing labor relations literature describing the nature and risks of pattern bargaining in the new economic arrangements of the early 1980s. A *Harvard Business Review* article in March 1982 titled "Last Rites for Pattern Bargaining" had noted, "Signs are evident that the established wage model has begun to fall apart. Unresponsive patterning is beginning to fragment and the wage-setting environment managers and unions are going to face will be quite new." The article urged a greater sensitivity by unions to new, often difficult, conditions in their industries.

Frank McKee had been correct in asserting that the copper industry did not suffer from the same woes as steel and autos, which faced deep, structural crises of lower-priced imports, quality, and depleted consumer demand. But such assertions did not change the atmosphere of uncertainty in which Phelps Dodge and the unions operated. The unions failed to pay sufficient attention to how an entire range of pressures (from third world restructuring to the negative press on Phelps Dodge to the promotion of Richard Moolick) would influence the company's behavior in 1983, particularly its willingness to lash out. As one observer has suggested, with the onset of pattern bargaining and union coalitions, labor relations went from a game of checkers, with companies and unions periodically "jumping" each other, to a much more complicated and intriguing game of chess. Frank McKee rejected the chess game, as did other unionists during the 1980s (the 1985 strikes at the Minnesota-based meatpacker, Hormel, offer another example). Taking into account the new, more complex rules would have meant measuring realistically the likelihood of success given the position of the workers and the state of the law, and then factoring in the costs of defeat. It would have meant examining the ratio of supervisors to workers, the changes in skill levels needed to operate the mine, and the depth of membership support for a life struggle. Solidarity required strategy *and* community.

There is also a deeper and more intimate layer to this discussion of solidarity—the meaning of the Phelps Dodge strike in the context of hard rock mining history. The Steelworkers, although the central power of the union coalition, were not really its soul. At the time of the strike, only fifteen years had passed since the Steelworkers had absorbed forty thousand members of the International Union of Mine, Mill and Smelter Workers, a union linked in its development to the earliest organizers in the copper camps. A surprising irony operates here: Mine-Mill, whose leftist leaders had clearly favored a monolithic, institutional agenda for the unions, was forced by history to operate as a democratic, diverse institution that promoted the local priorities of its workers. This reality shaped the continuing identity of many union members at Clifton and Morenci, who, in the 1983 strike, reasserted their own terms of struggle when the central Steelworkers authority had failed them.

The Steelworkers, on the other hand, political liberals, created a top-down structure that ultimately stifled local, democratic representation. The voices of Clifton and Morenci were smothered by the combination of Steelworkers procedure and personality. That institutional authority sometimes bordered on arrogance. One Steelworkers official from outside Arizona commented on the strike by saying of the local leadership, "We made these damn guys. We turned them into heroes." This international leader might be surprised to hear the lament of many of the local union leaders who no longer feel welcome in their home counties as organizers for other unions because of their reputation as losers in 1983.

The role reversal between Mine-Mill and the Steelworkers illustrates a practical conundrum for labor in the revolutionary but anti-ideological 1990s: solidarity and union democracy, both bywords of American unionism, are increasingly in conflict with each other. Unions that insist on solidarity in the modern, "coalition" or "pattern" sense may sacrifice democratic process. Unions that insist on local democratic process may forfeit the dream of broader union unity.

To understand why a new focus on union solidarity is necessary today, a comparison might be instructive. A labor conflict at Hormel's Minnesota meatpacking plants in 1985, two years after the Phelps Dodge strike, presented another test of modern union solidarity. (The Hormel strike became familiar to many Americans as a result of the 1991 Academy Award-winning documentary *American Dream*.) At Hormel, as at Phelps Dodge, the conflict involved a large international union, a concessions trend in the industry, and a local union steeped in tradition. Local union leadership rose up with fierce independence, and the rank and file followed these leaders in rejecting the international union's recommendation for a "reasonable" pattern aimed at achieving common contracts throughout the industry. The union (known as "P–9") didn't want to see its wages sacrificed for the greater good of the international.

At Phelps Dodge, the local members' voices were muted, limiting democratic choice; at Hormel, local voices were amplified, limiting union unity. In both the Phelps Dodge and Hormel strikes, the ideal of solidarity failed because local members and international union authority could not establish a common ground. Some commentators have suggested that to find that common ground requires a departure from modern vertical union hierarchies and a return to general interest unions, like the 1930s Minnesota-based Independent Union of All Workers. But such backtracking ignores the genuine successes that sectoral unionism has achieved. Union structures evolved into their present institutional form because they could best restrict wage competition, industry-by-industry. Better wages were, and will always remain, a paramount concern of American workers. There is much to recommend in a broad, social issues emphasis of unions; but such a system offers limited economic power.

Instead, local and international unions need to reexamine their democratic structures, the ones that provide voice to the rank and file. In the Phelps Dodge strike, the International Steelworkers needed to have a better understanding of what its workers were ready to give up—and why. Frank McKee's insensitivity to dissent was only one part of the problem. The Steelworkers needed to take a page from Mine-Mill, the page that had emphasized local education and participation, even at the expense of some of the core strength of the leadership. (A step in this direction was the Steelworkers' move under Lynn Williams to restore procedures for local democratic decision-making on economic issues.) Some other form of unionism—call it "basic" unionism—would recognize the conflict between local and institutional unionism and attempt some kind of case-by-case correction. Such a correction is urgently needed. For with strikes like Phelps Dodge and Hormel, unionism in America has suffered historic losses that weaken future attempts at organizing.

In fact, after the Phelps Dodge loss, copper unions at other Arizona mining companies began decertifying themselves even without strikes. Former copper union members at Cyprus Minerals Company, for example, explained their decertification votes by asserting that company labor relations officials had become more responsive than the representative union leadership. More than ten years after the Phelps Dodge strike there is still no hint of resurgent unionism at Phelps Dodge's Arizona properties. Some part of this local resistance to unions stems from a corporate willingness in good times to buy off prospective union members with bonuses. Still, the extent to which loyalty has gone up for sale should, itself, be a message to labor.

Strikebreaking and Its Sponsors

Local and international unions, however, need not suffer the complete burden of failure. The death of solidarity was by no means simply a union affair—in fact, a substantial part of the unions' decline was made inevitable by U.S. industry's refinement of legal ways to fight off and even kill unions. Since the 1980s, companies have made permanent replacement workers into a lethal weapon of economic warfare. Leading up to the Phelps Dodge strike and in the years that followed, this old weapon was upgraded and modernized in ways that tilted the playing field in favor of management and brought back with a vengeance the "fungibility" (or replaceability) of labor. With recent studies about diminished blue-collar wages and with increasingly public fights between labor and management over issues ranging from permanent replacement to plant relocation to layoffs, the degraded relationship between U.S. labor and management has finally been brought into national focus. President Bill Clinton's blue ribbon Commission on the Future of Worker-Management Relations has taken on the task of exploring this relationship and offering recommendations for the 1990s and beyond. The commission would do well to consider the antagonisms at the root of the 1983-86 Phelps Dodge strike.

The Phelps Dodge strike represented a kind of harmonic convergence of conservative forces that massed their resources to fight unions. From the ivory tower, one of the Wharton School's senior scholars, Professor Herbert Northrup, picked up the copper industry's cause just after the first pattern bargain was struck in 1967. From that time on, his professional interests became increasingly tied to antiunion campaigns. Indeed, Northrup's Research Advisory Group (RAG) academic team at the Wharton School tailored its work to Phelps Dodge's and other companies' express requests. Northrup originated a study of how the unions' most powerful weapon—the strike—might work against the unions and then he spread the word: in the 1980s, far from pressuring a company to terms, a strike with replacements could ensure a company's victory.

Nor did Northrup stop there. With the participation and financial support of Phelps Dodge, the RAG devoted attention to investigating and providing consultant services on other antiunion fights. The legacy of the Phelps Dodge decade (described in greater detail in the footnotes) includes such Wharton-RAG efforts as:

- Surveillance of and resistance to the National Association of Working Women's "9 to 5" union, also known as District 925 of the Service Employees' International Union, led by Karen Nussbaum (now the AFL-CIO's chief advocate for working women).

- Letter-drafting for industry on promanagement appointments to the National Labor Relations Board.

- Providing information and speakers on antiunion campaigns in textiles, chemicals, and other industries.

As to Phelps Dodge, Northrup regularly devoted space to the strike in his RAG memoranda, bringing it up in four consecutive mailings between October 1983 and July 1984. In a December 13, 1983, memorandum, he referred to the Phelps Dodge strike as a "case study" and noted that company officials would be present at the next RAG meeting to give their report. Presenting his own view, Northrup consistently blamed the unions for the company's difficulties and on at least one occasion he misreported the company's financial status, writing to RAG members that Phelps Dodge had shut down for a year because of the depressed copper market. (The company actually closed its Morenci mine for five months). In another memorandum, Northrup offered Phelps Dodge and Steelworkers-produced videos on the strike for sale to RAG members. On the whole, the RAG memoranda suggest that Wharton researchers saw themselves as management's mercenaries in a battle against labor.

When asked about his role in the RAG and the resulting aggressiveness of some companies in fighting unions, Northrup told me: "I thought I would never live to see it. . . . I figured I was some kind of Cassandra. I'd get up in these meetings and say, "I don't understand this foolishness,' and they'd say 'you can't win a strike' and so forth.

I was surprised it did happen. And it was good for the country that it did happen."

About his role in advising companies, Northrup said that he stayed away from negotiations and didn't get involved in "the 'keep the union out' stuff." His memoranda, however, contradict this.

Wherever the new aggressiveness of companies came from, it is clear enough that the Phelps Dodge replacement action became a model elsewhere. Northrup said he got calls about it even from companies outside the Wharton group. Phelps Dodge officials, too, were asked to speak about their replacement of union strikers. The first attempt to replicate Phelps Dodge's success took place within a few months of the company's replacement program—right down the street from Phelps Dodge's Phoenix tower.

"Greyhound [in 1983] followed us and used our techniques," said Moolick. "But then they chickened out down the road and didn't protect the guys that came in. You've got to protect the people that fight for you." (In 1990, Greyhound again used permanent replacements—and didn't relent.)

An increasingly familiar litany of replacement actions followed after Phelps Dodge, just as union representation was plunging toward 10 percent of the private American work force: Greyhound (1983), Continental Airlines (1983), *Chicago Tribune* (1985), International Paper (1987), Eastern Airlines (1989), Greyhound again (1990), *New York Daily News* (1991), Holsum Bread (1991), and Caterpillar Tractor (1992). Moreover, companies gradually perfected a "no-tolerance" approach to strikes: where Phelps Dodge waited a month before hiring outside replacement workers, International Paper in 1987 waited only thirteen days and Greyhound, in its second effort in 1990, began replacing drivers the very first day.

In one of the few notable wins for labor during this period, miners at Pittston Coal fought off a permanent replacement action. (Federal mediators intervened after the company's action had been declared an unfair labor practice.) Even there, the stamp of the 1983 Arizona strike emerged: the president of Pittston, Paul Douglas, who pushed the permanent replacement tactic, had been a director of Phelps Dodge at the time of the Phelps Dodge strike.

By the mid-1980s, as high profile companies in more labor-friendly regions than Arizona were beginning to use the permanent replacement tactic, the U.S. Congress finally began to take notice—and action. In 1990, when International Paper replaced its work force less than two weeks into a strike, Congressman Joseph Brennan of Maine introduced a bill in the House of Representatives to limit the right to permanently replace strikers. Congressional hearings soon began to bring to light evidence of a sharp rise in strikebreaking by permanent replacements dating from the early 1980s (most of the evidence available was anecdotal because the U.S. Department of Labor inexplicably never kept statistics on the use of replacements). The influence of programs like the Wharton School's may be evident in the results of one study that pointed out that far more companies would consider using permanent replacements now than in previous years, and that two out of every three employers' representatives believe that permanent replacements were used more often or even "far more often" in the late 1980s than in the 1970s.

By 1992, the U.S. labor movement had made changing the laws allowing permanent replacements its number one legislative priority.

In a turnabout from the Reagan and Bush administrations, President Clinton expressed support for new laws on replacements, but the Congressional response has been mostly gridlock. In a March 1993 Senate hearing, U.S. Secretary of Labor Robert Reich testified in favor of the "Workplace Fairness Act" (House Bill 55 and Senate Bill 5): "Look at the Phelps Dodge strike in 1983. Look at a list of strikes, of work stoppages . . . [T]he most important point here is that you cannot have a partnership in which one partner is bullied and intimidated into relative quiescence. That's not what I would call a partnership."

Twice the U.S. House of Representatives has passed bills limiting or forbidding permanent replacements. Despite a Senate majority in favor of passing the "Workplace Fairness Act," opposition from conservative Democrats and threatened filibusters by Republicans have killed the bill both times, most recently in the summer of 1994. During debates on the Senate floor in July 1994, Senator Edward Kennedy referred to the Phelps Dodge strike as a low point in the poisoned labor relations atmosphere of the 1980s. Congress's inaction leaves American labor law in a shameful state. So-called permanent replacement "doctrine" began as dictum—a non-binding comment by the 1930s Supreme Court, suggesting that, in economic strikes, replaced workers have no right to get their jobs back when replacements are necessary to continue operations. Congress could have picked up the issue then and decided whether and when it was "necessary" during strikes to permanently replace workers. Instead,

Congress abdicated that task and allowed the law to be shaped by judges, case to case and decade to decade. The result has been heavy restrictions on unions during strikes and progressively greater freedom by companies to replace workers. So unions rarely strike anymore, except when they can get back in the door before they are replaced, as when American Airlines flight attendants launched a brief strike in late 1993, or when replacing workers becomes an overwhelmingly complicated task for managers, as when major-league baseball players, UPS employees, and auto workers struck later in the decade. For all intents and purposes, industrial peace has arrived in America, Phelps Dodge style.

Industrial Justice

Industrial peace should result from correcting—not emulating— the errors of the Phelps Dodge strike. In congressional testimony (and his books) Labor Secretary Reich has called for a labor-business "partnership." Former Labor Secretary John Dunlop has also encouraged such a partnership in his blue ribbon committee's review of U.S. labor relations. But a fair balance of power must be reached between labor and business before partnership can go forward. To redress the imbalance, unions, companies, and public decision makers all have a role to play.

The unions must continue their self-search on how to apply both bottom-up democracy and top-down authority to a complex new industrial and service industry landscape. A new commitment to democratic procedures is an important start—but only a start. To enter into cooperation or partnership with companies, unions must also decide how to approach the reconfigured workplace and world economy. For example, there is little chance of putting off wage competition with workers elsewhere on the globe who benefit from the vastly improved mobility of capital and technology. Unions must join the struggle for broader labor standards and forge a new solidarity with workers beyond their traditional constituency rather than reflexively opting for protectionism. A lesson in hindsight from the Phelps Dodge strike is the importance of original and flexible thinking for the enhancement of union membership and programs.

Companies, too, need to commit to a similar kind of soul-searching, particularly with respect to their duties to their workers and the general community. Phelps Dodge celebrated itself as an independent, lean company determined to make economic decisions without the interference of labor unions. Its decision-making mechanisms became so intensely responsive to new demands for performance that any hint of "values" other than on a return-on-equity basis became almost irrelevant. When Governor Babbitt appealed to the company to consider the public stake in the negotiations, the leadership responsible for the Arizona strike positions had already rejected such an approach. No action was required, however, by the board of directors, and shareholders had no say at all in such decisions.

In a publicly centered world, Phelps Dodge instead might have paused to examine its checkered history with Mexican-Americans; it might have seen that its own debt to the public interest (when the federal government helped build the Morenci mine and, later, regularly forgave delays in environmental improvements) recommended public considerations during the crisis of 1983; and it might have recognized that union workers had provided the muscle that would reap a tremendous windfall for the company through new technologies. Such a public outlook, in turn, might have backed the company away from permanently replacing the union members. Instead, Phelps Dodge seemed to interpret "public trust" as whatever trust it could win from public authority. Public institutions were harnessed in the name of the private: a university that benefits from public funds provided advice on how to fight unions; state undercover officers used techniques to gather information about the unions; the state police and National Guard provided protection at the company gate; the federal labor board bent over backwards to enhance the company's chances of victory. Such tactics, multiplied across industry, can offer little hope of future cooperation. Cooperation must include course corrections to management's labor relations policies, to union concepts of participation and planning, and to government's role in balancing the differences.

Route 666

Permanently replaced engineer Ray Isner and I were driving from Clifton to Tucson along Route 666 at dusk in 1990. The steering was loose on his Chevy camper, kicking the vehicle occasionally across the yellow lines. Ray's mood made the steering feel even looser, especially when he was talking about Phelps Dodge. "They were out to break our asses," Ray said, just as a rabbit darted across the road.

The camper shimmied between the two lanes of the highway, but, from the ensuing calm, it seemed that the creature had survived.

As Ray spoke of it, life for the strikers sometimes felt just as precarious: a road, a vehicle with unpredictable steering, solidarity wagered, solidarity lost. We had been to Clifton for a reunion of sorts. The time had come to dedicate the historical miners' mural. No ceremony had taken place earlier because no one wanted to dedicate a symbol of defeat. Now, in spring 1990, the miners were ready to look back, and the testimony in the suddenly-revived union hall rang with emotion. A salsa band, the same one that had played half way through the riot on the strike's one-year anniversary, performed in front of the mural and the American flag. One of the band members recalled that when the state troopers came into view, they had planned to play "La Cucaracha." Then the teargas began to fly. After the attack, they christened themselves "Teargas and the Wooden Bullets." From Fillmore Tellez on the saxophone to Mike Diaz on the bass, each performer was a replaced or retired union member.

Dozens of strike "survivors" slowly advanced past the mural, some stopping to sit and meditate. Francisco Andazola, who had retired during the strike, stopped by to view the mural. So did Frank Andazola, Jr., whose raised fist was one of the mural's central images. Bobby Andazola had a job tending bar at the Refrigerated Cave up the street, so he couldn't be there. (His one-man protest didn't make it onto the mural because "some families didn't think it would be appropriate," he said.) One by one, as if at a wake, the strikers memorialized the defeated unions and their struggle.

Said one, "All of a sudden, you're without a job, without a house, no education. So you go out to find a job, and you look at another mine but it's not hiring."

Said another, "We knew how to eat cactus if we had to. At least we weren't going to die from hunger."

And another, "They say that time heals all wounds. Well, I don't know. This strike was so vicious . . . "

Then mural painter David Tineo told the group, "This mural is done on a wall. But it's not to be contained as if it's in a museum. It's for public viewing . . . so those who weren't there can know what took place, so it won't be forgotten."

But at the end of the ceremonies, after the salsa music and the tamales and the speeches, the lock was clasped again on the door of

Morenci Miners Local 616. Except for retirement meetings, the lock hasn't come off since.

Postscript

Like the Arizona mining unions that grew up alongside it, the Arizona segment of U.S. 666 no longer exists. In 1992, citing continued community opposition to the numbering and a plan to extend a different marker from Canada, the state of Arizona quietly decommissioned Route 666. It was redesignated Route 191.

 *Epilogue*

Life after Death?

Epilogue to the Second Edition, 1998

> *If you have signed a Decertification Card, ask for it back. If you know
> someone who has [signed], explain to them what they are gambling with.
> Brothers and Sisters, now is the time: stand up and show your colors.
> Let's fight this together!*
>
> —United Steelworkers pamphlet during the 1996
> decertification fight at Phelps Dodge in Silver City, N.M.

> *We, the working people, are, after all is said and done, still the salt of the
> earth.*
>
> —Local 890 President Don Manning, before the life-or-death
> vote on the future of his union

I returned to the United Steelworkers of America subdistrict office in
Tucson for the first time in years just before Labor Day, 1997. Since
the end of the 1983 strike, Alex Lopez, the chief negotiator, had been
riding the Steelworkers' southwestern circuit—as staff representative in
Arizona and New Mexico, district director in Los Angeles, and, finally,
back to Tucson as special assistant on organizing and negotiating to
Steelworkers president George Becker. From Lopez, who has one of the
few uninterrupted institutional memories in southwestern copper, I
thought I might get an update on copper unionism and antiunionism
during the last punches of the twentieth-century time clock. Of course,
I also wanted Phelps Dodge's views. When I called company human
resources director and vice president Stuart Marcus for an interview, he
mistook me for a union activist also named Rosenblum. When I corrected him, he still protested. The company had not received fair coverage in the first edition of *Copper Crucible*, he said. Why should they
speak to me for a second edition? Then he said he would have to call
me back. A few days later, I received the following voice mail message
from Marcus: "We have thought about your request to meet with us
again . . . but having thought about it, we are not interested in engaging
in further discussions." So much for Phelps Dodge on the millennium.

I found Lopez, true to form, in the Tucson office under a poster
calling on the public to "Support the Copper Workers!" As we

greeted each other, I congratulated him for not abandoning the past, even if the 1983 strike contained bitter memories. He corrected me. The poster, in Spanish and English, wasn't from the 1983 strike or any other time in the past—it was to support a current fight. Lopez explained that more than three hundred union members in Silver City, New Mexico, workers at an old union mine with a newer antiunion owner, were at this very moment trying to rebuild solidarity from the ground up in order to win a contract. That "newer antiunion owner" was—guess who?—Phelps Dodge. Of course, Phelps Dodge had obliterated unions in Arizona in the early 1980s. But the Chino mine, an acquisition from Kennecott Corporation in 1986, was another story. Quite another story. If I wanted to see the future between unions and Phelps Dodge, Lopez said, then I had to go to Silver City.

As it turns out, Local 890 possesses a cachet unlike any union in the nation. It is the birthplace of *Salt of the Earth*. In preparation for the first edition of this book, I couldn't help but hear about the 1950s edition of Local 890—it had been an inspiration during the 1983 strike to the Morenci miners and the women's auxiliary. That local had been synonymous with the achievement of basic rights for Chicano workers, including the end of inferior "Mexican" pay scales and separate facilities, and the advent of greater mine safety. Local 890 also had been the site of an inspired women's auxiliary that took over the picket lines in a protracted 1950–1952 strike at Empire Zinc after the men were threatened with arrest. At nearly the same time as that strike, a group of blacklisted Academy Award–winning filmmakers were establishing an independent film company to produce social dramas based on real stories of struggle in American life. Producer Paul Jarrico heard about the strikers during a vacation visit to New Mexico and convinced the film team that the plight of the miners and families of Silver City, Bayard, and Hanover, New Mexico, should be their first subject. Although the U.S. House of Representatives' Committee on Un-American Activities labeled the resulting movie "subversive" and theater owners refused to show the film, *Salt of the Earth* would eventually be recognized as one of the great U.S. achievements in the genre of social realism—including a slot in the prestigious U.S. Library of Congress Registry of Films. Union leaders and other local residents were featured in several of the major roles. Screenwriter Michael Wilson, who had won his Oscar for *A Place in the Sun*, and would later (anonymously, due to the blacklist) co-author the films *Bridge on the River Kwai* and *Lawrence of Arabia*, spent weeks among the miners, eventually emerging with his script and the famous title, taken from the lines in Matthew 5:13, in which Jesus blesses "those who are persecuted for righteousness' sake. . . . You are the salt of the earth."

Midway through the movie, the miners, faced with an injunction against "union members," must choose between fighting defiantly on the line one last time (with arrest and the failure of the strike certain to follow) or conceding picket duty and jail cells to their wives, a choice they feared meant loss of their machismo. Esperanza Quintero, the movie's heroine, reverses a familiar adage in uttering one of the film's most famous lines: "I *don't* want to go down fighting," she says. "I want to win." By that, she meant that the struggle could only be won (and, in fact, was won) as a community effort, with the full participation of women. Some thirty years later, with the sale of the Chino mine to Phelps Dodge, one of the nation's most historic unions had ended up on a collision course with one of the nation's most historic union killers. Local 890's membership and supporters reencountered Esperanza Quintero's dilemma. They wanted to fight, but didn't want to go down fighting. They wanted to win. So I scribbled the directions and a few names from Alex Lopez and—instead of sitting down to update the previous chapters of this book—I found myself on the road again, to Silver City, to have a look at *Salt of the Earth*, the sequel.

A Reckoning

An air of ferment—well-worn floors, newly minted picket signs, the bustle of protest line leaders—permeated Juan Chacón Union Hall of Steelworkers Local 890. Local president Don Manning greeted me with a hard-squeezing union handshake and showed me around. The walls of the main hall were adorned with work and protest drawings from the past fifty years. Juan Chacón was an early Local 890 president and also earned fame as a lead actor in the movie. The present struggle resounded from the central bulletin board, where letters to the editor decried Phelps Dodge's decertification campaign and a handwritten sign played off the old nuclear attack test signals on the radio (which aired frequently in New Mexico) to criticize the company's recent position at contract negotiations: Phelps Dodge's position at the table, the sign said, must surely be a "test" and not a real contract negotiation. If this had been a real negotiation "you would have been granted a raise, benefits, and a sign of appreciation." Instead, Phelps Dodge appeared to treat the ongoing contract negotiations as yet another opportunity to kill a union—in this case, a very prized trophy.

Despite the midday bustle, I had arrived during a relative lull in the storm. It was the Friday before Labor Day, 1997, and the company had ceded the moment to workers. Union officers and rank-and-filers shared the latest lists of participants for the Friday afternoon "honk for a contract" rally at the company's administrative office, and they exchanged addresses for the weekend events. It was a time for the union to take account, and there was much to add up. In 1995 Phelps Dodge had earned the highest profits in its more than 150-year history—$747 million—and added a $462 million profit in 1996, despite a dip in copper prices. Such a profitable state of the company contrasted markedly with the status of the union contract, under which Phelps Dodge workers had become the lowest paid employees of any major copper producer. Hourly workers received about a 7 percent raise from 1993 to 1996, plus small bonuses tied to copper prices—in all, just enough to stay even with inflation. By 1997, union employees at Chino were making, on the average, $2 an hour less than their counterparts at the top four other copper producers (and even lower yet when lower pension ratios were figured in). Meanwhile, worker productivity had gone up about 14 percent during the three years— meaning that efficiency improvements alone had covered the cost of the wage increase and bonuses. As at the Morenci mine, that efficiency at Chino had come in part because the company· was reprocessing rock that had been mined by previous generations of union workers, running it through an inexpensive liquid extraction process. Union labor had created the boom. Yet, the company mostly treated the combination of high copper prices and productivity as a windfall, with neither current nor past wage earners getting their share.

So who received the profits? As might be expected, Phelps Dodge CEO Douglas C. Yearley and mining division president Steven Whisler, got theirs: stock options and other bonuses of more than $1.5 million and $760,000, respectively. Yearley's bonus more than doubled his salary. With the executives at Phelps Dodge, shareholders got their share: an investor who bought Phelps Dodge stock in 1993 and sold it in 1996 collected a 54 percent return on investment. At the 1996 contract expiration, Phelps Dodge stood as a prime example of the 1990s trend of undervalued hourly workers and overvalued executives and stock holdings. The growing gap between wage earners and their bosses did not escape the attention of some who followed the industry. The editor of the pro–copper industry publication, *Pay Dirt*, wrote in a 1995 column that "executive compensation borders on being obscene" and added that unionization in the long run was likely to rise because "most management is reluctant to . . . pay fair wages [and] treat employees fairly." But while *Pay Dirt*'s words addressed the industry as a whole, Phelps Dodge had always considered itself *sui generis*: the company, in fact, was counting on further reducing unionization.

As of the time of my arrival in Silver City, on August 29, 1997, the company had thrown three consecutive low blows at Steelworkers Local 890: (1) a mere three weeks after its all-time record profit report in early 1996, the company announced a decertification campaign to rid the company of the Steelworkers; (2) in its June 1996 contract negotiations, the company presented only cutbacks for its 1996 contract "offer" (union president Manning called it "an insult" rather than an offer); (3) in spring 1997, Phelps Dodge, with a number of nonunion workers, announced another decertification effort, despite the fact that employees voted in 1996 to keep the union. It wouldn't have taken a paranoid person to conclude that Phelps Dodge was out to get Local 890 president Don Manning and his union.

❧

To the Morenci-trained ear, the attacks on Local 890 still rumbled with aftershocks of the 1983 strike. In 1983, under company president Richard Moolick, Phelps Dodge abruptly rewrote its relationship with the Arizona copper communities. Three or more generations of families had fed the great mine machine—and bought their bread at Phelps Dodge Mercantile. In the Moolick view, something had gone terribly awry in that system—company reliance on local families had combined with unionization in such a way as to confuse loyalties: workers were forgetting to whom they really owed their progress. Moolick's strike leadership helped transform the company from a kind of feudal lord (tangling with union-inspired "serfs") to a sponsor of carefully controlled individual freedoms. One key prerequisite for the Moolick approach was that the company had to abandon any role as job-producer for local families. Such a community role might stoke unionism and undermine tighter management control over the workplace. This change of operations in the aftermath of the 1983 strike was bluntly expressed by a supervisor who told me it was time "to bring to an end all this grandfather to father to son stuff." When the company permanently replaced the Clifton and Morenci (and Ajo, Bisbee, and Douglas) strikers, it also permanently ended many of the family ties to the company (recall the Torrez family from chapter 5, with more than 150 years seniority at the company). In the early 1990s, company president Len Judd was still telling associates: "We just don't want to be big daddy anymore." The "new" Phelps Dodge would promote certain worker-oriented initiatives (such as establishing a workplace "teamwork" scheme and offering 401(k) benefits) in exchange for complete control over its management decisions and property.

The company's efforts at promoting individual rights, including a kind of nonunion "democracy," had mixed results. Benny Ybarra, a union member originally from a New Mexico mine, got an inside view of the revamped Phelps Dodge when he was assigned to Morenci after cutbacks at home. One day Ybarra received a notice from the company inviting him to vote at an upcoming referendum. The issue was whether to extend the regular work day to twelve-hour shifts. Although Phelps Dodge evidently wanted the new schedule, the company didn't want to upset the miners by implementing the schedule outright (this was the heyday of the "team management" concept) and certainly didn't want to kindle new interest in unions. So Phelps Dodge announced that if 80 percent of the workers at the mine's ore concentrator approved, then the company would implement twelve-hour shifts (only Phelps Dodge knows how the company decided on 80 percent, but Ybarra suspects the number came from a New York psychiatrist the company hired to enhance team morale). Only 67 percent of the workers approved the plan, so it failed. Soon thereafter, to Ybarra's surprise, he was called to vote again. Mine management announced that this time a 67 percent approval rate would be enough to change the shift schedule. Confounding the company further, only 58 percent supported the change at that vote. So a third vote was called—within about a month of the first vote. Phelps Dodge had apparently decided that the problem was not with the work schedule, but with the electorate. So, in the best tradition of the "vote until you get it right" brand of democracy, management added electricians and tailings dam workers to the concentrator workers' voting pool. This time, according to Ybarra, 69 percent of the workers approved, and the twelve-hour shifts were implemented. (But when the Steelworkers Local 890 bargaining committee, an elected body, rejected Phelps Dodge's contract offers in 1996 and 1997, Phelps Dodge management attacked the decision as unrepresentative. The workers didn't have a chance to vote, the company complained to the press.)

Ybarra, who now works at the Chino mine and is a member of Steelworkers Local 890, recalled another incident during his first days at Morenci that made very clear Phelps Dodge's restrictions on permissible forms of worker representation:

> [A foreman] got into my truck as I drove toward the conveyor, and he says to me, "Benny, you know we don't have any unions here in Morenci."
> I said, "Yessir."
> He says, "Benny, we don't want anybody to start any such thing as a union. Do you know where I'm coming from?"
> I said, "I don't know anybody here."
> So he says, "But when you do, Benny. . . . See, I know what kind of union man you are."
> I said, "I believe you."

❋

Until 1987, when Phelps Dodge bought the Chino mine, workers there had been untouched by the Phelps Dodge revolution. But the company soon put its stamp on the work force. Union officials began to notice a decline in Phelps Dodge's hiring of local high school graduates—the sons and grandsons of union members—and increases in the numbers of out-of-state license plates in the mine parking lot. More ominously, decertification campaigns began brewing against the half-dozen unions that represented some twelve hundred Chino employees. In a matter of a few years, workers represented by the Machinists, Boilermakers, and Pipefitters had decertified their unions. The company also extended to nonunion workers an unsubtle pay package that originated in its nonunion mines. Special bonuses called "union-free" appreciation payments were ostensibly based on good economic performance and were paid out to the several hundred employees in the mine divisions that had decertified their craft unions. By all appearances, Phelps Dodge had begun a kind of hostile takeover of the unions, rewarding some workers with bonuses and supporting union decertification votes.

Enter Steelworkers Local 890 president Don Manning. When he first sought (and won) the union presidency in 1994, Manning knew as well as anyone that novel strategies, crafted under crisis, had made Local 890 famous in the 1950s; he also knew that there hadn't been a union strategy written that assured victory against Phelps Dodge. Though he posed for all the essential photographs with *Salt of the Earth* heroes, Manning, a stocky, balding mechanic, was also intent on avoiding the nostalgia that he felt sometimes afflicted union thinking in Silver City. During my visit, Manning took me for a drive around the vast mine property in his Buick and reflected on the union's struggles—avoiding decertification, maintaining union morale, winning a contract. We headed south out of Hurley, where a silver smokestack still advertised the old mine owner, "Kennecott." For miles into the desert, the highway paralleled drifting slag heaps, mountains that had been pummeled and seared into a long, low effluent. With the precision of an environmental engineer, Manning described the diminished water tables, the blowing mine debris, and the company's efforts at avoiding responsibility for both. Manning arrived at the subject of the union's struggle at Phelps Dodge with the studied words of someone accustomed to working in tension with toxic elements (he had once been a uranium miner). "We've had to get smarter," he said. "When they use politics [to advance a claim], we use our own pressure. When they use claims about stockholder profits to insulate them from community obligations, we go to the stockholders and force them to take on the issue. We have to approach them from all sides—PR, government, stockholders."

Manning has also approached his own union with a new eye. When nonunion workers circulated decertification cards, Manning took it as a test of whether Local 890 was capable of adapting to new times. If a majority of workers voted to decertify the local, more than fifty years of union history would come to a crashing halt. "One of the things we learned was that . . . we were about to lose a generation of membership. Young kids didn't know a damn about what was going on. We were ending up with a 35- to 55-year-old union." The union was also suffering under a reputation as a union for "Mexicans," with few new Anglo workers signing on. Manning, whose family roots in New Mexico went back centuries (most of his ancestors came from Spain, though the "Manning" came from Ireland), insisted that the union reach out to all workers. The decertification campaign against the union offered a case study in Manning's "smarter" approach to unionism—and perhaps the toughest test of all. He would have to recapture the attention and imagination of workers and the public. And he would have to persuade them all that union membership in the coming millennium could be as good a guarantor of economic progress as it had been for earlier generations—and a better path than anything Phelps Dodge could offer.

David v. Goliath

Cecil Waldrip, a fifty-six-year-old truck driver and never a union member, initiated the first decertification effort in the summer of 1993. Waldrip employed a surprisingly sophisticated strategy, immediately raising union suspicions of company sponsorship. He arranged for fellow workers to submit their petitions to the National Labor Relations Board from separate sectors of the mine rather than from the entirety of workers represented by the Steelworkers (the customary route to a decertification vote). In that way, antiunion workers could seek to divide and conquer various shops at the mine rather than face the whole union. Because Waldrip's approach also created an immediate legal dispute, Phelps Dodge's attorneys were permitted to step in and lead the decertification litigation (a role that, inexplicably, the labor laws do not consider formal company "sponsorship" of decertification, which would be illegal). Thus, with relatively few signatures from petitioners, Phelps Dodge could announce its backing of decertification by sending in its attorneys. Predictably, the NLRB rejected the petitions, but Waldrip and Phelps Dodge had sent a message that decertification of the Steelworkers was a major company priority. I reached Waldrip in January 1998 and asked him about his communications with Phelps Dodge on the decertification issue. "The only thing I've ever done as far as the company is concerned," he said, "is ask their permission, or ask them if this is a problem with the company if I try for decertification. I always ask if it's something they're okay with." Phelps Dodge's response? "They said, 'Go ahead and try it.'" Waldrip added that Phelps Dodge indirectly may have helped decertification along because the company no longer hired as many local workers as Kennecott: "A lot of [the truck drivers] have worked at other jobs in other regions, and they have less of a connection with the union. In other years there was a higher local proportion." Thus, the concentration of outsiders willing to decertify the union was rising.

Under the labor laws, when his 1993 effort failed, Waldrip had to wait nearly three years, when the union contract was nearing expiration in 1996, before again soliciting decertification. Again, Waldrip's effort gained strength from an unusual corner. This time, he was joined by a smelter worker who had arrived at Chino just a few years earlier after having been a strikebreaker in Ajo, Arizona, during the 1983 Phelps Dodge strike (the Ajo strikebreakers, like those at the other Arizona properties, decertified all the union locals). In April 1996 that ex-Ajo smelter worker, Scott Huish, and Waldrip gathered 167 signatures of support for decertification. Huish, then twenty-seven years old, explained his antiunionism in interviews with local newspapers. "[U]nions are a thing of the past," he said. "People now need to think of their families first." He added that unions are "a business, . . . [and] in it to make money." Waldrip told me that he was advocating decertification because he would "rather just talk with the company." He added: "The union has served a good purpose. Laws that we have today were established through the union's efforts. But now the laws have been established and we can use them. It's unnecessary to pay [the union's dues] for having those laws to guarantee our employment." Tink Jackson, another truck driver, gave an even blunter economic account of why he wished to decertify Local 890: "It's a matter of economics for all of us. Nonrepresented people here have better insurance, make better wages, and participate in the company's bonus plan," he said. "Represented employees don't get the bonus."

As a result of the petitions solicited by Waldrip and Huish, the National Labor Relations Board announced on April 30, 1996, a five-week "campaign" during which the pro- and antiunion forces would vie for workers' votes. The campaign would be followed by a two-day referendum on June 5 and 6, 1996. Although labor laws required unions to leaflet outside the workplace or to go house to house (or phone to phone), the company could conduct "captive audience" meetings at the mine. Patty Young, a newly hired ore hauler, learned firsthand what it meant to be "captive" to Phelps Dodge. Her foreman stopped her one day as she rumbled along in her 240-ton Caterpillar dump truck on her way to pick up a load of ore. She thought she must have broken a work rule. He climbed up the fifteen-foot ladder to the cab, sat himself in the passenger seat, and proceeded to shout over the engine noise that she should vote against the union. She had no right to throw him out, so she politely listened and kept her cussing to herself. Young said she later learned that Phelps Dodge was aiming its message at women because the company assumed that women saw the union (despite the *Salt of the Earth* legacy) as a men's club. But Young had expressly joined Local 890 out of respect for—and an interest in keeping alive—its legacy. In her childhood, she had met one of the women's auxiliary members from the "Salt of the Earth" strike, Virginia Chacón, and felt a special commitment to those early activists. Young was critical of the union's "old ways" of excluding women—but she thought it better to change the union from within than to abandon it. When Young shrugged off the Phelps Dodge foreman's antiunion lobbying, the foreman returned a few days later with the same message. And again a few days later. And again and again. "It seemed like he was riding [in the truck] every day for a month before the decert vote," she said. "Me and one other woman were hit really hard." Phelps Dodge invitingly put the 401(k) plan and nonunion bonuses before them as an incentive, but the women not only decided to vote to retain the union but also helped rally community support. In a modern twist on the *Salt of the Earth* themes, Young's husband, who is disabled, often directed the union support group.

To supplement the "captive audience" meetings, mine manager Bill Brack wrote a decertification newsletter, conducted newspaper interviews, and oversaw a regular antiunion mail campaign, all under the slogan "Moving Forward at Chino Mines Company." Brack's "moving forward" campaign included both friendly cajoling and thinly veiled threats (such as the loss of job security). For example:

> Our nonunion employees know that job security comes from . . . working directly together as a team with common goals. (May 1, 1996)

> I do not believe that we can establish the common goals and teamwork we will need in the future with the current climate. (May 9, 1996)

> [W]hile unions may have had a purpose in the past, that time is gone. (May 23, 1996)

A vote for decertification is a vote for a stable future for you and your family. Don't hold us back. . . . (June 3, 1996)

To counter the letters and the speeches to captive audiences, union president Manning mobilized his own door-to-door campaign teams, training them in the how-to of winning local elections. They carried lists of questions and index cards for rating union support on a scale of one to four. Members visited "99.6 percent" of the more than five hundred workers officially represented by the Steelworkers, said Steelworkers staff representative Manny Armenta, including those nonmembers who had expressed a strong antipathy toward the union (the 0.4 percent, according to Armenta, were the two decertification petitioners, Huish and Waldrip). Manning used the campaign as a chance to hear what workers felt was wrong—as well as to speak out on what was right—with unionism. If workers said the nonunion 401(k) plan was tempting, the campaign supporter reminded them that without the union there might never even have been any pension at all. If they said that the company was more responsive than the union, the campaigner reminded them of Phelps Dodge's "responses" to workers in the Bisbee deportations of 1917 and the Morenci wage cuts and replacement of workers in 1983. High school students with driver's permits were asked to paint their cars "Union Yes!"—and garish shoe polish hues suddenly bloomed on car windows all over Cobre High School. Letters of support—including one by the county sheriff—dotted the editorial pages of the two local newspapers. Union members even split up responsibility for the local watering holes to ensure that the bars were on their side. Noted Manning, "It says something when even the drinking has strategy."

The union also countered the NLRB decertification petition with a "recertification" petition of its own; in place of the anonymous decertification signers, hundreds not only signed their support of the union but published their signatures and photographs in the newspaper with the statement:

We signed this pledge voluntarily, and we were not intimidated by anyone as P.D. states. We are your co-workers, so don't listen to P.D. Ask us. . . . WE ARE THE REAL SALT OF THE EARTH. JOIN US!

On Saturday, May 31, 1996, five days before the vote, approximately a thousand supporters, in more than four hundred decked-out cars, conducted a raucous parade of honking, chanting, and waving from union headquarters in Hurley to the designated "Union Park" in downtown Silver City. There, just down the street from the Phelps Dodge general offices, members young, old, and retired, as

well as surviving leaders from the "Salt of the Earth" women's auxiliary, exhorted workers to remember that their community and their
union were one and the same. The next day, a local newspaper reporter recording these events posed a question that hung heavily over
the union: "Will Local 890 go the way of 39 other Phelps Dodge
unions and fade into history? Or will the vote go the other way, allowing the union to go beyond these troubled times and regroup for
the future?"

In the waning days before the vote, the company scheduled several
mandatory meetings in a final lobbying effort against the union, but
union supporters became so raucous at one of the sessions that mine
manager Brack decided to call them off. Then, when Brack sought to
schedule company vans and supervisors to take workers to the polls,
the union arranged to have its supporters vote before work and avoid
any last-minute company influence. No company move against the
union had gone without an equal or stronger union response. Finally,
on the afternoon of June 6, 1996, the union's survival came down to
the ballot markings of 544 copper miners. Steelworkers staff representative Manny Armenta, who had helped lead the door-to-door campaign, witnessed the official NLRB tally. At a surprisingly early moment in the count, the prounion totals topped the magic 50 percent
threshold of 272 votes. Armenta could no longer maintain the election
room decorum; he yelled out "Bingo!" "You should have seen the
faces of Phelps Dodge's attorneys drop," he said. Phelps Dodge had
won every decertification vote since the 1983 Morenci strike. Now its
streak was broken. The union won by a count of 389–155, more than
a two-to-one margin. As the Local 890 victory celebration continued
into the night, union volunteers to the county rescue squad comman-
deered a fire truck and drove through town sounding the siren for
victory.

Current Events

From a perspective of community support and union morale, the
campaign and election were restorative events, bringing the union
back in touch with its activist roots, said union president Manning.
The election campaign "made our members and the people around us
aware that . . . we make ourselves stronger when we fight together."
Manning's "smart" unionism had helped win the day: combining the
nuts-and-bolts skills of precinct workers with passionate appeals to
community and history, Local 890 had prevailed against the odds.
The "Salt of the Earth" lived on. But, as a practical matter, the union
had won only the right to enter into the next battle at Phelps Dodge.

That challenge loomed directly ahead: the three-year contract was expiring on June 30, 1996. Could Local 890 now return to producing positive victories?

Through the last days of proofreading this epilogue, the outcome was still in doubt. As of mid-August 1998, Phelps Dodge had steadfastly refused the slightest increase in basic wages at contract negotiations. It offered instead a wage freeze, with a continued copper price-based bonus—a bonus that, in good times, would average about the rate of inflation. The rest of the "offer" was a call for concessions: more nonunion subcontracting, reduced retirement benefits, twelve-hour shifts, and, at one time, even the elimination of Memorial Day. (The company eventually dropped the demand for a reduction in holidays and then called the package a "final offer.") When I wrote a column in the *Los Angeles Times* criticizing the company's refusal to offer a wage increase, Phelps Dodge finally "responded" to my request for interviews. The company still wouldn't talk directly, but mining division president Steven Whisler wrote in a letter to the editor on Christmas Day, 1997, that my column was "an attempt to mislead readers and malign Phelps Dodge" and that the Chino miners were "among the best paid in New Mexico." He left out the fact they were among the worst paid in the entire U.S. copper industry. Meanwhile, the company was also openly taunting the union, with CEO Douglas Yearley telling an interviewer on CNBC television that "if they really feel as strongly [about the contract] as they have demonstrated, they ought to strike."

Phelps Dodge's challenge puts Local 890 on a collision course with its own heritage. In the 1950s, although a strike was initially disfavored, the members eventually decided to walk out, and they won their demands through an all-out community struggle. Today, union leaders—international Steelworkers leaders as well as local president Manning—have worked overtime to avoid a walkout. Under the 1983 Clifton-Morenci permanent replacement precedent, a strike, they argued, would be suicide. As the union attempted to carry forward its contract fight from inside the mine, members and supporters, past and present, have begun weighing again the meaning of the words of Esperanza Quintero: "I don't want to go down fighting. I want to win."

The Chacóns and the Floreses

Virginia Chacón, 80, widow of former Local 890 president Juan Chacón, sat at the dining room table in a white block house on the Mimbres River, about ten miles past where the Phelps Dodge slag heaps dropped off into desert. Over her shoulder, a framed poster stood out on her living room wall: it was a promotion for *Salt of the Earth*, featuring the heroine Esperanza Quintero (Rosaura Revueltas was the Mexican actress), when the film won an international film award decades ago. Chacón's late husband, Juan Chacón, presided over the union for nearly twenty years, starred in the movie, and, for a time, commanded the kind of loyalty in copper country that Cesar Chavez drew among farmworkers. Virginia Chacón was blunt about what Local 890 now had to do to stay true to its roots: "Strike." But might that mean "going down fighting"—the end of the union? Esperanza Chacón, Virginia's daughter, interrupted from another room. She was born during the filming of the movie and was named for the film heroine. When she was a few days old, she appeared in the movie in a baptism scene. "Esperanza would have said, 'Hell, we've already done it once and won. Why can't we do it the second time and win again?' They would still have it in their hearts, that fire, that struggle to make it some way. Their determination was very strong." Virginia nodded her own agreement and added that if the union attempted to wait the company out instead of striking, it might only be a matter of time before it was decertified. "You stick to your strides," she declared.

Then I tracked down Arturo Flores, 79, president of Local 890 in the 1960s. He recalled the days when being Mexican American meant "you had to work on the track" instead of in skilled jobs at the mine, and payday meant a mandatory kickback to your foreman. His father and brother helped support the "Salt of the Earth" strike while he was working as an organizer for the International Union of Mine, Mill and Smelter Workers in Arizona. Now retired near Albuquerque, Flores has stayed in touch with union activities via the internet and e-mail. He said that the current Local 890 did just what it had to during the company's decertification attempt: "The organizers got out there, and they told others about the consequences of not having a union, and the benefits." But Flores expressed concern that the union might still face extinction. Beyond the decertification vote, Local 890 hadn't maintained sufficient contacts with nonunion workers and with the community at-large, he said. "What we used to do is educate all the workers, let them all know how they needed the union. I think they're failing in that—not just in letting members know, but in the community, too. . . . I don't see the leaflets." Flores later sent me a follow-up e-mail that seemed to offer a new riddle in response to the challenge of "how to win" at Phelps Dodge: "If my ship was sinking," he wrote, "I would not contemplate drowning, I would take to the lifeboats and try to harass the attacker."

Flores' criticism of insufficient community activism couldn't help but be taken personally by union members—his son Ernest is a current member of Local 890 and a past vice president. But Ernest Flores has diagnosed the primary problem somewhat differently. The union has reached out to the community—even if imperfectly, he said. The labor laws are more skewed now against unions than those passed during his father's activist days. Companies like Phelps Dodge are more strategic and spend more money in their union-fighting. "In times past, you could go on strike and put a stop to the company's profits without fear of being replaced," he said. "The strike was an effective tool. We don't have that tool any more thanks to [President] Reagan, a weak National Labor Relations Act and a dumb Congress." Flores said that the strategy to stage protests but continue working was the only way the union could hold on and still fight another day—when the laws were changed or when (and if) the union got a favorable ruling in unfair labor practice charges filed before the NLRB.

❦

As the union–Phelps Dodge struggle approaches a second century, this epilogue closes without a conclusion. In late 1997, the international Steelworkers launched a corporate campaign to publicize Phelps Dodge's refusal to grant a fair contract. The union has attempted to cast Phelps Dodge as the uncaring outsider, willing even to degrade the "Kneeling Nun," a natural eighty-foot-high stone monolith that union president Manning pointed out on our tour of the mine. "The Nun," as it is called, is considered sacred by area residents but is located near an ore body that Phelps Dodge is seeking permission from the federal government to mine. Fulfilling the call for more community action by retired Local 890 president Flores, the union is leafletting the entire county—and drawing huge crowds to community meetings—about the risks that "the Nun" may one day fall victim to company blasting. The union has also alleged that the company's current production violates environmental laws. As to the contract, in January 1998 the NLRB issued complaints against the company alleging a failure by the company to bargain in good faith. The complaint means that the union has a fighting chance to protect jobs in the case of a strike, provided that the NLRB and courts ultimately agree that the company committed an unfair labor practice. Meanwhile, Cecil Waldrip has pursued yet another decertification petition against Local 890. In early June 1998, union president Manning again led a pro-union campaign, winning by a 333–170 margin. But as long as the contract remains unsigned, Waldrip or anyone else can annually renew the decertification effort. Finally, by the time of the company's annual shareholders meeting in the spring of 1998, market conditions made it even less likely that Phelps Dodge would agree to union demands: although Phelps Dodge was still on track to turn a significant profit, the decline of Asian economies had depressed the price of copper.

In all, Local 890 stands at a dangerous precipice. Pattern bargaining in the copper industry is still moribund—where once there was strength in numbers, now the numbers are low. The unions that once gave voice to Phelps Dodge workers in Arizona are still dead. The lack of a contract can wear down even the most dedicated union member. What lives on is the belief of former Morenci Local 616 president Angel Rodriguez—incarnate in Local 890 president Manning— in a coming day of judgment and the resurrection of unions at Phelps Dodge. The members and supporters of Local 890 know the Morenci story now the way Morenci once knew the Silver City saga. In my Labor Day visit, the members of this last Phelps Dodge Steelworker stronghold in mining expressed the hope that their victory against decertification will rekindle the fires of once and future unions at Phelps Dodge, and that—if they must strike—the world will take note that the "Salt of the Earth" are again calling for justice.*

---

*Realizing that *Copper Crucible* remains an open book, I asked Arturo Flores, the Local 890 ex-president, if he would be willing to update readers on the fate of the Chino struggle. He said he would. His e-mail address is arturo78@juno.com. When he can't answer the correspondence, he will pass it on to his son Ernest, the current Local 890 member. For identification purposes, anyone writing to the Floreses might wish to label the inquiry "Salt of the Earth II." A Phelps Dodge web site has also been established by environmental activists at www.envirolink.org/orgs/PhelpsDodgeWatch. Phelps Dodge's own web page is listed at www.phelpsdodge.com.

Source Notes

This book is based upon hundreds of hours of personal interviews, as well as newspaper, magazine, and television accounts and various books and journals. While I have opted for a somewhat informal style of notes (for example, no footnotes appear in the text), I have attempted in most cases to maintain an academic substantive standard. Quotes from books are cited with author, title, publisher, publication year, and page numbers. When a person is quoted for the first time, I give the date or dates of my interviews. In some instances, when the person is reintroduced, I also refer to the date of the interview. Newspaper and magazine quotes are referred to by publication name and date. On some subjects, I occasionally provide additional background information. These notes provide both documentation of sources and an extension of the body of the book where I did not want to interrupt the flow of the text.

Introduction. Critical Conditions

The state troopers' "book" **(p. 3)** was called the "Unusual Occurrence Control Task Force Operations Plan" and was dated June 1984. It eventually became known as Exhibit No. 41 in a successful federal lawsuit against the state. Bobby Andazola's account, as well as the quotes from his father, Francisco **(pp. 4–5, 6)**, are from my interviews of June 4 and June 19, 1988. Parts of the introduction are adapted from my article in the *Arizona Republic* of June 26, 1988 entitled "Labor's Last Stand." Mining companies recruited married couples from Mexico to work in Clifton **(p. 5)**, according to Victor Ciuccio's Ph.D. thesis, "Political Change in a Mexican-American Community" (University of Pennsylvania, 1975) at 25. I heard the description "uncapping the mountain" **(p. 6)** from retired company engineer Spike Pendleton while on a tour of the Phelps Dodge mine in the summer of 1990. In 1983, *Fortune* magazine listed Phelps Dodge as America's 300th largest corporation, with $1 billion in annual sales, twice that much in assets, and 9,100 employees. **(p. 6)** The industry publication **(p. 9)** is Standard and Poor's *Metals-Nonferrous Industry Survey* (1982–83). Portions of this section are adapted from my *Wall Street Journal* article of April 16, 1992, entitled "The Dismal Precedent That Gave Us Caterpillar." U.S. Supreme Court Justice Sandra Day O'Connor **(p. 9)** is from Duncan, Arizona, a few miles down the road from Clifton. The labor law case she wrote is *TWA v. Independent Federation of Flight Attendants*, 489 U.S. 426 (1989). Harvard labor law professor Paul Weiler drew my attention to O'Connor's language. The reference to Phelps Dodge, superstar **(p. 10)**, is from *Engineering and Mining Journal*, January 1987.

Chapter 1. Workers of the World and Copper in Arizona

For a complete guide to U.S. 666 near Clifton and Morenci, Arizona **(p. 13)**, see Arizona Department of Transportation Application Report "Coronado Trail Scenic Road," September 1988, and *Arizona Highways* magazine, July 1992. For an account of the Apache dance **(p. 13)**, see *Arizona Republic*, October 5, 1962, "Coronado Trail Ceremony Tomorrow." On the impossibility of getting an Arizona vanity license plate "666" **(p. 13)** resident Marguerite McIntyre requested the plate for her car on my behalf and was given the described reply. I spoke with Arizona traffic engineer Dennis Alvarez **(pp. 13–14)** on September 18, 1992. I consulted geologist Roy Grumman for the description of copper deposits **(p. 14)**. The Clifton-Morenci mining district's history **(p. 14)** is set out in Clifton's "Community Profile" of July 1975. On the number of motors in homes **(p. 14)**, one estimate in *Forbes* (October 24, 1983), puts the average number of electric motors at more than one hundred, but because I assume they must be "Forbes" households, I have used my own random polling to arrive at twenty. The average American stores $9.93 in pennies at home **(p. 15)**, according to a poll reported in the *Chicago Tribune*, May 23, 1994.

The Ralph Martinez description **(pp. 15–16)**comes from my interview of August 1, 1990. The quote from *At Work in Copper: Occupational Health and Safety in Copper Smelting* (Inform, Inc., 1979) **(p. 16)** by Manuel Gomez, Richard Duffy, and Vincent Trivelli is at 201. I spoke with Andrés Padilla **(p. 16)** on August 3, 1990.

The references to Phelps Dodge history **(p. 16 et seq.)** are from Robert Glass Cleland, *A History of Phelps Dodge, 1834–1950* (Knopf, 1952) and James Byrkit, *Forging the Copper Collar: Arizona's Labor-Management War of 1901–1921* (University of Arizona Press, 1982). The Phelps names **(p. 17)** are explained in Cleland at 4. The Wyatt Earp/Doc Holliday account **(p. 17)** is found in the *Phoenix Gazette*, December 3, 1979, "Earp's Other Career Glossed Over." Phelps Dodge pointed out in publicity for its one hundredth year in Arizona that the gunfight at the OK Corral in Tombstone took place in the same year as Phelps Dodge arrived in Morenci—1881. The story of George Warren **(p. 18)** is from Byrkit at 15. The quote about "Copper" **(p. 18)** is from Cleland at 154 and the company's output figures **(p. 18)** are from Cleland at 158–59. The indictments of Phelps Dodge officials **(p. 18)** are from Byrkit at 54 and 288 and Cleland at 58. Byrkit points out in a footnote at 352 that Phelps Dodge had industrial lead and zinc from Europe cast "into thousands of crude Dianas and Venuses and Mercurys" **(p. 18)**.

James Douglas **(p. 18)** is described in Michael E. Parrish, *Mexican Workers,*

Progressives, and Copper: The Failure of Industrial Democracy in Arizona during the Wilson Years (University of California Press, 1979) at 4. The Protestant ethic of the families **(p. 18)** is described in Cleland at 21 and the contributions to various institutions **(p. 19)** are described at 34, 73, and 153. The skills of Mexican workers **(p. 19)** are referred to in Rodolfo Acuña, *Occupied America: The Chicanos' Struggle toward Liberation* (Canfield Press, 1972) at 90, and the proportion of Mexican workers **(p. 19)** is in George Leaming, *Labor and Copper in Arizona* (College of Business and Public Administration, University of Arizona, 1973) at 13. International diplomacy in Arizona **(p. 19)** is described by Byrkit at 52–53. For a fascinating account of Joe Hill's demise **(p. 19–20)**, see Philip S. Foner, *The Case of Joe Hill* (International Publishers, 1965). I would make this book required reading for law school evidence classes. Mother Jones writes a whole chapter on Governor Hunt **(p. 20)** and describes him in Mary Harris Jones, *The Autobiography of Mother Jones* (C. H. Kerr, 1925) at 174. The 1903 strike **(pp. 20–21)** is described in Acuña at 96–97 and Leaming at 5. The "other study" **(p. 21)** is Acuña at 96. The Arizona Supreme Court case about the foundlings **(pp. 21–22)** is *New York Foundling Hosp. v. Norton* 9 Ariz. 105, 79 Pac. 231 (January 1905). The ethnicity of the families **(p. 21)** is at 109; the long citation **(p. 21)** is *Norton*, 9 Ariz. 105, 110; Superintendent Mills **(pp. 21–22)** is described at 111 and his "remonstrances" **(p. 22)** are at 113; the court's own description of the children **(p. 21)** is at 111. The U.S. Supreme Court case **(p. 22)** is *New York Foundling Hospital v. Gatti*, 203 U.S. 429 (1906). The Court's reasoning **(p. 22)** is at *Gatti*, 203 U.S. 429, 438–41.

These average wage figures **(p. 22)** are somewhat unreliable as a result of shifting rates and poor historical record keeping. The average mining wage is from Leaming at 9; the "Mexican wage" is from Acuña at 97; the average national wage is from U.S. Department of Labor, *Employment and Earnings: 1909–1972*. The bribe and rent premium **(p. 22)** is described in Acuña at 97. Accounts of the 1915 strike **(pp. 22–24)** are found in Byrkit at 55–62 and in James Kluger, *The Clifton-Morenci Strike: Labor Difficulty in Arizona, 1915–1916* (University of Arizona Press, 1970). The Hunt speech **(p. 23)** is reported in Byrkit at 58. Mother Jones's comments and speech **(pp. 23–24)** are in Jones, *The Autobiography of Mother Jones*, 172–75. The articles and letters war in *The New Republic* **(p. 24)** are from Byrkit at 62 and 67–68. The first *New Republic* article appeared on January 22, 1916, at 304–6; the Walter Douglas response came in the March 18, 1916, issue, and the letter from Governor Hunt appeared in the April 15, 1916, issue. The long Byrkit quote **(pp. 24–25)** is from Byrkit at 72. Thomas Campbell and the 1916 election **(p. 25)** are described in Byrkit at 91 and in an unpublished work by Timothy J. Eckstein, *The Hunt for a Better Arizona: The Arizona Gubernatorial Election of 1916* (B.A. thesis, Pomona College, 1992). Governor Hunt was later returned to office when a court ruling nullified a number of disputed ballots that had been counted in favor of Campbell. The prominent historian **(p. 25)** is Michael Parrish, *Mexican Workers, Progressives, and Copper* at 8. The quote attributed to Phelps Dodge **(p. 25)** is from Cleland at 180; the quote of Walter Douglas **(p. 25)** is from Byrkit at 184, and the testimony **(p. 25)** about Douglas's role in the deportation is from Cleland at 188.

The Bisbee Deportation **(p. 25 et seq.)** is the central subject of Byrkit's book, especially beginning at 192, and is also described and analyzed by Philip S. Foner in *Labor and World War I, 1914–1918*, vol. 7 of his *History of the Labor Movement in the United States* (International Publishers, 1987). The testimony about Walter Douglas **(p. 26)** is in Cleland at 188. The *New York Times* quote **(p. 26)**, cited in Byrkit at 224, is from July 14, 1917. The deportation was recorded in Stephen Vincent Benét's first work, *The Beginning of Wisdom*, but it has been ignored by most history books. Katie Pintek **(p. 26)** spoke in a documentary film, *The Wobblies* (First Run Features, 1979). President Wilson's communication **(p. 27)** is in Byrkit at 210. Byrkit notes the gap **(p. 27)** in Wilson and Cleveland Dodge's letters at 279–80. I spoke with Professor Link **(p. 27)** on November 3, 1993.

I owe much of this account of Felix Frankfurter's trip to the Arizona copper mines to Michael E. Parrish, *Felix Frankfurter and His Times: The Reform Years* (Free Press, 1982). All of these letters may be found in the Frankfurter Papers, Library of Congress. Frankfurter's letter **(p. 27)** to Marion Denman is quoted in Parrish at 92; the letter about the "marooned outpost" **(p. 27)** to Katherine Ludington is quoted in Parrish at 87–88. A view of Frankfurter's script and these letters **(p. 27)** is available in the Frankfurter Papers, Library of Congress. The letter to Learned Hand **(pp. 27–28)** is quoted in Parrish at 93. The Mediation Commission report **(p. 28)** is presented in *Report of President Wilson's Mediation Commission on the Bisbee, Ariz. Deportation*, Official Bulletin vol. 1, no. 170 (November 27, 1917). The letters to Brandeis and Denman **(p. 28)** are quoted in Parrish at 95. The description from the railcars **(p. 28)** is in Parrish at 92. The alleged attack on Frankfurter's Jewish heritage **(p. 28)** is described in Byrkit at 265. The quote from Dubofsky **(p. 29)** is from Melvyn Dubofsky, *We Shall Be All: A History of the Industrial Workers of the World* (Quadrangle Books, 1969) at 418. The Roosevelt letter **(p. 29)** is quoted in part by Parrish at 99; I have sometimes used different extracts of the letters than Parrish. Frankfurter's response **(p. 29)** is referenced in Parrish at 99; again, I have selected a different portion of the same letter. The U.S. Supreme Court case on the Bisbee deportation **(p. 30)** is *U.S. v. Wheeler*, 254 U.S. 381 (1920). Byrkit wrote of the approval for Sheriff Wheeler **(p. 30)** at 292–93. For a succinct account of the IWW arrests **(p. 30)**, see Richard O. Boyer and Herbert M. Morais, *Labor's Untold Story* (United Electrical, Radio and Machine Workers, 3d ed., 1975) at 198–99.

My interviews with Padilla and Velasquez **(p. 30 et seq.)** were on August 3, 1990, and July 27, 1990, respectively. The account of the Mine-Mill victory followed by the setback **(pp. 31–32)** is from my interview with Padilla. The quote about labor unions as "anathema" **(p. 32)** is from Cleland at 73. The source for the 1935 Bisbee organizing drive **(p. 32)** is the U.S. Supreme Court case, *Phelps Dodge v. Labor Board*, 313 U.S. 177 (1941). The Kitchel argument **(p. 32)** is at *Phelps Dodge*, 313 U.S. 177, 179–80. The Frankfurter language about "textual mutilation" **(p. 33)** is from *Phelps Dodge*, 313 U.S. 177, 186, and the long quote **(p. 33)** is at 185. The U.S. Government funding to Phelps Dodge **(p. 33)** is in George Hildebrand and Garth Mangum, *Capital and Labor in American Copper, 1845–1990: Linkages between Product and Labor Markets*

(Harvard University Press, 1992) at 90. I have also used this important text for general accounts of the structure of the copper industry and for various statistics. The account of Mine-Mill's communism problems and Maurice Travis **(p. 34)** can be found in Vernon Jensen, *Nonferrous Metals Industry Unionism, 1932–1954: A Story of Leadership Controversy* (Cornell University Press, 1954) at 248–49. Jensen's description of the rank and file as "good CIO unionists" **(p. 34)** is at 268. *Salt of the Earth* and Howard Hughes **(p. 35)** are referred to in a United Press International article of March 27, 1982. The quote about Mine-Mill communism **(p. 36)** is in Hildebrand and Mangum at 210. The "red" quote from the Steelworkers **(p. 38)** is from a draft of a paper by Russell W. Gibbons given me by Steelworkers publicist Cass Alvin.

The wage figures for Arizona **(p. 38)**, provided by the Arizona Department of Economic Security, are inexact because they are derived indirectly from reported wage and payroll totals. The state did not begin reporting to the Department of Labor until many years after 1967. The U.S. and industry averages **(p. 38)** are from U.S. Department of Labor, *Employment and Earnings* (1972) and from newspaper accounts. The account of the unity conferences **(p. 38)** is in William Chernish, *Coalition Bargaining: A Study of Union Tactics and Public Policy* (University of Pennsylvania Press, 1969); the bargaining language **(p. 38)** is from Chernish at 181. The "charades" quote **(p. 38)** is from Chernish at 167. The "classic case" **(p. 38)** is from Chernish at 168. Chernish refers to the "highest common denominator" **(p. 40)** at 181. The Cass Alvin quotes **(p. 40)** are from my interview of April 3, 1990. The ASARCO replacement effort **(p. 41)** is reported in the *Baltimore Sun*, February 22, 1968. The "gentleman's agreement" **(p. 41)** about replacing strikers is referred to in Bruce E. Kaufman, *The Economics of Labor Markets* (3rd ed., Dryden Press, 1991) at 562–63. The goals of uniformity in the industrywide strike **(p. 41)** are described in Hildebrand and Mangum at 230–35.

The Willard Wirtz quote **(p. 42)** is from Chernish at 189. The Joseph Molony statement from the 1967 strike **(p. 42)** is from Chernish at 195. President Lyndon Johnson **(p. 42)** is quoted in a page-one story in the *New York Times*, March 2, 1968. Pat Scanlon **(p. 42)** is quoted in the *Arizona Republic*, March 18, 1984, and President Johnson is again quoted **(p. 42)** in the *New York Times*, March 5, 1968. Phelps Dodge's opposition to the Nonferrous Industry Conference **(p. 43)**, as well as the NLRB decision on the matter **(p. 43)**, is described in Hildebrand and Mangum at 240–41. The central court case **(p. 43)**, reversing the NLRB, is *AFL-CIO Joint Negotiating Committee v. National Labor Relations Board* 470 F.2d 722 (3rd Cir. 1972). On Professor Northrup **(p. 40)**, see pp. 60–63 and 222–24.

The account of negotiations after 1967 **(pp. 44–45)** is from Hildebrand and Mangum, beginning at 244. The source of the "inside" picture of Phelps Dodge **(p. 45)** is the late company counsel, John Boland, Jr., from my interview of May 8, 1990.

Chapter 2. Hard Places

The *Business Week* article **(p. 47)** appeared on July 26, 1982, at 58–60. The same article referred to Richard Moolick as "abrasive" **(p. 48)**. The Moolick quotes dispersed throughout the book **(and here at p. 48)** are from interviews of April 7 and 20, 1990, August 13, 1990, and April 12, 1992. The reference to Phelps Dodge as "ruthless" **(p. 48)** came from the *Wall Street Journal*, November 24, 1989. The Official NBA Basketball Encyclopedia reports that guard George Munroe **(p. 48)** played the 1946–47 season for the fledgling National Basketball Association with the St. Louis Hawks, averaging 7 points per game. The next season with the Boston Celtics, he averaged 3.4 points per game. Perhaps one reason for his decline in the second season was that he was studying at Harvard Law at the same time. The *Arizona Republic* **(p. 48)** article is from October 2, 1983. The Bruce Babbitt quote **(p. 49)** is from my inteview of May 11, 1990. My interview with Munroe **(p. 49 et seq.)** was on April 21, 1990. The quote about the company's "corporate citizenship" **(p. 50)** is from the July 26, 1982, *Business Week* article. My interview with John Coulter **(p. 51 et seq.)** was on April 22, 1990, and with William Seidman **(page 51 et seq.)** on August 15, 1991. The quotes about Western Operations **(pp. 51–52)** are from the July 26, 1982, *Business Week* article. Munroe's comments about the "easy life" **(p. 53)** are from my April 21, 1990, interview. The quotes from the Ajo speech **(p. 53–54)** are from a text dated May 8, 1982, that was distributed by Munroe in Ajo and provided to me by the Morenci union local. The Jack Ladd comments **(p. 54)** are from my interview of November 26, 1991. The Munroe comments on the shutdown **(p. 55)** are from my April 21, 1990, interview; Seidman comments **(p. 55)** are from my August 15, 1991 interview. The supervisor who referred to the psychologist **(p. 56)** spoke on background and requested not to be identified. The quotes about Seidman's departure and Munroe's troubles **(pp. 56–57)** are from *Business Week*, July 26, 1982.

The Wharton School memoranda **(p. 61)** are available at the school's Industrial Research Unit library. The quotes about provisions for replacement workers **(p. 62)** are from Charles Perry, Andrew Kramer, and Thomas Schneider, *Operating during Strikes: Company Experience, NLRB Policies, and Governmental Regulations* (Industrial Research Unit, Wharton School, University of Pennsylvania, 1982) at 135. The introduction points out that "Overall, technological and institutional conditions in the early 1980s appear to favor expanded exercise of the right to operate as an asset to management power in collective bargaining. Thus, this seems an appropriate time to reassess the use of usefulness of operating during a strike." The Wharton School book **(p. 62)** is Steven A. Sass, *The Pragmatic Imagination: A History of the Wharton School, 1881–1981* (University of Pennsylvania Press, 1982). The quote from this work is at 302. The account of Lemuel Boulware **(pp. 62–63)** benefits also from the article "Boulwarism at GE" from the *Wall Street Journal*, August 31, 1964. My interview with Northrup **(p. 63)** took place on August 19, 1993. The newspaper quote of Northrup **(p. 63)** is from *Newsday*, May 3, 1992. Coulter's comments about spy Rudolph Abel **(p. 64)** are from my interview of April 22, 1990. My interview with Frank McKee **(p. 65 et seq.)** took place on May 3, 1990. McKee's speech **(pp. 66–67)** was delivered to the Nonferrous Industry Conference (NIC) on February 9, 1983, and was titled in full: "Mucking Out Some Myths: Planning for the 1983–84 Nonferrous Industry Negotiations and the Future of Our Industries." The William Winpisinger view of the 1983 contract negotiations **(p. 67)** was noted by Cass Alvin in my interview of April 3, 1990.

The Richard Pendleton quote **(p. 71)** is from the *Washington Post*, May 1, 1983. The plant episode and Jack Ladd's comment **(p. 72)** were recounted by Carl Morris in a September 17, 1992, interview. The union proposal **(p. 72)** and all subsequent references to the negotiation sessions are taken from Angel Rodriguez's union minutes. The Ladd, McKee, Petris, and Ghearing comments **(pp. 72–73)** are from the minutes of May 4, 1983. The Ray Isner quote **(p. 73)** is from my interview of March 25, 1990. The Scanlon quote about communicating Phelps Dodge's contract terms to employees and the union response **(p. 77)** are from the negotiations minutes of June 25, 1983.

The Frank McKee quote **(p. 78)** is from my May 3, 1990, interview. The Pat Scanlon quote about the Greeks **(p. 78)** is from my interview of May 3, 1990. The Chernish quote **(p. 79)** is from William Chernish, *Coalition Bargaining* (1969) at 185. The Angel Rodriguez quotes **(p. 79 et seq.)** are from my interview of March 23, 1990. The Frank McKee strike decision and quote **(p. 80)** was related by a Steelworkers official (not Alex Lopez), who was present and spoke to me on background.

Chapter 3. *Midnight at Morenci*

I interviewed Ralph Martinez **(p. 81)** on August 5, 1990. I base the old-timers' characterization **(p. 81)** on Martinez's account. I spoke with Lydia Gonzales Roybal **(p. 82)** on August 15, 1990. The *Time* magazine article **(p. 82)** appeared on January 5, 1970. The Sorrelman quote **(p. 82)** is from my August 14, 1990, interview. I interviewed Mike Cranford **(p. 82)** on August 3, 1990. I interviewed Leo and Ray Aguilar **(p. 83)** on August 1, 1990. I interviewed Mike Martinez **(p. 83)** on July 27, 1990. The quote about the union response to Phelps Dodge **(pp. 83–84)** is assembled from Martinez's account, but is not a direct quote of Martinez. The Abel Peralta account **(p. 84)** is from my interview of August 1, 1990. I spoke with Pete Castañeda **(p. 84)** on March 3, 1990. The John Bolles letter **(p. 86)**, which was just one of many, was addressed "To Each Employee Who Is Still On Strike, And Each Laid-Off Employee Who Has Not Yet Returned To Work" and was dated August 2, 1983.

Don Harris's article **(p. 86)** appeared in the *Arizona Republic*, July 10, 1983. The Angel Rodriguez quote **(p. 86)** appeared in the *Arizona Republic*, July 20, 1983.

Chapter 4. *Copper Wars*

The *Arizona Republic* editorial about the Chandra Tallant shooting **(p. 89)** appeared on July 29, 1983. The Babbitt quotes **(p. 90 et seq.)** are from my interviews of May 11 and August 25, 1990, except where otherwise noted. Cass Alvin's comment **(p. 90)** is from the *Arizona Republic*, August 3, 1990. The John Coulter quote **(p. 90)** is from my interview of April 22, 1990. The Pat Scanlon quotes **(p. 91)** are from the *Arizona Republic*, August 3, 1983. The Richard Moolick quote **(p. 91)** is from my interview of April 7, 1990. All subsequent quotes are to this interview or interviews of April 20 and August 12, 1990 and April 12, 1992. I spoke with Jack Ladd (p. 91) on April 7, 1990. The account of the Doubletree meeting (pp. 92–93) is from Coulter and Moolick. The description of the "day that everything stops" (p. 93) comes from the *Arizona Daily Star*, August 9, 1983. Other accounts from the day are from the *Arizona Daily Star*, August 7, 1983. John Bolles's status at Morenci (p. 93–94) is from my Moolick interviews; the Bolles response to the coming clash (p. 96) is from my interview of July 30, 1990. The employment office and highway descriptions (pp. 94–95) come from interviews of Rick Melton on November 24, 1991, and John Bolles, as well as assorted newspaper reports and interviews on background. The interview of Conrad Gomez (p.95) was with a union member who requested that he not be identified by his real name. The Babbitt account (pp. 96–98) is from my interviews cited above.

Pat Scanlon and Angel Rodriguez provided accounts of the courthouse meeting (pp. 98–99). I interviewed Scanlon about the menacing crowd (pp. 99–101) on May 3, 1990; the quotes attributed here to Rodriguez about being unable to control the crowd (p. 99) are from Scanlon's recall. I spoke with DPS officer Dave Boyd (pp. 100–101) on September 30, 1991. The words of Angel Rodriguez on the bullhorn (pp. 100–101) were captured on television news videos (henceforth, "strikers' videos") of August 9, 1983, that were recorded by strikers and which I viewed at the Andazola home; the station identifications were not preserved. The descriptions of Sheriff Gomez and the state intelligence officer (p. 101) are from my interviews with former state intelligence officers George Graham on November 28, 1991, October 20, 1992, and June 30, 1993, and Steve Kuykendall on June 30, 1993. I interviewed John Boland, Jr. (p. 103), on May 8, 1990.

The quote of John Munger (p. 104) is from the *Arizona Daily Star*, August 12, 1983. The quotes of Jim Bush and Arthur Kinneberg (p. 104) are from the *Arizona Daily Star*, August 10, 1983. Federal mediator Sam Franklin's press conference (p. 104) was recorded in the strikers' video collection. The Cass Alvin comment, as well as comments by Sam Franklin and Robert Petris (p. 105), are reported in the minutes of August 11, 1983; Scanlon and Petris's exchange (pp. 105–6) is from the minutes of August 12, 1983; the Petris exhortation of the union members and the Franklin visit to the union committee (p. 106) are from the August 15, 1983, minutes. The Frank McKee quote about his meeting with Moolick (p. 106) is from the *Arizona Republic*, August 17, 1983; the Moolick quotes (p. 106) are from my interview of April 8, 1990. The Scanlon quote about "abnormal wear" of gloves (p. 107) is from the August 20, 1983, minutes.

The account of the Babbitt meeting (pp. 107–9) is from interviews with George Britton on November 28, 1991; Ronnie Lopez on December 21, 1991; and Ralph Milstead on August 24, 1991. The *Arizona Republic* article (p. 109) ran on August 26, 1983. The account of the Arizona Criminal Intelligence System Agency infiltration of the unions (pp. 109–13) is from my interviews of George Graham on November 28, 1991, October 20, 1992, and June 30, 1993; Steve Kuykendall on June 30, 1993; and Frank Navarrete on June 30,

1993. The *Arizona Republic* article that quotes Andrew Hurwitz and Frank Navarrete **(pp. 109–10)** ran on August 26, 1983—a week after the company restarted operations (with the National Guard at the gate) and three weeks into the undercover operation.

The Rose Mofford anecdote **(pp. 113–14)** is courtesy of eyewitness Andrew Hurwitz. The Bruce Babbitt quotes, **(p. 114)** other than those attributed to newspapers, are from my interviews of May 11 and August 25, 1990.

Chapter 5. Hard Times

The background to the song "Open Pit Mine" **(p. 117)** is described in Tom Miller's article, "The Working Man's Romeo and Juliet" in *Arizona Trend* (February 1989), at 75–77. My thanks to Tom for bringing this article to my attention (and for lending me his tape of this catchy tune). Just for the record, the song peaked on the country/western charts at number thirteen. The anthropologist's account of Clifton **(p. 118)** is by Victor Ciuccio, *Political Change in a Mexican-American Industrial Community* (Ph.D. diss., Pennsylvania State University, 1975) at 61. The Ciuccio quote **(p. 118)** is from Ciuccio at 66. I interviewed Josephine and Antonio Rivas **(pp. 118–119)** on August 3, 1990, and spoke with them regularly while they were my landlords in Clifton during the summer of 1990. The George Britton quote **(p. 119)** is from *The Arizona Republic*, August 20, 1983. I spoke with Grace Carroll **(p. 119)** on October 4, 1991; Roy Gann's comments **(p. 119)** were on news reports of August 19, 1983, compiled on the strikers' video; the member of the strike auxiliary **(p. 119)** spoke to me on background.

I interviewed Tony Tellez **(p. 120 et seq.)** on December 21, 1991. The Jim Krass quote **(p. 121)** is from the *Arizona Daily Star*, August 20, 1983. The accounts of the strikebreakers **(p. 121)** are from the *Arizona Republic*, July 31, 1983. The Babbitt quote from the negotiations **(p. 122)** is from the *Arizona Republic*, August 25, 1983. My account of the special union meeting in Phoenix **(p. 122 et seq.)** is based on interviews with Duane Ice on September 22, 1992, and December 4, 1993; and with Robert Petris on November 22, 1990, and November 14, 1993. Among the options floated at this meeting, according to Petris, were a return to work at Phelps Dodge without a contract, or a "freeze" (rather than termination) of cost-of-living adjustments. Frank McKee strongly believed that such proposed concessions would break the pattern contract already signed with the other companies. Scanlon **(p. 123)** presented the Supreme Court case *Belknap v. Hale*, 463 U.S. 491 (1983), at the negotiations of September 21, 1983, according to the minutes of that date.

The peaceful atmosphere at the Morenci mine gate after the National Guard's arrival **(p. 123)** belied the tensions simmering below the surface. On August 23, 1983, Scott Thomas, a 19-year-old weapons buff from the nearby cotton farming town of Safford, was shot in the back when a DPS officer accidentally discharged his weapon during a botched sting operation. Thomas had been set up through a DPS and ACISA informant to deliver hand grenades to undercover officers—although no grenades were ever produced, and Thomas was never found to have violated any law. (Two years later, according to an article in the *Arizona Daily Star*, November 17, 1985, a permanently disabled Thomas received $98,000 in a settlement, after a $60,000 payment to his lawyers.) On August 24, 1983, striker Paul "Larry" Gonzales was critically beaten outside the Oasis, a Clifton bar, after an altercation inside between strikers and strikebreakers, according to the *Tucson Citizen* of August 30, 1983. His head injuries were so serious that he was never able to identify the attacker or attackers—or even say for sure whether they were the strikebreakers—and he died of his injuries later in the year.

The most serious law enforcement incidents connected to the National Guard's mobilization were, ironically, caused by the Guard itself. First, a tractor trailer carrying supplies and driven by a Guard member swerved out of control on one of the many curves along Route 666, plummeting three hundred feet down a ravine and causing two injuries. In the other incident, according to Guard records, travelers at the Picacho, Arizona, rest stop complained that the members of the Guard were causing trouble: while "men, women and children were around," according to a complaint, fifteen Guardsmen were reported to have urinated outside.

The law enforcement assault on Ajo **(pp. 124–25)**, including the alleged role of company officials and the justice of the peace, is described in *United Steelworkers of America v. Phelps Dodge Corporation* 865 F.2d 1539 (9th Cir. 1989) and in the Phoenix alternative newspaper *New Times*, October 12–18, 1983. Moolick's promotion of Forstrom **(p. 125)** was described in my interview with Moolick on August 13, 1990. The Frank McKee quote **(p. 125)** is from my interview of May 3, 1990.

In the "Profiles in Pain" section **(p. 126 et seq.)**, I interviewed "Fred Torrez" **(p. 126 et seq.)** (whose name has been changed) on August 17, 1990. I interviewed Chito and Livia Tellez **(p. 128 et seq.)** on July 24, 1990. I interviewed Mary Beager **(p. 130 et seq.)** on August 18, 1990. I interviewed Father Mike Martinez **(p. 131 et seq.)** on July 27, 1990. I interviewed James Carter **(p. 134 et seq.)** on October 1, 1991. The *Tucson Citizen* article **(pp. 134–35)** is from May 24, 1984, but the claims made in the article had surfaced in Clifton and Morenci much earlier. I interviewed Father John Bardon **(pp. 135–36)** on October 4, 1991. I interviewed Nancy Foster **(p. 136)** on August 16, 1990. Alex Lopez told me about his copper price dream **(p. 137)** in an interview on March 21, 1990.

I interviewed Marty Montoya about the flood **(pp. 137–38)** on August 18, 1990. The flood issue of the *Copper Era* **(p. 138)** appeared on October 3, 1983. The *Arizona Daily Star* article **(p. 139)** appeared on October 4, 1983. The *Arizona Daily Star* quoted the unnamed company official **(p. 139)** on November 17, 1983. The *Copper Era* published Bill Thompson's poem **(p. 139)** on October 11, 1984. The decisions at Duval copper **(p. 140)** were reported in the *Arizona Daily Star*, October 5, 1983.

I interviewed Dr. Jorge and Anna O'Leary **(p. 140 et seq.)** on June 5, 1988. The *People* article **(p. 142)** on Dr. O'Leary appeared on January 16, 1984. The quotes from Paul Brinkley-Rogers's interview **(p. 142)** quotes are from an unpublished manuscript. Other quotes are from my interview with the O'Learys. I owe a debt of thanks to reporter Brinkley-Rogers for supplying his articles and other material on Dr. O'Leary. The Women's Strike Auxiliary account **(p. 143 et seq.)** comes largely from my interviews with Fina Roman on November 11, 1991; and with Anna O'Leary on October 2, 1991. I spoke with Toni Potter **(p. 144)** on September 15, 1992. Fina Roman's letter to the *Copper Era* **(p. 146)** ran on September 7, 1983. The quotes from Barbara Kingsolver's book **(p. 148)** are from *Holding the Line: The Great Arizona Mine Strike of 1983* (ILR Press, 1989). The "blow his damn head off" quote **(p. 148)** is from my interview with auxiliary member Shirley Randall on October 1, 1990. The Kingsolver quote of Alicia **(p. 149)** is from *Holding the Line* at 138. Roman's speech during the corporate campaign in New York **(p. 150)** was delivered on September 29, 1984. The Kingsolver "laundry basket" line **(p. 151)** is at 187.

Chapter 6. Hard Change

The Standard and Poor's account **(p. 156)** is from the *Metals-Nonferrous Industry Survey* (1982–83). The U.S. Chamber of Commerce report **(p. 156)** is from the *1983 U.S. Industrial Outlook* at 19–2. The *Engineering and Mining Journal* predictions **(p. 156)** are from the March 1983 issue. I interviewed Kennecott's Judd Cool **(pp. 156–57)** on April 6, 1992. I interviewed ASARCO's Douglas Soutar **(p. 157)** on April 16, 1992. The union-company argument over exact savings **(p. 158)** began in the *Arizona Daily Star* on July 2, 1983. The company's $25 million figure **(p. 158)** surfaced in the *Arizona Republic*, August 21, 1983. That amount rose to $50 million **(p. 158)** in the *Arizona Republic*, August 25, 1983—five days after the arrival of the National Guard. The one-year-after appraisal (based on the company's reported savings after one year of its new terms) **(p. 159–60)** appeared in the *Arizona Daily Star*, July 1, 1984. Timothy Greaves's testimony before the NLRB **(p. 160)** was reported in the *Arizona Republic*, August 15, 1984, and was reflected in the September 11, 1984, NLRB decision (see Phoenix NLRB case 28-RM-490 at 20) rejecting the unions' claim of ineligibility of laid-off workers for the decertification vote.

For George Hildebrand and Garth Mangum's argument **(p. 161 et seq.)**, see especially their *Capital and Labor in American Copper: 1845–1990* (1992) at 252–55. For Professor Ruth Bandzak's argument **(p. 161 et seq.)**, see especially "A Productive Systems Analysis of the 1983 Phelps Dodge Strike," *Journal of Economic Issues* (December 1991) at 1113–15. The citations on productivity **(p. 163)** are found in Hildebrand and Mangum at 253–54, and in Bandzak at 1115 and 1121. I have used a more complete source on productivity in the industry, *The Primary Copper Industry of Arizona in 1986* (Arizona Department of Mineral Resources), "Table XIX: Employment, Earnings, and Hours in Copper Mining in the United States and Arizona." The Price Waterhouse evaluation of Phelps Dodge productivity **(p. 164)** is dated July 22, 1983, and was presented at the 1983 annual meeting. The Bandzak quote **(p. 165)** is at 1115.

Chapter 7. Wars of Attrition

This account is generally based on February 26, 1992, and October 19, 1992, interviews with Ray Rogers, as well as on Union Corporate Campaign documents and interviews with United Steelworkers officials. One academic source that gives Rogers credit for the modern corporate campaign **(p. 166)** is *Union Corporate Campaigns* by Charles Perry (Industrial Research Unit, Wharton School, University of Pennsylvania, 1987), especially at 1–2. I interviewed McKee **(p. 169)** on May 3, 1990. The *Village Voice* quote **(p. 169)** appeared in the article "Copper War" on March 19, 1985. The federal discrimination lawsuit **(p. 170)** is *U.S. v. Inspiration Consolidated Copper Company* 6 EPD 8918 (April 9 and September 25, 1973) and is discussed by Hildebrand and Mangum in *Capital and Labor in American Copper, 1845–1990: Linkages between Product and Labor Markets* (Harvard University Press, 1992). My interview with Alex Lopez **(p. 170)** was on March 24, 1990. In 1991, the International Labor Organization's Committee on Freedom of Association **(p. 171),** for which I worked in 1992–93, found in ILO Governing Body 278th Report, Case No. 1643, paragraphs 60–3 (1991, no. 2) that U.S. law allowing permanent replacement failed to adequately protect the freedom of association. Jack Ladd's comments **(p. 171)** were in the *Arizona Republic,* November 21, 1983. The Wharton School's *Operating during Strikes: Company Experience, NLRB Policies, and Governmental Regulations* **(p. 171)** discusses medical benefit options at 17. The decision on medical benefits by arbitrator Leo Kotin **(p. 172)** was described in the *Arizona Republic,* December 16, 1983. The report by Congressman William Clay **(p. 172)** was issued in a news release dated December 20, 1983. *People* magazine **(p. 172)** published an article on the strikers in its January 16, 1984 issue.

Frank McKee announced his candidacy **(p. 172)** to Steelworkers membership in December 1983. References to the election campaign **(pp. 172–73)** are quoted from *And the Wolf Finally Came: The Decline of the American Steel Industry* by John Hoerr (University of Pittsburgh Press, 1988) at 403–11. Williams's quote **(p. 173)** is at 400 and McKee's **(pp. 172–73)** are at 406.

Angel Rodriguez and Jack Ladd's comments **(p. 174)** on the new union contract proposal were reported in the *Arizona Republic,* June 9, 1984.

The *Cinco de Mayo* events **(p. 175)** are described in the *Arizona Daily Star,* May 6, 1984.

The account of the June 30, 1984, anniversary rally **(p. 175 et seq.)** is based on court depositions and conversations with attorney Michael McCrory regarding the case *United Steelworkers v. Ralph Milstead et al.* 705 F. Supp. 1426 (1988) and on supplemental memorandum opinion and order No. Civ. 84-649 TUC CLH (January 27, 1989) as well as on assorted interviews. I owe special thanks to McCrory for sharing his boxes of documents, exhibits, tapes, etc. from the court cases. For parts of this section, I have adapted sections from my article "Labor's Last Stand" in the *Arizona Republic* of June 26, 1988. The company literally attempted to get in the last word **(p. 176)** when, in July 1984, Phelps Dodge Mercantile Co., Morenci, posted a policy at its mercantile stores announcing that "There will be no Spanish spoken between employees in any department while working." According to the *Arizona Republic* of August 17, 1984, the policy stemmed from an incident at the company store in another town where two employees speaking Spanish had allegedly insulted a patron. The company later modified the policy to require only that employees speak English in the presence of English-speaking customers.

The corporate campaign announcement with Lynn Williams's speech **(p. 177)** was published, among other places, in the October 15, 1984, Morenci Miners Local 616 newsletter. The Bruce Springsteen solicitation on behalf of the copper miners **(p. 178)** was reported by Dave Walker in the Phoenix alternative weekly *New Times*, November 21, 1984. The *Business Week* article **(p. 179)** quoting the bank response to the corporate campaign appeared on September 24, 1984, and is cited in Perry's book *Union Corporate Campaigns* at 99. The Kamber Group memorandum on Babbitt **(p. 180)** was dated March 14, 1985.

Lynn Williams's comment on the corporate campaign **(p. 182)** is quoted from the Morenci Miners Union report, July 1985. The Albert Shanker/American Federation of Teachers angle on the corporate campaign **(p. 182)** comes in part from *Union Corporate Campaigns* and in part from the *Village Voice* article, "Copper War" of March 19, 1985. Shanker's comments **(pp. 182–183)** are quoted from the text of his press release dated February 19, 1985. The *New York Times* article quoting Shanker and Kamber **(pp. 183–84)** ran on February 23, 1985. Angel Rodriguez's comments **(p. 184)** are from my interviews.

Chapter 8. Slant of the Law

The Frank Fitzsimmons account **(pp. 185–86)** is from friends of the union with direct knowledge of the Fitzsimmons visit with President Reagan. The exact date of the meeting is difficult to determine because presidential logs do not list meetings that the president requests to be kept off them. Top Fitzsimmons aide Walter Shea, who was not the source for the account of the meeting, has a notation on his calendar records of a February 10, 1981, meeting with the president, probably the date of this meeting.

For Price's reputation **(p. 186)**, see *Engineering News Record* (January 15, 1981) at 7. The *Arizona Republic* editorial supporting Price **(p. 187)** ran on March 20, 1981. These accounts of Price **(pp. 188–89)** come from a series of interviews with NLRB officials, past and present, as well as practicing Phoenix attorneys. In most cases, these officials and attorneys asked not to be identified. One of the reasons my sources (as in the "board employee" on **p. 188**) would not identify themselves was that NLRB general counsel Jerry Hunter expressly refused my request to authorize officials of the Phoenix office to speak with me on the record. His written response of October 14, 1992, stated, among other things, "There is a likelihood that the neutrality of particular board agents or the board itself, could be compromised by the public disclosure of personal opinion concerning either the case processing itself or the circumstances surrounding the case." Although I suspect Hunter's response was meant to be applicable to all NLRB cases, it was particularly appropriate regarding the Phelps Dodge strike.

I interviewed former NLRB investigator Martin Dominguez **(p. 192)** on October 21, 1991, and October 16, 1992. The account of the switch in investigators came from two Phoenix attorneys with direct knowledge of the change. The account was initially denied by the Phoenix office of the NLRB, but a check of internal files 28-CA-7521 and 28-CA-7534 produced the handwritten office cards showing that Dominguez's name had been crossed off after the investigation had begun, with Jorgensen's name penned over it. The decision signed by Peter Maydanis **(p. 192)** came in Case 28-CA-7521 and was issued on September 2, 1983. The unfair labor practice charge filed by the unions **(p. 192)** is quoted from Case 28-CA-7584 filed by the unions on September 2, 1983. The decision by Milo Price in the same case **(p. 193)** was issued on October 14, 1983.

The Moolick quote **(p. 194)** is from my interview of April 8, 1990. The Seidman quote **(p. 194)** is from my interview of August 15, 1991. The Boland quote **(p. 194)** is from my interview of June 5, 1992. Boland died of cancer on August 13, 1992. I interviewed Gerald Barrett **(p. 195)** on October 1, 1991.

The quotes of NLRB officials **(p. 194 et seq.)** are, again, conditioned on anonymity. The Rodriguez and McWilliams quotes **(p. 196)** are from an Associated Press article dated October 9, 1984. The Carl Forstrom quote **(p. 196)** is from his undated letter distributed during the decertification campaign in October 1984. The unpublished ruling by Judge Earldean Robbins **(p. 197)** was issued on June 28, 1985, and is filed with the NLRB branch office in San Francisco as document JD(SF)—111—85. The article detailing the conflict-of-interest and ethics allegations against Price **(p. 198)** appeared in the *Arizona Republic* on June 15, 1986. The citations to federal law and NLRB rules **(p. 198)** also appear in that article. A follow-up article ran in the *Arizona Republic* on June 20, 1987, disclosing a settlement in which Price did not admit any wrongdoing.

Conclusion. Angels and Demons

The Angel Rodriguez letter of March 16, 1986 **(p. 202)** was supplied to the author by Rodriguez.

The strike results also had multiple meanings to the institutional union leadership **(p. 203)**. Steelworkers spokesman Cass Alvin said that, paternalistic as it was, Phelps Dodge might once have cared about compromising with workers to keep the community together. Now the Steelworkers had "discovered that Daddy is a prick." Interview of April 14, 1990.

The quote from Hildebrand and Mangum **(p. 204)** is at 263. The 1986 negotiations are laid out as well in Hildebrand and Mangum **(pp. 205–6)** at 265–66. This account is supplemented by my interviews with Edgar Ball on August 9, 1990, Robert Petris on November 22, 1990 and November 14, 1993, and Lynn Williams on August 9, 1990. My description of industry and company views about the strike **(p. 207)** is a summary of dozens of interviews with industry consultants and company officials. In print, the company officials refer in shorthand to the strike as "history" or as PD "doing what it had to do" as in *Arizona Trend*, August 1987. The *Wall Street Journal* article **(p. 208)** appeared on November 24, 1989. My visit with Arthur Kinneberg **(pp. 208–9)** occurred on December 1, 1991.

The quotes of labor writer John Hoerr **(p. 211)** are from *And the Wolf Finally Came: The Decline of the American Steel Industry* (University of Pittsburgh Press,

1988) at 404–5. The Moolick comments **(p. 213 et seq.)** are from my interview of August 13, 1990. The analysis of Phelps Dodge stock share value by Stephen R. Sleigh, Michael Kapsa, and Chris Hall of City University of New York **(p. 213)** was reported in Bureau of National Affairs, *Daily Labor Report*, November 5, 1992. I spoke with Ron Collotta **(p. 215)** on April 2, 1990. The *New Times* article on Bruce Babbitt **(pp. 215, 216)** appeared in the October 12–18, 1983, issue. The video "meeting" between Babbitt and the AFL-CIO **(p. 215)** was described in the *Arizona Daily Star*, May 6, 1987.

The Phelps Dodge reference **(p. 217)** in Thomas A. Kochan, Harry C. Katz, and Robert B. McKersie, *The Transformation of American Industrial Relations* (Basic Books, 1986; ILR Press, 1994) is at 135 and in Bruce E. Kaufman, *The Economics of Labor Markets*, at 563. The Kingsolver short story is "Why I Am a Danger to the Public," in *Homeland* (Harper Collins 1990), pp. 226–44.

The article on the death of pattern bargaining **(p. 219)** is Audrey Freedman and William E. Fulmer, "Last Rites for Pattern Bargaining," *Harvard Business Review*, (March–April 1982) at 30. The labor observer **(p. 219)** is Chicago attorney Joseph Ferguson. The off-the-cuff comment about the local "heroes" **(p. 220)** is from one of many Steelworkers officials with whom I spoke on background. The Hormel strike **(pp. 220–21)** is noteworthy because it has been the subject of at least three books, Dave Hage and Paul Klauda's *No Retreat, No Surrender: Labor's War at Hormel* (William Morrow, 1989), Hardy Green's *On Strike at Hormel: The Struggle for a Democratic Labor Movement* (Temple University Press, 1990), and Peter Rachleff's *Hard-Pressed in the Heartland: The Hormel Strike and the Future of the Labor Movement* (South End Press, 1993), and an Academy Award-winning documentary, *American Dream*, by Barbara Kopple. None of these adequately examines the issue of pattern bargaining in the context of larger American union movements.

The decertification of unions at Cyprus Minerals Co. **(p. 222)** is described in the *Wall Street Journal*, August 8, 1989.

The references to Herbert Northrup's work at Wharton **(p. 222 et seq.)** come from his memoranda, which, rather than a Research Advisory Group title, bear the letterhead: "UNIVERSITY OF PENNSYLVANIA" and "The Wharton School." Northrup's tone was especially strident on women's issues. In a Wharton memorandum to companies on December 13, 1983, Northrup pointed out to the ninety members of the Research Advisory Group (RAG), which included companies such as Eastman Kodak, Nestlé, and Consolidated Foods, that women's organizations allied with unions were attempting to organize "your office employees." He characterized this organizing as "causing . . . considerable effort and trouble" and stated somewhat nefariously that "we have been able to collect a considerable file on 925 and other women's groups." He urged companies that had a potential problem with organizing by female clerical workers to contact the Wharton School for information "and assistance." In another memorandum, he informed members that 925 leader Nussbaum had been, in his words, "induced" to speak to a Wharton class, and that information gleaned from that visit would be reported to a later RAG meeting.

Northrup also reported to the business membership on a new AFL-CIO national polling project to determine the likelihood of workers joining unions. Northrup wrote that, as with the women's organization, this union project had been the subject of an "investigation," and he indicated that the unions had learned that a description of their polling technique had been leaked to what Northrup sarcastically referred to as "unfriendly hands." Northrup distributed the polling information with his memorandum, apologizing that "we could not get a clean copy." References to the "9 to 5" women's group **(p. 223)** included the December 13, 1983, memorandum as well as memoranda of March 27, 1981, October 4, 1982, and December 7, 1982. The AFL-CIO polling project **(p. 223)** was described in the December 13, 1983, memorandum. The accounts of the Phelps Dodge strike **(p. 223)** included memoranda of October 4, 1983, December 13, 1983, March 20, 1984, July 3, 1984, March 12, 1985, and July 2, 1985—from nearly the beginning of the strike through decertification. The reference to Phelps Dodge as a "case study" and the inaccurate description of the shutdown **(p. 223)** came in the December 13, 1983, memorandum; the Steelworkers and Phelps Dodge video sale **(p. 223)** was announced in the July 2, 1985, memorandum.

I spoke with Northrup **(pp. 223–24)** on August 19, 1993. The testimony by U.S. Labor Secretary Robert Reich **(p. 225)** took place on March 30, 1993, before the Senate Subcommittee on Labor.

Senator Kennedy's floor speech **(p. 225)** was delivered on July 12, 1994. Although a majority of fifty-three senators favored passage of the "Workplace Fairness Act," a cloture vote fell seven votes short of the sixty necessary to end debate. The statistics on the use of permanent replacements **(p. 225)** come from the *Daily Labor Report*, March 24, 1993, and from *Labor Management Relations: Strikes and the Use of Permanent Strike Replacements in the 1970s and 1980s*, (General Accounting Office: HRD-91-2, January 1991). The U.S. Supreme Court case **(p. 225)** is *NLRB v. Mackay Radio and Telegraph Co.*, 304 U.S.222 (1938).

My ride down Route 666 with Ray Isner **(p. 227)** took place on March 25, 1990. The mural dedication in Clifton **(p. 228)** took place on March 24, 1990.

Epilogue. Life after Death?

The quote from Don Manning on "salt of the earth" **(p. 231)** is from the Silver City edition of the April 19, 1996, *Sun-News* (Deming, N.M.). My visit with Alex Lopez **(p. 231)** took place on August 28, 1997. The creative origins of the movie *Salt of the Earth* **(p. 232)** are detailed in Henry Biberman, *Salt of the Earth: The Story of a Film* (Boston: Beacon Press, 1965) at 37 et seq. Esperanza Quintero's famous line **(p. 233)** may be found in the screenplay version of the movie, Michael Wilson and Deborah S. Rosenfelt, *Salt of the Earth* (New York: The Feminist Press, 1978) at 81. My first visit with Local 890 president Manning **(p. 233)** occurred on August 29, 1997. The dismal state of the union contract **(p. 234)** is detailed in economic analyses produced by the Steelworkers (and in the possession of the author). I confirmed their wage data with officials from other copper companies. The Len Judd comments **(p. 235)** were recalled by a Clifton-Morenci area resident who felt that the remarks referred to company cutbacks on corporate sponsorships in general, not family issues in particular; I find the quote significant—and use it—for its syntactical similarity to the company's restrictive position on family hiring. My conversation with Benny Ybarra **(p. 236)** took place on August 30, 1997. My drive around the mine property with union president Manning **(p. 237)** took place on August 29, 1997. I interviewed Cecil Waldrip **(p. 239)** on January 7, 1997. The quotes from Scott Huish **(p. 239)** are from the Silver City edition of the *Sun-News*, June 2, 1996. I interviewed Patty Young **(p. 240)** on November 21, 1997. The first comment on decertification by mine manager Brack **(p. 240)** was from the May 1, 1996, *Sun-News*; the rest are from letters to union members in the possession of the author. The newspaper reporter's question about Local 890's survival **(p. 242)** was posed in a June 2, 1996, *Sun-News* article. My op-ed column in the *Los Angeles Times* **(p. 243)** was published on November 23, 1997, and the Phelps Dodge letter to the editor ran on December 25, 1997. The quote from Douglas Yearley **(p. 243)** appeared in a *Sun-News* article of May 15, 1997. My interview at Virginia Chacón's house **(p. 243)** took place on August 31, 1997. My interviews with Arturo and Ernest Flores **(p. 244)** took place November 20, 1997, and I received Arturo's follow-up e-mail on December 2, 1997.

Index

Franklin, Sam, 104–107, 122, 254n
  role in strike of, 214–15
Freedman, Audrey, 261n
Fulmer, William E., 261n
Fungibility of labor, 222

Gann, Roy, 119, 255n
General Electric, 62
Gentry, D. T., 117
"Getting to No," 73
"Getting to Yes," 73
Ghearing, Edward, 73, 253n
Gibbons, Russell W., 251n
Gilmartin, Helen, 124
Goldwater, Barry, 186–87
Gomez, Bobby, 101, 107, 254n
Gomez, Conrad, 95, 254n
Gomez, Manuel, 248n
Gonzales, Lorenzo, 173
Gonzales, Paul "Larry," 256n
Government, U.S.
  historic relation with unions and management, 8–11, 27–45
  Labor-Management Relations (House subcommittee), 172
  legal issues of strikebreaking and, 222–26
  national security issues and, 42
Graham, George, 109, 110, 111, 254n
Gray, Johnny, 117
Great Western Produce, Inc., 198
Greaves, Timothy, III, 160, 257n
Green, Hardy, 261n
Greyhound strike, 224
Gruender, Dan, 189
Grumman, Roy, 248n

Hage, Dave, 261n
Hall, Chris, 261n
Hamel, Chris, 108
Hand, Learned, 27, 250n
Hard-Pressed in the Heartland: The Hormel Strike and the Future of the Labor Movement (Rachleff), 261n
Harris, Don, 86, 253n
Harvard Business Review, 219, 261n
Harvard Negotiation Project, 73
Hatch, Orrin, 186
Haywood, Big Bill, 19
Henderson, Edward D., Jr., 179
Hennebach, Ralph, 60
Higgins, George, 42
Highway 666, 3, 13–14, 95, 116, 120, 227–29, 248n, 262n
  geology of, 14
Hildebrand, George, 36, 44, 45, 68, 161–65, 204, 250n, 251n, 257n, 258n, 260n
Hill, Joe, 19–20, 249n
  song, 20
History of Phelps Dodge, A (Cleland), 17, 18, 26, 248n, 249n, 250n

History of the Labor Movement in the United States (Foner), 250n
Hoerr, John, 173, 211, 258n, 260n
Holding the Line (Kingsolver), 148, 257n
Holliday, Doc, 17, 248n
Holsum Bread strike, 224
Holy Cross Church, 133
Hormel strike, 220, 261n
Hughes, Howard, 35, 251n
Hunt, George W. P., 20, 23–24, 97, 249n
  election of 1916, 24
  referendum against, 24
Huish, Scott, 239, 263n
Hunter, Jerry, 259n
Hunt for a Better Arizona: The Arizona Gubernatorial Election of 1916 (Eckstein), 249n
Hurwitz, Andrew, 97, 103, 108, 109, 113, 255n

Ice, Duane, 122, 123, 255n
Independent Union of All Workers, 221
Industrial Workers of the World, 19, 25
  and One Big Union rhetoric, 40, 79
  World War I and, 28, 30
Inspiration Copper, 70, 76, 156–57, 204, 258n
International Association of Machinists, 67, 123
International Brotherhood of Teamsters. *See* Teamsters
International Paper strike, 224
International Union of Mine, Mill and Smelter Workers, 25, 30, 31, 33–37
  communism and, 34–37, 251n
  contracts of, 35–36
  ethnic diversity of, 35
  as the Mexican union, 32
  Mexican workers' benefits and, 37
  Morenci Miners Local 616, 31, 33–37, 139
  noncommunist oaths, 34, 38
Isner, Ray, 73, 100, 204, 227–28, 253n
IWW. *See* Industrial Workers of the World

J. P. Stevens, 166–67
Jackson, Robert, 191
Jackson, Scott, 121
Jackson, Tink, 239
Jarrico, Paul, 232
Jensen, Vernon, 251n
Job classification systems, 45, 56, 74
John Olin Foundation, 61
Johnson, Ernie, 95
Johnson, Frank, 28
Johnson, Lyndon, 42, 51, 251n
Joklik, Frank, 60, 69
Jones, George, 117
Jones, Mary Harris (Mother), 9, 20, 23, 27, 44, 80, 249n
  speech on unionism, 24
Jorgensen, Gordon, 192, 193, 260n
Judd, Len, 235, 262n

About the Author

Jonathan D. Rosenblum received his B.A. from Duke University
and his J.D. from Northwestern University School of Law. He has
worked as a journalist with the Waynesville, N.C., *Mountaineer, The
New Republic,* and *Time,* and as an attorney for the United Nations'
International Labor Office. He now practices law in Madison, Wisconsin.